In honor of all veterans both young and old, each Louch paperback sold results in a one dollar donation to <u>The Honor Flight Network</u> and an additional one dollar donation to <u>The Fisher House Foundation</u> for wounded veterans and their families.

Thank you for your support!

The author

[signature] 9/20/14

Louch
(Loo-ch)

A Simple Man's True Story of War, Survival, Life, and Legacy

By Lou Baczewski

For additional copies and information go to
louchthebook.com

Also available on kindle at
Amazon.com

Copyright pending
ISBN #9781492115809 - 90000
First Published via Createspace.com on 9/25/2013
Printed in the USA

This book is dedicated to Louis J. Baczewski, to the lessons of his life, and to all soldiers and fisherman like him.

Louis J. Baczewski (left) and his grandson Louis A. Baczewski (right)

Louis J. Baczewski
(November 7th 1922- May 20th 2013)

Upon reading this book, I asked him, "Well grandpa, what did you think?" He smiled with pride and said, "I liked it, it was really good." I replied, "Grandpa, it's a three hundred page book about your life, don't you have any comments or problems with it, I mean there has to be something that was off the mark?" He smiled once again and said adamantly, "No. I really liked it, it was really good!" He said no more, he just smiled.

My dad always said, "They broke the mold when they made him," and I agree, for it seems like they just don't make men like that anymore. He was a man among a generation of great men and women who for their part strove to lead simple and noble lives.

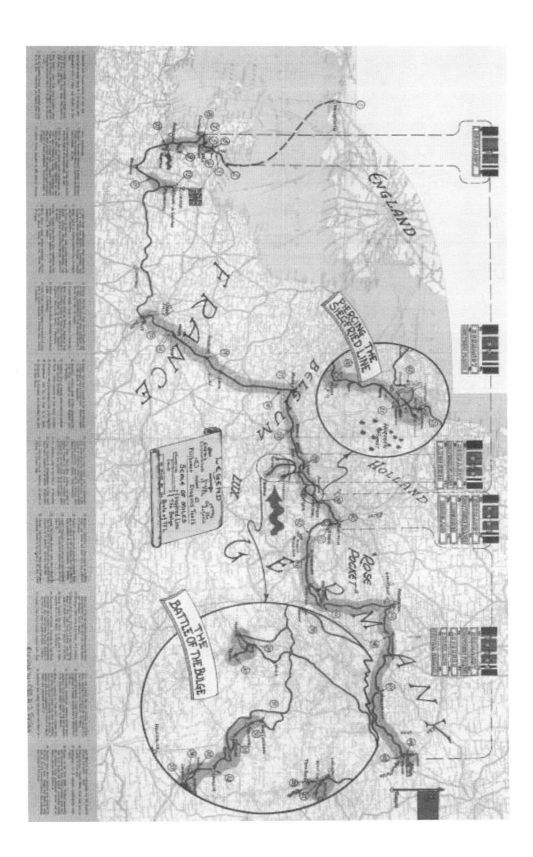

Acknowledgments

Were it not for the following people this book would not have been possible, and the order by which I mention them in no way denotes the importance of their support or guidance throughout this titanic endeavor. I have to thank Louis J.Baczewski, Les Underwood, and Dave Pagan, for without their survival and willingness to tell their story, there would have been no story at all.

When I started this project many years ago, I received immediate encouragement and support from my long time mentor and friend, Dr. Ed. Wehrle. After coaching me through my initial slipshod battle through editing and publication, Ed guided me all the way, and ultimately helped me make this book possible.

In this one giant run on sentence, I want to thank all of the following people: Ed and Elizabeth Anderson for encouragement and the dessert "bag," Leslie Baruffi for driving all that way, Mrs. Underwood for finding a pencil and being a nice person, My Mom for always telling me that I could be a writer, Cassandra Suggs for advice, aid, and encouragement, Stanley Baczewski (my father) for changing his mind about me being a writer and helping me all the way, Judy my second mom, for her encouragement, open ears, and distinct intolerance for people who make fun of *"The Sound of Music,"* Ann Smith for asking us to sing when we drank too much, Bruce Chapman for use of his cabin, providing endless information on invasive species, and for being Bruce Chapman, Bob Hustava for information, Joe Baczewski for drinking "Irish car bombs" and legal advice (although not in that order), Penny Wilmesherr and Lisa Coffman for listening to all of my stories, Bob Vieluf for giving me the "fascist" perspective on all manner of things, Dr. Jon McEligott for helping encourage me to write and teaching me volumes, Tom Haas for aid and encouragement, the folks at Central Illinois Honor Flight, and Franklin County Honor Flight, Chris Prom, Dan Raymond, Angela Jordan, and the University of Illinois Archive Staff, Vic Damon and the 3rd Armored Division Historical Foundation, Aunt Mary Kay for info and potato salad, Uncle Dave for running the lines all night, some scrutiny over toilet paper usage, and for always bringing enough ham, and Shawn Wallace for support, an open ear, and *Oreo Cookie* day in shop class.

Introduction

The name is Baczewski. In truth, no one really is sure how to say it or if it has any meaning. A professor of mine in college, who spoke fluent Polish, once told me that it is correctly pronounced, Baa- chef – ski. So essentially, I and all of the members of my family pronounce our own name wrong, as we have become accustomed to saying Ba – zest – ski. Ah, what the hell. Pronunciation has never been a big issue with us, or grammar, or basic English structure for that matter. So, when faced with the constant mispronunciation of my name everywhere I go, I always greet it with a certain acceptance. After all, it is our own fault. In any event, I am proud to have the name regardless of how it looks or sounds. My name is Louis Andrew Baczewski. A lot of people call me Andy, and some call me Lou - among other things.

I hear that "Baczewski" is just another everyday name in both Poland and Chicago. I have heard that our last name is basically the Polish Smith. However on the Illinois side of the St Louis Metro area, our name is an oddity. In general, I receive two types of reactions when people are faced with the name Baczewski: Either there is a long awkward pause followed by a butchered attempt at pronunciation, or there is an instant acknowledgement of the name. If you know, or have met somebody designated as a Baczewski, it tends to stick with a person – from my experience. Whether it is for good or bad reasons, the name sparks a reaction. Whatever the case, I am either greeted with a frowning head shake and a verbal response such as "Baczewski huh," or more commonly, I receive something like, "oh yea! I know a guy named Baczewski, I use to drink with him." To those who know us well I think we are considered a decent bunch of people. I guarantee that you can find at least one person in each and every local tavern that will speak up for most of us.

A few years ago, I began to wonder how it was that we Baczewski's ended up living in and around the St Louis area in the first place. When I thought about the region, I pondered why anyone would choose to live here at random. Of all the places to go in the country, my great grandfather decided that moving here would be a smart move for some reason or another. Here, it is cold and windy in the winter, hot and humid in the summer, flat and boring in the sense of landscape, and our muddy rivers sludge through pastures and industrial areas, not through breathtaking canyons and plains. Despite all this, Stanislaws Baczewski made this place home. There are no mountains here. There are no majestic views. To reach an ocean it is thousands of miles in each direction. There is little here, but people, crumbling industry, and highways intersecting. All of which, is surrounded by a seemingly endless expanse of cornfields, bean fields, and winter wheat. I do have to say though, that there is nothing more beautiful than a huge green hilly field of winter wheat. On a wet spring morning when the wind sales across it, the wheat ebbs and flows as if it were waves upon the sea – it truly has to be seen.

In any case, why did he leave Poland and come here, and for that matter eventually settle in a hole-in-the-wall town called Pocahontas, Illinois; located about an hour outside St Louis. What was our family story anyway? The bits and pieces of the story that I knew or saw first-hand, were filled with humor, history, war, poverty, compassion, hard work, true fishing tales, and sometimes family tragedies, yet they were excellent tales. These were stories that had to be told, but they were only the tip of the iceberg. Just from knowing my pieces of this story alone, I knew that

10

in the living memory of all of our family from grandparents to great-grandkids, that there was not just a good story here, but a great one. I have procrastinated, I have stalled, and I have found reasons to do a million other things, but I know in my heart that the most important thing for me to do is to tell this story. This is more than just a mere story, it is legacy, and it is a task that I must complete. I was born into a good family and our origins derive around the little town of Pocahontas Illinois and a very muddy creek which I will speak more of.

So, my story starts here as it should – on the muddy banks of the Shoal Creek. This creek flowed through my grandfather's life and into the lives of his grandchildren. My grandfather, Louis "Louch" Baczewski, and five friends grew up during the Great Depression battling the muddy grungy creek named Shoal. It was on this stream in rural Illinois, that they fished with only the crudest methods to seize the roughest of fish. They lived off the creek in a style similar to the fabled stories of Huck Finn and Tom Sawyer. All five of these friends would end up fighting in Europe in the US First Army- Louch and two others would ultimately survive. They were from a small town of only 800 people, but all their paths crossed during the war; some in absolutely miraculous ways.

Along the banks of Shoal Creek, my grandfather would tell me stories of his life, while he also taught me the same fishing methods that he and his friends and brothers had learned so long ago. Although they were arduous and archaic, I chose to never forget them. There was wisdom and stillness to be gained from fishing Shoal Creek. There was an ethic of life and hard work taught to me and all my family there. Fishing Shoal helped my grandfather forget the war, just as it eventually helped me throughout my own life. The word "shoal" itself means shallow, yet this creek ran deep through our family history, and it is the tie that binds this

11

vast story together. This book flows from Pocahontas Illinois, to WWII Europe, and back home again. Louch survived five major European campaigns, battled "Hitlers Own" SS Division in the Battle of the Bulge, liberated the Dora-Mittlebau concentration camp and V2 missile factory, only to return home and tangle with mob run unions and desperate times. He was one of only a handful of men in his entire company to survive the war.

Shoal Creek is the axis of this story. It bound my grandfather's boyhood friends together before they went to war, and it comforted those who were lucky enough to return home. The creek stood and still stands as that hollowed place, that savored place, that place where all the loss and strife and turmoil of Grandfather's life faded away. In time, the creek's lessons would help me through my own darkest days. Once I grew older, and came to realize all the wisdom and history that flowed out of this stream, I knew I had to write it all down. This is a true story of amazing coincidences, survival, friends, family, and war. It is a tribute to my ancestors and to all of the lessons we should garner from their struggles.

Driven by the gods of poverty and war, Louis Baczewski made a journey through an unfathomable series of events, only to return to Shoal Creek and relive the simplicity of his youth. Thus the tradition still goes on to this day and it will go on, just as long as there are those who choose to heed the lessons of Shoal. For many reasons, this story came terribly close to not being told at all, and I therefore feel very privileged to be the one to tell it.

Chapter 1
Why would anyone do this?

If you are going to tell people the truth, you better
make them laugh; otherwise they'll kill you

George Bernard Shaw

My shoes had about a pound of sand in them already. My back and arms ached from carrying countless buckets full of water and bait. There was no shade to be found in the middle of the creek. The August sun both poured onto us from above and reflected from the water and the aluminum jon boat below. We were in a crossfire. The direct beams of sunlight were scorching, and here and there they shot through the tree line. The humidity hovered around one-hundred and twenty percent, and the bugs as usual were there to meet us in force. Our attempt to thwart them with spray was to no avail and I believe for the bugs it was the equivalent of putting gravy on a biscuit. It was just beginning, and I was already tired. My arms and legs felt like they were about to burst into flames from the stinging nettles. Additionally, the gashes I received when cutting willow poles in a swamp seemed to have become red and infected almost immediately. I hurt everywhere. Yet honestly, I didn't even think about any of it. I was just too excited and I believe I speak for most of the family when I say this, "I live for this stuff." Why? I don't know, but I do. I am quite certain (and have seen evidence of this following fact on a few occasions) that no rational person would ever do this – at least not multiple times. However, here we were again. We represented three generations of polocks crammed in a twelve foot jon boat - my grandfather, my father, and I.

The boat itself was only a boat in the sense that it sort of floated. Beyond this, there was nothing positive to say about it. I think at one point it was blue in color, but the paint had chipped off or scratched off in various ways. It was in mixed stages of decay throughout. The transom was rotten and falling apart. There was a huge dent in back from where it hit a tree in a severe storm. The plug leaked, the rivets leaked, and there was either a small caliber bullet wound or puncture of some kind in the bow. When water leaked in through this hole it looked like the creek was peeing on us in a steady stream. Every year we would forget to fix it. About ten seconds and a caulk gun would have done the job, but it just never did get done. Yet there was always talk about fixing it for next time. There were no seats, rod holders, depth finders or amenities of any kind. There was pretty much nothing done to the boat over the years besides damage. But, for the intents and purposes of this gig, the boat did the job.

As for the creek itself, it wasn't much to look at either. After all, it was just a creek. The going perception in the area was that fishing it was a waste of time. It was a muddy grungy creek of fair width in places. Its depths were by no means vast, and a great percentage of the creek was merely a foot or so deep, if that. There were periodic holes however, which could go to five or ten feet deep, perhaps even deeper under log jams. Such jambs were common place and the cause of many good fishing holes. The banks of the creek were shrouded in trees of various types. Close to the waterline willows and maples would grow, but as one rose up the steep banks and back from the creek, the tree line would be a mix of weeds shrouded by groves of oaks, cottonwoods, sycamores, and hickories. The lower banks were many times sandy and as distance from the waterline increased the sand would turn to mud, willows, and weeds. Life abounded on the banks and a consistent hum of insects and birds

14

would fill the air all day, only to change to a different but familiar din of creatures at night.

On that particular hot summer day, as our jon boat slowly crept around the creek bend, we could all see that there was a fish on. Sticking out of the sandy bank before us, one of our many crudely fashioned willow fishing poles slowly bent up and down breaking the surface of the water. To anyone else it would just look like a stick with a string on it. The weight of the fish bent this particular pole almost double. It became quickly apparent that this was a rather large fish. We paddled toward the commotion in all possible haste. Dad shifted and knelt over the bow in anticipation. Upon arrival, he reached out for the end of the pole while his other hand searched for the landing net. Our small craft swayed and listed forward as Dad seized the pole's end and struggled to place the landing net in the proper "fish landing" location. Water splashed over the bow of the boat in the ensuing commotion. A desperate scene unfurled, amidst the combination of an angry fish and a large awkwardly fumbling man. Mayhem reigned. Expletives flew.

True, Dad's size alone made it a show. Some say his shadow alone weighed a good thirty pounds. The best way to describe him aesthetically I guess, would be to say that he looked something akin to Grizzly Adams. He didn't seem to fit in – by that I only mean the he didn't fit in a small boat hunkered over the bow. In any case, the battle raged for a good minute or so. Sweat poured down the brave bowman's face. And to the chagrin of the other jon boat passengers (my grandpa and myself) there before us, a plumbers crack grew ever larger as the struggle between man and fish continued.

Suddenly, Grandpa yelled at the sight of the tail which swashed the top of the muddy water, "that's a twenty pounder." And if anyone could

15

tell the weight of a fish by just this mere event, it was Grandpa. Knowing this, our hearts beat faster and the bowman struggled on. Yet in a split second, the great fish came loose and plunged into the depths of Shoal Creek, never to be seen again. A bitter silence followed, only to be punctuated by Dad's long but muffled "ssshhhiiiiittt."

Grandpa was one to hold a grudge about such things and unfortunately for Dad many years of reminders now awaited him of this incident. He took fishing very seriously. Grandpa was in his 70's at the time with few trips left to take, but no one aboard our chewed up little boat knew more about creek fishing and fishing in general. He was a fairly skinny man with dark hair that never dulled in color. Even in his 70's he was agile and strong and could outwork men a quarter of his age. He had fished this creek at early age and taught his sons and grandsons to fish it just as he had learned so long ago.

I don't remember the exact year this was, or how many we caught that particular time, but this incident is locked in my mind among thousands of similar little stories. Perhaps, I can never explain it to anyone else what these stories mean to me and why, but it is the intent of this book to try. One might argue (and many have) that there is nothing sublime about this creek I refer to, or our muddy and exhausting struggles to catch catfish. These fishing expeditions have admittedly been similar to Thomas Hobbes's explanation of the state of nature, "nasty, brutish, and short." They were always "nasty" due to the nature of the muddy Illinois creek itself. They were "brutish" because they demanded a good deal of beast like activity, an abandonment of self-preservation and after a few beers, many involved have acted like cavemen – myself included. They were also "short" because frankly no one besides grandpa could take the torture involved for more than a day or two.

16

Seriously, I have only known a few people in my life, other than family, who have fished in this manner for it really is a Paleolithic undertaking. On one trip to Shoal Creek, a friend of my dad's once commented that, "I feel like I'm in a National Geographic special or something." He was astonished with the archaic tasks we needed to perform and he continually stated in confusion, "We need to cut sticks to fish with?" It seemed perfectly normal to all of us, He mumbled that statement over and over to himself, "sticks to fish with." All the while, we cut more sticks to fish with. We didn't think much of the primitive aspects, as we were accustomed to it. After all, we were all raised doing it. We learned how to fish like this because of Grandpa, and it is for that reason that I and others will carry on this tradition despite the ardors, strange comments, strange looks, and overall degradation of it.

There was nothing glamorous about fishing Shoal Creek. It is not a majestic river in the mountains. It is not akin to the Montana trout stream which "ran through it" in Norman McLean's book. On the contrary, this creek gurgled and slumped through it and still does; it meaning, cow pastures, corn and bean fields, and under highway overpasses - which consequently serve as good campsites. The wildlife around the creek was and is in many cases abundant. Deer, possums, raccoons, coyotes, squirrels and other interesting wildlife frequent the banks of the mighty Shoal. However, there are also frequent sightings of a few non-indigenous species of Frigidaire, Kenmore, Hoover, Firestone, Goodyear, and various other radial brands, and on rare occasions Maytag. There's even a car stuck in the bank just south of the Interstate 70 Bridge just outside of my grandfather's hometown of Pocahontas, Illinois - AKA "Pokey."

Car embedded in the Shoal Creek bank, south of I70

Years ago, in my grandfather's youth, the water was a bit cleaner and fewer appliances lived on the banks. Yet, this was always a muddy Illinois creek filled with predominantly ugly fish and requiring only the crudest methods of fishing. There was never the need for depth finders, GPS or fancy fiberglass boats that sparkle when the sun strikes their sides. Not even the simplest rod and reel or tackle box is necessary here. The beautiful dance and display of a fly fisherman has most likely never been seen on this stream, for it would only take about five minutes for a guy to lose about all his tackle and break a rod or two trying to fight his way into a good hole. This is a sophisticated sportsman's worst nightmare.

The mere frustration of trying to fish with a rod and reel would kill most guys. The average person upon the sight of the creek would assume that there were few if any fish to be had in there. I have heard on many occasions a slur of jokes and condemnations related to fishing this creek. However, it was attitudes such as these that helped keep much of the competition away. Then again, the biggest deterrent in our favor was how we fished in the first place. Truthfully, I don't even know if it is legal in a lot of places.

Creeks like ours, were spots that most people didn't go to. It was as if there was a whole different world out there that we were privy to; one that no one else seemed to care about. They weren't areas that were pretty enough to attract hikers or canoeists. It may well have been that many times we were sort of trespassing, at least while getting bait. That may have been part of our problem. Many people thought we were dumping trash or doing something sinister if they saw us in their creek. So, we tried to stay out of sight and out of areas with a lot of people. It seems like nowadays if people see a bunch of guys who happen to be dirtier than Frenchmen knee deep in a small muddy creek that couldn't conceivably have anything good in it – then therefore they must be disposing of toxic waste, appliances, or bodies. We were not guilty of any of these things, but seining bait with a two man net is so far apart from people's normal modern things to do, it is always assumed that we are felonious individuals just by the shear act of being where we are. Can't blame people I guess.

The reason that we bothered to do this stuff in the first place was that we were raised doing so. One of my oldest memories of the creek was the sight of a train crossing the railroad bridge east of Pokey. The conductor waved to us while my sister Ann and my cousins Mike and Chris and I played on a sand bar in the middle of Shoal creek. I could not have been more than six or seven years old. Many of the fondest memories of my life have been from the banks of that creek.

As far as I could remember we fished the creek every year. It took at least a week to prepare. The week consisted of assembling the gear, sharpening and prepping the banklines, checking if the aerators and bait equipment was intact, cutting small willow trees for poles, and getting bait. There was a certain manner of doing things that was necessary, just as much as it was tradition. From making the banklines to where people sat in the boat, there was a system to it. I learned this system slowly over the years as I moved up in the hierarchy of tasks and positions. This system was designed and perfected by my grandfather. The various tasks and roles were never really stated outright, but the system was no less apparent despite it. Things were always done a certain way – Grandpa's way. His methods had been tested and perfected over a few lifetimes, and they worked. Such things were done without question because everyone realized the system made sense and it caught fish. Ultimately the process was the most important thing. If the process was followed correctly, even when conditions were poor, you would always catch some fish.

Literally everything we knew about fishing the creek came from Grandpa. He had learned it as a boy. It was just a part of growing up poor in the country. He had to make his own fishing line and poles from what he had, because he didn't have the money to buy a real fishing pole. He had discovered at an early age that a green willow tree had enough snap to catch a fish, and was limber enough not to break from even the weight of a large fish. Some old men in Pokey showed him a few tricks on fishing with willows. He wasn't the first to come up with the idea by any means, but he made a science out of it.

So as the gritty and violent Prohibition and Depression era raged and as war brewed in Europe and Asia, Grandpa, and his brothers and friends lived their summer days running their willow lines on the banks of Shoal Creek. My grandfather fished the creek for weeks at a time accompanied by his brothers, Joe and Ed, and close friends, Dave Pagan, Mel Weber, John Hustava, Bill Kalous, and Stanley Cravens. Day to day, my grandpa "Louch," his brothers, and his friends lived as if they were characters yanked straight out of a Samuel Clemens tale. They lived off the creek. They lived off its fish, squirrels, and whatever else they could scavenge from their gardens and neighboring farms. The creek was their boyhood home away from home and I have never heard my grandfather speak about Shoal without seeing him grin and glow over the time he spent there. Shoal Creek flowed throughout my grandfather's life. So it came to pass, that this same stream would weave its way into the lives of his sons and grandsons.

Grandpa (Louch) and his grandson Nick standing over a mess of fish from Shoal Creek

Chapter 2
"You mind moving there bub?"

"I never fight for a cause to try to change my enemies – I fight to keep my enemies from changing me."

Donny Schmeder

Grandpa and I headed slowly down the steep bank balancing ourselves carefully. I had learned from him to walk on the sides of my feet in such occasions. If you walked straight out, you would wipe out for sure. We walked awkwardly as we carried our cane poles and buckets and so on. As it was late summer, it was hot as usual. The sharp sounds of the birds and the bugs made my ears ring. The weeds stood at least five foot tall in places and as we trudged through them, sweat beaded on our brows and ran down our faces. The saw grass would cut you like a razor and the itch weed if it made contact, would burn like a snake bite. Yet, we had a purpose here. Despite nature's usual effort to kill us, injure us, embarrass us, or just frustrate us in general, we were out here once again. This creek writhed with life – it was full of bait fish. We aimed to catch as many as possible for the coming trip to Shoal Creek.

Once we made our way to the actual bank of the small creek, it was a shear drop for about three feet. Below us lay a small trickle of a stream which was about four feet wide in places. Grandpa, (who had to have been over seventy at the time) climbed down it like it was nothing. He then turned, and watched me carefully as I made it down as well. I suppose, I was about thirteen or fourteen at the time.

Once we were set on the creek bottom, we turned towards the square concrete tunnel before us. Now and then, a car roared past on Keebler Road above and the sound resounded in a hollow tone as it passed over and around the vast culvert. At our feet, the murky water ran on towards the cement cavern - we were obliged to follow. On the other side of the culvert there was a surprisingly large pool. The shallow stream formed itself into a relatively deep cut just large enough to maintain a breeding population of small bluegill, creek chubs, shiners and the sought after "perch" AKA "pumpkinseed." The mission before us was to catch these small fish with a cane pole, a short length of line, a tiny hook, and a very aptly named "red wiggler" worm. Grandpa walked ahead in his usual steady saunter. He moseyed more than he walked. He was quite bow legged – so much so, that one day his doctor told him, "Lou you are so bow legged that you couldn't catch a pig in a ditch." He still gets a kick out of telling people that to this day.

The tunnel was like a near death experience. We were surrounded by black and we headed toward the light. This light was however nothing too special, it was merely the sun's glow from the other-side of Keebler Road. We walked on as our feet splashed around in the shallow stream running through the culvert. Just before we reached the other end and as the light began to grow stronger, Grandpa began to look to his right. He was apparently studying the side of the tunnel. He slowed down and he paused before me. His bucket hung from one arm and his cane pole from the other. He was a few paces ahead, so I could not see what he was looking at. He said nothing, but was obviously deep in thought as he gazed at the side of the culvert. He was frozen for a moment as if in a trance. When I came closer, I looked up to see the thin rays of light exposing some figure in red spray paint. Someone had painted something

24

in red and grandpa was transfixed on it. The sparkling waves of light washed over the symbol as they were reflected from the nearby pool in the creek.

I walked a few steps closer and realized that standing before me was a huge swastika painted across the side of the tunnel. The swastika was at least six foot high. Grandpa starred at it in silence all awash in reflected glints of light. He studied it for quite some time, emotionless and silent. He said nothing. I said nothing. His face was flat and almost purged of expression as if he were somewhere outside of himself – as if he were long far away.

Eventually he spoke without turning his head from the bright red symbol. His head and body never moved a millimeter as he spoke. He said in a flat and slightly hush voice, "Now I bet that kid who painted that, didn't have the slightest idea what that God damned thing means." Now, I have heard that back in the day Grandpa was quite the cusser, but as I knew him, he rarely cussed and more importantly to him, he rarely blasphemed. He use to always say things like "Son of a biscuit" or "that sapsucker" rather than actually cuss.

Truthfully at that age, all I saw on that culvert was a little known symbol painted in red on a concrete wall. It was fairly innocuous to me. Grandpa as I would later learn however, saw far more than I did. Within that paint there was an ideology, a conception of reality which was forged of unimaginable hate and destruction, there was a world at war, and there was a personal horror of war. Behind his eyes there was a vision, a vivid memory of so many deaths and losses that it makes me ill to think of it.

How could those ignorant kids have known that what that symbol meant when they sprayed it? How could they have known that what they painted would later be seen by a man who knew all too well its true meaning? A man who lived no more than ten houses down the road, who had been drafted at age 18 and shipped half way around the world to fight a war against what that paint symbolized.

It was moments like these that made me want to know more about my grandfather's life. At the time, I knew he had been a tank driver in the Second World War and that he had fought through poverty and war and all manner of battles throughout his life. I grew up listening to his stories about the war, Prohibition, gangsters, and the Great Depression, but little did I know how much my grandfather had truly seen and lived through until I had started researching this book. That swastika was not an ancient cryptic symbol to Lou Baczewski. As I would grow to learn, the struggles of his youth and his entire life were significant enough, but his experience in the war and his dealings with the Nazis and SS were truly remarkable. He knew deep down in his soul what that Swastika meant, for he had seen the carnage laid before it firsthand. Through his own eyes he had witnessed enough death and destruction to last a thousand lifetimes. Yet miraculously he had somehow survived to become the calm patient man I knew. Somehow he became the quiet man who taught me how to fish.

Many nights when the sun had long since gone down and as we sat around the campfire waiting to run the lines on the creek again, Grandpa would tell stories about the war. On the banks of Shoal Creek many times camped under a railroad trestle or an old highway bridge, we would listen intently as Grandpa would revisit his experiences. Sometimes he would tell stories about fishing with his brothers and friends and how they grew up poor in the country. He would tell stories about the gangsters running his town during Prohibition, while other times he might delve back into details about the war or perhaps the mob run union he battled when he returned home from Europe.

26

Once I grew a bit older and hopefully smarter, I finally started transcribing conversations and interviews with my grandfather. Initially I wanted to know about his life and experiences, just to document them for our family. Yet as I dug deeper, I found that my grandfather survived history and hardship on an almost unimaginable scale. The vast lessons of his life drove me to write this story. Grandpa had always been a quiet stoic man of few words, but it seemed like his life story just became too large to be kept to himself or even within our family, at some point it had to be told.

Once I dug deep enough, I knew that I had to write it all down. So, I started half ass writing in 2003. By 2008, I started using my whole ass. My initial years on the project consisted of infrequent attempts to gather info and some irregular interviews. I would sit many times with Grandpa and Grandma at their kitchen table and just ask questions with a tape recorder running. Whatever happened with the story or the book, that didn't matter to some degree, because at the least I spent all that time with Grandpa and Grandma, just listening to them talk about their lives. So, over numerous cups of coffee, dozens of homemade pieces of peach cobbler, apple pie, coconut cream pie, homemade cookies, stews, chicken and dumplings, fried chicken, and buckets of fresh vegetables and home canned you name it, we talked about everything under the sun.

The very dated kitchen with its white Formica table spattered with powder blue spots and matching plastic place mats was our setting. It was very 70's in that kitchen. A fake brick wall to the back of the table housed a myriad of pictures and miscellaneous items – pictures of Jesus, Mary, post it notes, family pictures, and numerous awards my grandmother received for her civilian service to the US Air-Force. There was even a folded American flag in a glass case that once flew over the US Capital

Building and was given to my grandmother for all of her years of work at Scott Air-Force Base. All around and on almost every wall or surface there were pictures of family.

On each visit to my grandparent's home I learned a little more about their past as well as my own. I found that Louis J. Baczewski had lived a boyhood that is non-existent today. He lived far more freely than any young boy today: free to be a boy. We learned how to fish from him in our own crude way, because he was too poor to do anything else. He grew up in Pocahontas, Illinois, a jerkwater town, nicknamed, "Pokey." It was home to Shoal Creek, a coal mine, a few stores, farms, the basic stuff, and little else.

Initially, I didn't know much besides a few bits and pieces in relation to his life, the war, and in reference to what my grandfather had done and seen. Before I started the project, what I did know in short was this; Grandpa was a tank driver in five major campaigns who still carried his tank driver's license in his wallet even to the present day. He was one of only 18 men out of 152 in his company to make it through the war and home without a scratch. He was the only combat tank driver in his company to make it through the entire war – most of the 18 others were cooks, truck drivers, and general rear echelon. He lost a tank commander, a driver, and a lieutenant in his tank alone. He went through many replacements and saw the bulk of his entire company killed in the Battle of the Bulge. He received a Bronze Star for his combat record and was put in for a silver, but the officer who wrote him up died before he could complete the paperwork. He is proud of his service and loves his country but detests war and questions any person who blindly desires to go to it, or especially force others to do so. He had seen the face of war and the price it carried, and he spoke little of its horrors until later in his life.

Louis (Louch) was the youngest of three brothers. His oldest brother Joe ended up working as a US Army cook in California throughout the war. He became a chef in later life and a character to say the least. His other brother Ed was listed as having bad eyes and thus "unfit for the service." Louch on the other hand was drafted shortly after he had finished high school. Unlike many WWII vets, Grandpa was not in a rush to get drafted, he just waited until it happened. According to him, it was the general consensus of his town - just wait for the draft.

Louch said, "I was a senior in high school when Pearl Harbor got hit. I went to a show in Greenville and that was when they bombed Pearl Harbor – they announced it in the theatre; that was in forty-one." I asked if there was anybody from Pocahontas that signed up immediately after Pearl Harbor. He replied, "I think most of them was drafted." In all honesty, I was surprised by his response, given all of the patriotic fervor associated with the war. In so many documentaries and movies, it is shown that men swarmed to enlist - to volunteer. In Louch's reality, he and others in Pokey were too busy being poor to worry about how this global situation affected them. They set their minds to basic living and having known nothing else; they put their heads down and worked.

When he finished high school, Grandpa took a job in a small arms plant in St Louis. He and others carpooled all the way from Pocahontas to St Louis daily. They bounced their way down the rough roads to St Louis in a Model T Ford, each and every day for more than an hour in either direction. Because he worked in Missouri, he was eventually drafted in Missouri. Louis J. Baczewski was inducted into the service at Jefferson Barracks. He said, "They gave me a choice, they said 'you wanta go into the Navy, or you wanta go in the Armed forces,' [having never laid eyes on the ocean] I said, well I don't know, I'll just go into the Armed forces, I guess. And that's how I landed in Kentucky. It was February of 1943." It was there in Fort Knox Kentucky that he would receive his basic training and begin his training in the M4A1 Sherman. He joined the ranks of the 1st Army 3rd Armored Division, 33rd Armored Regiment, D Company. The 33rd would later become the major armored force in the 3rd Armored's Combat Command B. As part of the 33rd, Louch was trained as a Sherman tank driver. Early on into his training, he was told by one ordinance officer, "Whatever you do, don't leave that tank. Take care of that tank. That tank costs $60,000 and you are only worth 10,000 dollars." At the time, a GI's life insurance policy was only worth $10,000, so the officer told Louch and his tank crew, "That tank is more important than you are!" He never forgot the monetary distinction of his worth and it was a dark reality to face as he began his training.

Louch during training

Louch inside the Sherman during tank training

During basic training he went through all the ardors of calisthenics, road marches, and the standard PT (physical training). Yet as a tanker certain parts of each day were dedicated to training in the tank and on the tank equipment. Target practice was specialized to the weapons on the tank and then also to the personal weapons carried by the tankers. Each tanker was armed with a 45 caliber pistol or a Thompson submachine gun. Each crew member trained with both weapons. Grandpa even smiled as he recalled that, "Them Thompson machine guns was shaky, but they really spit out the rounds!!" The crew also trained to fire the 30 caliber and 50 caliber machine guns. Additionally a great deal of time was dedicated to understanding the operation and maintenance of the tank itself, the crew was responsible for all field maintenance, re-supply, and fueling task. To this day, Grandpa still remembers every last part on the tracks of the Sherman, to the exact amounts of lubricants needed in each and every reservoir.

I asked him if he ever had any trouble in basic training, with the regiment and discipline and so on. He replied, "I pretty much toed the line." It sounded to him as a bit of an odd question, and he didn't complain

31

about the discipline, or the orders, or any of the training in any way. He felt that it was just the way it was. When asked whether he ever had any problems with particular officers or non-coms, he couldn't think of anything major. He did however recall an incident that was more odd than anything. At Fort Knox, he was given the task of scrubbing the barracks floor, on his hands and knees. As he progressed his way across the floor, cleaning all along on all fours, he looked ahead to see a corporal standing with his arms crossed and his legs firmly set in his path. He turned back to the floor and scrubbed along the floor. Yet as time went on and he made his way across the floor, he kept looking noticing that the corporal was still a stationary fixture in his path. The corporal just stood there staring at him. So, he just kept scrubbing that floor until he made it up to a shiny pair of boots. His head and eyes rolled up from the floor following the shiny boots to a tightly pressed uniform. Eventually his gaze met with the corporal's. The corporal's head loomed over him painted with a condescending sneer. The corporal said nothing and just stared down at him. After an awkward pause, Private Baczewski looked him in the eye and said, "Hey bub, how about moving, ya know."

The corporal immediately yelled down at him in reply, "I hope you know that you don't call me bub, I'm acting corporal!!" Pvt Baczewski quickly returned, "yes sir!" He instantly realized that the corporal had just stood there for the hell of it, just to see what he would say. It was an early lesson in the role of rank, because as Grandpa stated, " I was just in the service ya know; I didn't know what the heck was going on."

While stationed in Fort Knox, Pvt Baczewski continued his training and received further in-depth instruction in tank tactics. He was given the job of assistant driver in the M4A1 tank. This tank and other M4 versions would later become known as the Sherman. It was the British

32

who first dubbed the M4A1 the Sherman after the American Civil War General William Tecumseh Sherman.[1] The British then as now, typically knowing more about American history than the American's themselves, could recall names from history, and thus labeled all the American manufactured tanks with historical US Generals, namely Grant, Stuart, and Sherman.

Louch sitting on an M4 Sherman

Pvt. Louis Baczewski - Ft Knox Kentucky, 1943

Unknown 33rd Regiment tank Crew, Pvt. Baczewski's photo collection.

The M4 was close to 20 feet long and stood about ten foot high at the top of the commander's hatch. Designed for fighting the early German Mark IV tanks, the Sherman possessed similar armaments, firepower, and maneuverability. The frontal armor was two inches; the back and side armor merely one and one-half inches, the base was only one inch thick, and only three quarters of an inch protected the top of the tank.[2] Such armor stood up like aluminum foil to the German anti-tank guns. If these shortcomings were not enough, the top speed of the Sherman stood at just around twenty-four miles per hour. Initially thought to be substantial, the Sherman's speed proved barely adequate.

The Sherman tank crew consisted of five men; a driver and assistant driver, a gunner and assistant gunner, and the tank commander. Each crew member wore a tanker helmet similar to an old style leather football helmet as well as tanker's coveralls. These crash helmets provided absolutely no protection from shrapnel or small arms fire. If their tank was knocked out and the men ended up fighting on the ground, they were poorly protected, and easily distinguished as tankers.

Each platoon consisted of around three tank crews of five tanks and each company at full strength had 17 tanks. These original tank crews were trained in every aspect of the tank from maintenance to the battle operations. Later in the war, when tank crews began to lose men at staggering rates, replacement tankers were sent up to the front lines with little or no training. In combat, it was difficult to keep any company with 17 tanks let alone tanks filled with experienced crewmen.

Unfortunately for Private Baczewski and so many other tankers, the perception that the US had the best equipment quickly eroded once combat began. The tank and tanker crew losses in the European theatre were staggering. The Sherman tank was, as Belton Cooper called it, a "death trap." In fact, Cooper felt so adamant about this issue that his own war memoir was indeed titled, *Death Traps, The Survival of an American Armored Division in World War II*. Cooper served as an ordinance officer in the 3rd Armored Division Combat Command B (CCB). He was charged with removing damaged tanks from the battlefield, repairing them, and returning them as quickly as possible to the front line. In his memoir, he discussed how the outgunned and outmatched Sherman sadly turned into a quick means to kill five men, when met with German AP (Armor Piercing) fire or other tanks. As the 3rd Armored, pressed on through France, Cooper was forced to remove more and more damaged tanks from the field. He was confronted with the daily task of removing the bodies of burned and obliterated men out of the hulls of mangled and burning Sherman tanks. When met with the German tanks and anti-tank guns the weak armor of the Sherman and low velocity of its main gun could not compete.

The lacking armor and firepower were accompanied by an additional shortcoming; the tank did not possess the ability to make a quick pivot turn. The Sherman could take as much as eighty feet to make a complete rotation. In a firefight, the inability to turn caused numerous casualties and knocked out tanks. The M4 also had difficulty in a variety of terrain. Lt Colonel Wilson M Hawkins of the 2nd Armored Division bemoaned, "it had been claimed that our tank is more maneuverable. In recent tests, we put a captured German Mark V (Panther) against all models of our own. The German tank was faster, both across country and on the highway and would make sharper turns. It was also a better hill climber"[3] Even the German's heavy tank, the Mark VI (Tiger) weighed almost twice what the Sherman did, at sixty-two tons, (The Sherman weighed thirty-three tons) yet the Tiger, had the same top speed of twenty-four miles per hour. Additionally, the Tiger carried a high velocity eighty-eight millimeter (88mm) cannon as well and vastly superior armor.

If the lack of armor, weaponry, and mobility were not enough, the fact that the tank ran on high octane gas added an additional nightmare. The Sherman's engine was originally designed for the aircraft industry and the high octane gasoline it required, both ignited easier and burned hotter, thus increasing the risks for the crew members.[4] If this were not enough, the two gas tanks holding ninety gallons of gasoline each, sat on both sides of the personnel compartment. Tankers who were forced to operate these mechanized Molotov cocktails gave them the name "Ronson Cans" after Ronson lighter fluid – "because they always lit on the first strike." Due to the thin armor, when the Sherman was hit sometimes shells both entered and exited the tank. If the shell passed through the tank, it typically killed only those crewmen in that path. However, if the shell ricocheted within the personnel compartment, the men inside would be completely destroyed and fire typically engulfed the tank simultaneously. If the crew members survived a hit, the smoke and debris filling the tank made escape difficult to impossible. Few Sherman tankers had the time to evacuate before the tank's many flammable materials ignited. Between the paint, seats, insulation, fuel, ammunition, and oil; the Sherman was a time bomb.

The decision to use the Sherman tank was a mistake which could have been avoided, but big egos and bureaucracy turned tank warfare into an unmitigated disaster. There was an American tank that could have been deployed which would have been far superior to any German tank. General Rose, later commander of the 3rd Armored was against using the Sherman and advocated for the M26 "Pershing." The M26 Pershing tank carried a 90mm cannon and had better armor, traction, and was overall a better vehicle. However, Patton and other commanders pushed for mass production of the Sherman due to their perceived wisdom of tank tactics. They insisted that the Sherman would require less fuel and would be faster than their German counterparts, thus allowing them the ability to quickly overrun the German Panzers. Tankers such as Pvt. Baczewski would soon find out how flawed this logic was as he and so many other tankers rolled into the firefight.

Burning 3rd AD Sherman (3ad.com)

After his initial training, Private Baczewski left Fort Knox for Camp Campbell. After a short spell at Camp Campbell, he and the 33rd Armored Regiment soldiers relocated to a few different bases. Eventually he and the rest of his outfit made their way to the New York Harbor. In New York City, he boarded the John Erickson, the ship which hauled himself and most of the 3rd Armored Division to England. There, the 3rd

received further training and awaited the invasion of "Fortress Europe."
As he loaded the Erickson, he and the other 3rd Armored Division soldiers
could see the statue of liberty off in the distance. It was a bold reminder
that they were soon leaving American shores. "I think there was about
7,000 people on there. We was like sardines on there, all down in the
hole," he recalled. The rocking ship combined with the tight confines and
tensions resulted in widespread nausea among his comrades. "Oh yea,
vomiting all over the place." According to him, down in the "bowels" of
ship, the soldiers yaked all over themselves and each other - it turned into
a contagious barf-a-thon, all across the Atlantic.

For Louch in general though, the trip was long and uneventful. He
and his company remained stuck deep down within the ship for the greater
part of the journey. Once he and the rest of the 3rd Armored Division
arrived in England, they trained and prepared for the amphibious assault
and forthcoming land battle. On the English Salisbury Plain, he and other
3rd Armored tankers trained in tank tactics. During their training, he found
it difficult to avoid hitting a few Englishmen. He complained that the
roads were narrow and driving on the "wrong side" was an adjustment.
The tight curvy country roads were tough to navigate in a car, much less in
a column of tanks. He and his company invariably smashed a few allied
cars in the process of their training. "Of course a lot of them was small
English cars and they'd get by you, but heck we had to run into a lot of
Englishmen with them tanks," he grinningly recalled. The common
statement that the Yanks were, "over sexed, over paid, and over here," was
more than likely an insufficient insult to any Englishman who not only had
those issues, but a crushed car as well – courtesy of a Yank tank.

3rd AD Tankers training on the Salisbury Plains England (3ad.com)

In England, tank tactics were practiced in the open, and the roads were used mostly as roads are – as a means to get from place to place. However, the tactics would prove horribly useless as soon as the 3rd Armored landed in Normandy. Ironically when Louch and the other tankers were forced to avoid English cars, this may well have been the only training for how they would actually fight in Normandy and throughout the bulk of the war. Even when some of the tank training could have been utilized, the entire system was dumped and ignored. The adoption of a new column formation was enforced and used without exception, even when a reversion to earlier training could have saved lives. There was no fluidity. It seemed as if the bulk of choices related to tank design, manufacturing, armaments, tactics, and battle planning was utterly flawed and unreasonably rigid. The Normandy terrain was mostly to blame for the initial issues with tank tactics, as the tanks could not fight abreast given the sunken roads and thick shrubbery surrounding each and every Normandy field. The lush green walls of hedgerow plant life, some reaching a height of six to eight feet, stood atop of an earthen grid work of deep roads carved by thousands of years of use. Such terrain proved impossible for coordinated tank tactics, as the tanks were forced to move in single file columns.

"Actually tank tactics was that you fought abreast. Ya had five tanks. Ya had all this firepower, that's the way you was trained to fight; five tanks abreast, and that's the way it was." Louch declared. "We tried that over in Normandy and the terrain ya know, [with] them hedgerow fields and everything. It was so slow, that they decided to just go down the roads. So they took a column of tanks and only the lead tank had the fire power."

Even despite their former training, the tank platoons would not break out of their columns even in the thick of combat. Louch lamented, "We just kept on the roads. You didn't spread out or nothing. The next tank just went around ya, and if he got knocked out, then the next tank went around ya. Like if you came to a hill you were supposed to just pull up there and take turret deflate - where just you could see the targets or something just over the hill, not the whole tank exposed. You laid to where you could see what was going on - that was tank tactics. We didn't fight that way in Europe, it didn't do us no good. When we was in England that's the way we trained in the Salisbury Plains. We was in England eight or nine months ya know, for maneuvers and everything and heck we didn't practice what we did in Europe, we practiced tank tactics."

Even though the men knew it would be helpful to spread out, their commanders kept them in column formation, no matter the case. Louch adamantly disagreed with the tactics and questioned the logic, "I don't know why, but they just didn't do that. They didn't spread out. They just kept there. If they ran into something and a tank got knocked out; they tried to get the infantry up there. Ya know, they got the ground guys up there to feel it out, reconnaissance, ya know. They had a reconnaissance platoon to with the infantry, so they sent them out to try to feel things out."

The 3rd Armored tankers learned very quickly that due to the strict column formation, the Germans merely had to train their guns (zero in) on any crossroads and wait. The ensuing jam up of vehicles and easily flanked tank groups turned immediately costly. Louch angrily lauded, "We, just lost a lot a tanks! The main thing, when one tank got knocked out there was two waiting, ya know. We replaced it right away, there was no waiting and that's why I think we kept going. Otherwise you try to fight maybe with one or two tanks in a platoon ya know, you wouldn't have much firepower."

Eisenhower overseeing 3rd AD tank maneuvers - England 1944 (3ad.com)

He and the rest of his comrades would soon find out how useless a great deal of their training was and how vulnerable their tanks were. They worked feverishly on preparing the tanks for the actual transport and landing. "Just before the invasion, we had to water proof our tank. We put a 6 foot stack on the exhaust," Louch remembered. "You had to caulk everything on the inside. They had a big pit dug, so you drove the tank in there. So, you made sure that you really water proofed that tank; cause they told us if that water comes in, your gone. You'll drown. Well, heck that took a couple of weeks."

In a letter sent to, "Soldiers, Sailors and Airmen of the Allied Expeditionary Force," Supreme Commander of the Allied Armed forces and future president Dwight D. Eisenhower wrote the following:

You are about to embark upon a Great Crusade, toward which we have striven these many months. The eyes of the world are upon you. The hopes and prayers of liberty—loving people everywhere march with you. In company with our brave Allies, and Brothers—in—arms on other fronts, you will bring about the destruction of the German war machine, the elimination of Nazi Tyranny over the oppressed people's of Europe, and the security for ourselves in a free world.

Your task will not be an easy one. Your enemy is well trained, well equipped and battle—hardened He will fight savagely.

43

But this is the year 1944! Much has happened since the Nazi triumphs of 1940–41. The United Nations have inflicted upon the Germans great defeats, in open battle, man–to–man. Our air offensive has seriously reduced their strength in the air and their capacity to wage war on the ground. Our Home Fronts have given us an overwhelming superiority in weapons and munitions of war, and placed at our disposal great reserves of trained fighting men. The tide has turned! The free men of the world are marching together to victory!

I have full confidence in your courage, devotion, to duty and skill in battle. We will accept nothing less than full Victory!

Good Luck! And let us all beseech the blessing of almighty god upon this great and noble undertaking.[5]

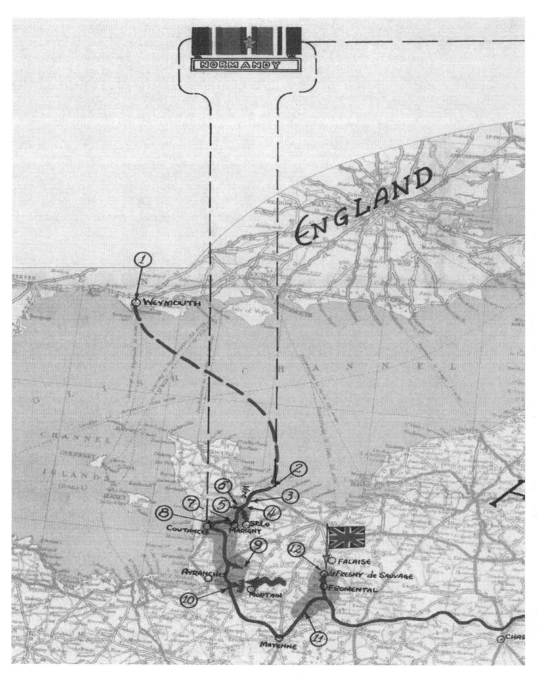

Detail of the Lovelady Taskforce Campaign Map – Normandy Campaign
(#1 of 5 Campaign Stars)

Chapter 3

"I wouldn't move this tank for you, or General Eisenhower!"

3rd Armored Division Sherman tanks disembarking on Omaha beachhead (3ad.com)

LOG BOOK OF THE SECOND BATTALION 2190−G
<u>201650</u> departed from Warminster, Wiltshire, and proceeded via Shaftsbury, Blanford, Dorchester and Weymouth to marshalling camp D−14, 3 miles west of Portland, arrived 2220, having covered 57.6 miles in 5 hours and 30 minutes. <u>21 June 44</u> Spent day waiting to load.

<u>22 June 44</u> 0400 Dq., H2, and "D" Co. proceeded to Portland naval base, a distance of 3 miles and at 1040 loaded onto U.S.S LCT 532. Left harbor at 2040 and proceeded to anchorage in Weymouth Bay. Set out for Omaha Beach at 2200 in convoy with numerous other craft.

<u>23 June 44</u> Arrived off Omaha Beach at 1100 and anchored. At 1230 weighed anchor and proceeded to "Fox Red" portion and beached itself to await low tides to disembark vehicles. Unloading started at 1740. 1820 arrived in transit area #5 approximately 4 miles south of Omaha Beach. 2205 Hq. and Hq. Co. and "D" Co. departed from transit area to assembly area and bivouacked at T502815.[6]

On June 23rd 1944, Pvt. Baczewski and his company rolled their tanks off an LST, Landing Ship, Tank. Their tracks sank into about four foot of water as they headed into the English Channel. D Company landed with relative ease, because of the efforts of so many American men, too many of whom paid the ultimate price. Seventeen days prior, the men of the initial invasion faced absolute hell to make this very foothold. On Omaha beach alone, tallies reached an estimated 2000 casualties, and somewhere between 2500 and 5000 Allied men died in the invasion of Normandy.

Despite the passage of many days, the front line fighting stood no further than a few thousand yards inland. Artillery could be heard in the distance. The initial attack stalled only a short distance away, and fears of a World War One like stalemate spread throughout the allied forces. By the time Pvt Baczewski arrived on Omaha Beach, he and his comrades faced only the logistical chaos of a makeshift port. Under the command of Sgt Cady, Louch's tank crew made its way into an endless foray of soldiers and machines. According to the account of Eaton Roberts, a surgeon in the 33rd Armored Regiment, the beach resembled a "beehive" of activity. Everywhere around, above, and before them mechanized activity raged about. The LST's (Landing Ship, Tank), LCT's (Landing Craft, Tank), and LCI's (Landing Craft, Infantry), that carried the massive loads of men and equipment were surrounded by DUKWS (amphibious vehicles) moving back and forth from the shore. On the beach, bulldozers paved out roadways for the innumerable infantrymen, jeeps, trucks, tanks, half-tracks, and self-propelled artillery pieces. Overhead massive barrage balloons and a constant cloud of air traffic carried on. While flying in all directions, massive and seemingly unceasing waves of C 47 transports passed above. Once off the beach, the columns of tanks and equipment made their way as MPs (Military Police) guided the mishmash of vehicles to their proper staging areas. All of the vehicles eventually made their home under gigantic camouflage nets, in order to hide them from German air attack.

Eaton Roberts described the country side as a mix of small fields, dairy farms, and orchards, all locked in with tall hedgerows on earthen fences; as he stated, "the terrain was impossible for tanks." So as they sat idly for fifteen days the 33rd Armored Regiment listened to the roar of fighting ahead of them and looked out onto the patchwork of jungle like land. Commanded by Colonel Dorrance Roysden, the 33rd made up the armored workhorse of Combat Command B, which served as one of two division combat commands. Unsure of what lay ahead, Roysden and his men sat on the side lines waiting and wondering. There on the bluffs above Omaha beach they reviewed their training and prepared their gear.

Each Sherman crewman knew that he had a job to do, and a specific spot to fill. Once mounted, the driver and assistant driver sat side by side behind the front hull and were separated by the transmission. The driver and assistant driver both had a hatch and a hatch mounted periscope above them. In the driver's area there sat an instrument panel to his upper left, a periscope in front, and the controls before his hands and at his feet. The assistant driver, sitting to the right of the driver had a 30 caliber ball mount machinegun to operate.

The other three tank crew members were called the "turret crew" which consisted of the following; the gunner, assistant gunner, and the tank commander. The gunner and assistant gunner operated the main cannon and fired various types of 75 millimeter shells along with the top mounted 30 or 50 caliber machine guns. Louch's tank crew lucked out by having a more powerful high velocity 76mm cannon on their Sherman, most crews had just 75mm guns.

As for the job of the tank commander, he could sit and command the tank from within, but, quite often he had to stick his head out of the turret. Visibility was limited when using the periscope and commanders could not easily see to their rear or flanks if they stayed in the turret. Because of this, good tank commanders were constantly exposed and therefore killed at staggering rates.

The commander could speak to his crew through a radio microphone. Each tanker had earphones and a microphone to communicate with each other and their company of tanks. If the tank was hit, the turret crew was forced to work their way out of the commander's hatch alone, while the driver and assistant driver each had their own hatches. Sadly, far too many turret crew members burned to death, because they only had one means of escape. Once in France, Private Baczewski would see this happen far too many times.

Each platoon of tanks was also supported by a nine man squad of infantry soldiers. The soldiers supporting Combat Command B (CCB) were part of the 36th Armored Infantry Regiment. These soldiers had the difficult job of scouting out ambushes and targets while also protecting the tanks from enemy infantry. When in combat, these men would follow the tanks or work ahead of the tanks on the ground. When the fighting died down, and the tanks were set to push toward a different location, the infantry squadrons would then mount up on the tanks and ride. However, in the hedgerows there were few occasions of this; for the infantry support in Normandy, fighting was bitter, field to field, and sometimes hand to hand. The job of armored infantryman was at times far more dangerous than the job of the tankers themselves. Louch witnessed all of his infantry support utterly destroyed on various occasions throughout the war. Years later when I asked Louch if he felt that it would have been safer outside of the tank, he looked at me quite befuddled and adamantly replied, "No!" Despite all of the Sherman's issues, Louch never wished to be in the infantry; he watched far too many of them meet their end through his periscope.

Louch and his tank crew

The 33rd Armored Regiment, Combat Command B (CCB) would begin fighting once they crossed the Vire River in Normandy. The 33rd made up roughly half of the 3rd Armored Division and part of the US VII Corps of 1st Army. They would not stop fighting until a relatively small group of original tankers, along with many replacements reached the Mulde River in Central Germany, some ten bloody months later. Men of the 33rd were lucky to get out of the hedgerows, much less make it all the way to the Mulde.

On July 8th, deployment orders arrived in the evening and the division's once stationary and still bivouac turned into a blaze of movement. Colonel Roysden summoned the officers to the Command Post (CP) and informed them of their mission. After the briefing, Captain Stallings made his way under the camouflage tents and back to inform his men. Captain Stallings, D Company's Commanding Officer (CO), called his tank crews together. He made a speech that Lou Baczewski never forgot. Stallings informed them that from this point on, "All of them were moving out, but a lot of them were not coming back." As he stated this warning, little did he know how right he was. Out of the 152 men he commanded in D Company, only 18 would be left at the end of the war. "We went to an area where they briefed us on everything before we went into combat." Louch recalled. "They briefed us on what we had to do and where we was going. They already knew what German outfits were there from reconnaissance. They briefed us there, then from there, we took off and we fought all the way from there into Germany."

Watches were synchronized and commanders told to move out at 1930. Hundreds of tanks fired up, crews loaded up, and infantry support clamored into formation. In the darkness Lou and his tank crew began their bloody mission. The massive columns formed around them and the taskforce now fully assembled crossed the Vire River Bridge. Almost immediately the column halted as artillery broke the silence and tore at the roads and hedges before them.

The dense foliage and cleverly placed German defenses proved immediately horrible for the green American tankers. It was next to impossible to determine who held which field. Farm to farm and dense hedge to hedge, each square of land was as much in German hands as Allied. The hellish shriek of artillery and the burning flesh and machinery soon engulfed the men and machines. For the first time, the men of the 33rd heard the screams of wounded men, watched their friends fall about them, saw their tanks burn amongst the shrubs and heavy underbrush. The lead in the air scattered its specks and balls of light amidst the darkness. Tanks and men appeared and then disappeared in the flash of the guns. The only consistent light to be found roared from the burning hulks of tanks and the fiery remains of homes and buildings in the nearby city of Aire. Some tank companies took heavy casualties the first night, while others found themselves victorious without even knowing why. Disorder and confusion reigned.

In their first night of hedgerow combat, D Company knocked out five Mark IV tanks before dawn, while only losing one tank of their own. Despite this seemingly easy and quite successful entrance into combat, Louch recalls the incident with a very sobering sensibility: "Yep that was the first day, we got one tank knocked out. That was our first encounter. We fought all night. Our gunner, every place he saw a flash, that's where he fired his gun. We was green, we didn't know what was going on. On that first night of combat, I thought I am never gonna make it back to the states, I was gonna die there. I was certain I wasn't gonna live through it, after seeing that first night. The most amazing thing was that I survived."

On that first night every crew member was jumpy, and so new to the chaos of war, that even tank commanders like Cady seemed unable to know what to do. Luckily their first engagement involved a tangle with Mark IV tanks, which were in-fact the type of tanks that the M4 Sherman was designed to fight. It would be one of the few times during the war that the odds were stacked in D Company's favor. Mark IV tanks represented 1939 technology, yet German engineers had learned a great deal since then. By 1944, the Sherman was basically the sad equivalent of a mechanized jello-mold in comparison to the German's newly designed Mark V and Mark VI tanks.

3rd AD Sherman passing a destroyed German Mark IV tank (3ad.com)

The first night offered no indication of what was to come. The German's, knowing that the terrain would necessitate the use of the roads, and aided by the confinement of the hedges, zeroed their guns in at any possible crossroads, camouflaged their equipment, and waited to ambush. They used every possible hedge as a temporary fortification and slowed the allied advance to a crawl. Only by sacrificing greater numbers of tanks and men did the 3rd Armored grind its way through the hedges. Historian Richard Tregaskis concluded that, "The thing that hurt American boys used to the idea of superior U.S. technology was finding out that German Panzers could only be defeated by superior numbers of tanks."

In addition to the problems with the Sherman's themselves, the natural barriers of the hedges presented a constant horror for the division. While flying over Normandy, aerial reconnaissance could see that hedges aligned almost every road in a tight grid work, but prior to the invasion, what they did not know was that these hedges were in many cases up to ten feet tall. The perspective point of the planes didn't allow for this understanding and when the initial attack forces arrived, they soon found themselves stuck in a World War One like setting. The earth and plants themselves had created a series of trench like systems and easily fortified positions, which the German army took to their full advantage. Attacks and counterattacks rolled in and out on both sides accomplishing little, but taking a field here and there. It was a bitter reminder of the useless carnage of the Great War.

In order to confront the problem, the 3rd Armored Engineers came up with a multi-bladed "hedge-chopper" and welded it on the front of certain tanks. Strangely no one had the forethought to consider this prior to the invasion. Even with the hedge chopper however, the Sherman was still busting a hole in the hedges, just to get a hole busted in the tank. The limited armor and the lack of distributed hedge-choppers made more problems, as the welding crews could not keep up with demand. Each tank that made it through a hedge opened itself up to antitank guns and other tanks. The tank platoons still could not support each other, due to the dense foliage and earthen dams along the roads. The hedgerows presented one big damn mess, and the casualties certainly showed how poorly we had been prepared for the terrain.

Louch's tank in hedgerow country (Lou Baczewski's personal photo)

M4 Sherman with hedgechopper attachment (3ad.com)

"One tank had to have that [the hedge-chopper], just one tank, and he busted a hole… The lead tank, he'd bust a hole through there and then back out and then the tanks would go through that hole and do the firing." Baczewski explained, "Them their fields, they had these hedgerows, just

56

like a dam all around these fields and you couldn't see what was on the other side. They was all growed up all around that field… You couldn't see what was in the next field, there might have been an 88 sticking in that next field to knock you out. Hell, couple times that tank busted a hole and backed out, and the next tank went in and Whamo!!! Ya know, he got knocked out. They had to make another hole, so that the other tanks could get the firepower, but that was bad. All of our firepower was with one tank. Five tanks in a platoon, but they couldn't help you a bit."

While advancing towards St Jean-du-Daye, 33rd moved slowly – incurring many casualties and paying heavily for every inch of ground. On July 11th D company's commander himself, Captain Stallings, lost his tank in a fire fight, played dead to avoid capture and made his way back to American lines only after dark. D Company, the 33rd Armored Regiment, and the bulk of the Division was getting pummeled. They were neither prepared for the horrible terrain, nor the skill and armaments of their German enemy.

They had trained to fight five tanks abreast and with five tank commanders searching for targets and supporting the others with fire. Yet in the hedgerows only one tank was able to fire, acquire targets, and determine where enemy fire was coming from. It was one tank and one tank alone. This Sherman rode at the head of a lumbering column and it took the responsibility and fire for the whole company at once. It was a horrible task and the duty was rotated amongst the tank crews. Those tanks that survived the day would rotate back and forth as lead tank.

"Like my tank took the lead one day and if I didn't get knocked out, then the next day, the next tank in the platoon took the lead. And then every day, if you were the front tank you'd take the chance of getting killed. We got hit a couple of times, but no damage." Louch gratefully recalled. Throughout the war, Louch was immeasurably lucky, as he was only forced to bail out of his tank once, because his crew thought the tank was penetrated. The great majority of Sherman tankers did not share his fortune. By war's end, Lou Baczewski was the only tanker in his company out of the few remaining original crewmen who could make this claim.

On July 11th, The German Panzer Lehr Division launched a counterattack attempting to split the American First Army, which included the 3rd Armored Division and D Company of the 33rd Armored Regiment. The German assault forces were composed of mixed armored groups possessing Mark IV tanks, Panthers, and massive heavily armored Jadpanther tanks which were supported by elite German paratroopers. If accomplished, the attack would have cut off 7th Corps of the First Army; the First Army would have been pushed back onto the Omaha beachhead.[7]

As early as the 16th of July and as tank losses mounted due to the German counterattack, the After Combat Report for the 33rd Armored Regiment listed twenty-four tanks totally destroyed by enemy gunfire, many from bazooka or "panzerfaust" fire. The panzerfaust could easily knock out a Sherman and despite attempts to bolster the armor with extra plate, sandbags, etc, the Germans could wipe out Shermans with little effort. The impact of the panzerfaust many times caused the men in the tank to literally explode from the concussion. Cleaning crews from the 3rd Armored retrieval squadrons faced a morbid task of cleaning out the river of blood and body parts strewn about the tanks after each panzerfaust hit. These tanks were washed out, the body parts were sorted in an attempt to keep the tanker's remains together, the impact holes were welded shut, the insides of the tank were repainted, and the tank returned to the front. Once the repaired tanks made their way back into the battle, the tanker crews loaded themselves into these mechanical tombs and pushed on.

German tank knocked out by the 3rd AD – courtesy of University of Illinois Archives

German Soldier holding a Panzerfaust – courtesy of University of Illinois Archives

A few days into the fight in France, Louch's tank crew faced an attack from a Panzerfaust and consequently lost a man. The column lumbered down a sunken road. D Company stalled once artillery and small arms raked the tanks and sent the infantry into action. Louch's tank could not move, it was stuck between two others and locked in on both sides by the hedges, which were erupting German fire. A panzerfaust round roared out of the brush and struck Louch's tank. "Yea, we got hit by a bazooka and a big flash came off, and my tank commander [Sgt. Cady] thought that we was hit and penetrated, and he said, 'bail out!' And ya know we was green in combat. We was green and jumpy, and scared, and you name it."

They bailed out in a panic. When they climbed out, they were immediately surrounded by small arms fire. Rounds bounced off the tank around them. They quickly ran to shelter behind the thick shrubs and earthen wall of a hedge. They were crouched down and unable to determine where the fire was coming from. The driver, Ingert, took a hit as he huddled right next to Pvt. Baczewski. A sniper round ripped through his skull and he fell dead next to his crewmates. Eventually, the fire died down. Cady's tank crew and infantry support made their way back to the American lines. When maintenance eventually retrieved the tank, they quickly determined that the tank hull was completely sound. No penetration occurred. They had bailed out needlessly. The flash from the panzerfaust scared Cady into thinking that the tank had been compromised, and about to burn.

As soon as maintenance made a report, Captain Stallings quickly addressed Cady and his crew, he asked, "Well, how come you guys bailed out.' Sgt Cady replied, 'Well captain, there was a flash from that bazooka, and I thought we was hit. I thought we was penetrated, and I just give the command to bail out." Baczewski remembered quite clearly how the whole crew felt when they abandoned the tank, "You know I mean we was green and scared. Ya know, we was scared to death. Hell, they had to understand that, cause everybody was on edge. You know after a while ya figure if you are gonna get hit, you are gonna get hit. Heck you are probably gonna get hit anyway. But then the first week or so you are in combat, there's guys getting killed, there's tanks getting knocked out, you wonder when your next. That's why we bailed out. We'd been in combat for about two weeks I guess."

The carnage witnessed each day by D Company was not isolated, the division as a whole was getting its ass handed to it. Between the 8th and the 16th of July, the 33rd Armored Regiment had lost twenty-four tanks on their own, but the 3rd Armored Division as a whole, lost eighty-seven tanks and this number did not include those that had been repaired and put back into the field.[8] Eight days into combat, the division had lost eighty-seven tanks - all of which were totally destroyed! More than ten tanks per day were knocked out in an effort to take roughly five miles of Normandy terrain. It was no wonder that tankers were jumpy.

The 3rd Armored suffered such losses during those early days of the war, that the Supreme Allied Commander, Eisenhower himself, was forced to change the leadership of the division. The 3rd had been under the command of General Leroy H. Watson, throughout the initial days of fighting. No doubt the men of the 3rd Armored were green to combat, but his command had not helped lessen the impact through wise tactical decision making. According to Tregaskis, "The Division's erratic moves and tentative maneuverings had been costly in casualties – something was wrong. Eisenhower, appraised the situation...[and] made his decision relieving Leroy Watson of command – who was reportedly cracking under the pressure."

On August 7th Major General Maurice Rose, former chief of staff for the 2nd Armored in Africa under Patton, assumed command of the 3rd Armored Division. Little to nothing is said about this man in history, but

Rose was considered an exceptionally able commander and tank tactician. Rose was the son and grandson of rabbis and was at the time the highest ranking person of Jewish origin in the US Army. He was an able leader and arguably one of the greatest generals of the war, but due to his modesty, and desire to stay out of the lime light, (unlike Patton) he never received the true credit due to him.

Many historians maintain that his tactical abilities surpassed Patton's by far. In fact, Rose had argued against Patton's choice of the Sherman, after leading a combat command of Sherman's against the panzers in Africa. Rose was adamant that the Pershing should be chosen as the main battle tank of the US Army rather than the Sherman.[9] However, such efforts were overridden by Patton's insistence, thus saddling divisions like the 3rd Armored with a substandard weapon. By the end of the war, The 3rd Armored Division alone had a tank loss rate of 580%. In other words, the division lost so many tanks that each and every one of the 232 tanks possessed by the division at full strength were replaced more than five times throughout the course of the war.[10]

Even despite the change in command, the Sherman crews certainly had plenty to fear as they pushed on through France. If it was not infantry with panzerfausts, often the tanks would face towed or self-propelled anti-tank guns set in place to thwart any advance. The most feared weapon that the German's possessed was the 88 mm cannon commonly referred to as the "the 88" which served as an anti-tank, anti-personnel, and anti-aircraft gun. The German "88" was a highly versatile and deadly weapon. According to Louch, "That 88, it was just something else. I seen several tanks where it went through one side and out the other – it had a great velocity." The comparably thin armor of the Sherman was no match for the speed and armor penetration of the 88mm cannon. Tankers lived in constant fear of this weapon. Although the German Panther tank did not possess an 88mm, it did have a 76mm high velocity cannon, which could also easily penetrate Sherman armor. The German Tiger tank not only had more armor, but it also possessed an 88 mm cannon.

Major General Maurice Rose (3ad.com)

Depending on the way the Sherman was penetrated when hit by an 88 or other German gun, the crew might not have a chance at all. The odds were not in the favor of the crew. Louch watched many tanks take hits from German fire. He recalled that when a Sherman was hit, "Well, the majority of the time they burst into flames, just about instantaneously.

I had several tanks knocked out in front of me and they just burst into flames. Ya got 90 gallon of gasoline on each side, and ya got 80 or 90 rounds of big ammunition inside. Well, you're bound to not get a chance - not get a chance to get out. Very seldom would all of them get out. Yea, it would explode or catch on fire. Some of them would get out of the tank, and some others they couldn't get out."

As tank losses mounted in the 3rd Armored Division General Eisenhower demanded to know why so many 3rd Armored tanks were still being destroyed even after Rose had taken command. This question was best answered by a letter in response to Eisenhower, written by General Maurice Rose. The letter included the following statement from a 3rd Armored tank gunner, "General, in order to knock out a German tank, I've got to get within 600 yards and catch him on the flank. They can knock me out at 2000 yards dead on."[11] According to Private Baczewski and most historians, the only way the American armor was able to keep up was because of the shear amount of tanks it could deploy, the effective distribution of supplies, and the support of the Air-force. As he stated, "If we had one tank knocked out, they had two or three waiting, see they replaced them right away. Ya didn't have to wait ya know. But the Germans they got one knocked out - they was out, cause them factories wasn't working. That's what kept us going was plenty of supplies." The ability of maintenance crews to repair tanks and get them back into the field in a short time proved astonishing. The German's had nothing to rival the mechanical prowess of the American retrieval and repair crews.

Louch recalled with pride that, "the Air Force was also very helpful to us. The P51 fighter planes, they done a lot of bombing runs and strafing ahead of us. Like when you hit a crossroads or something and you was stalled, well then they called them P51's and P 38's… They'd call the

Air Force and they'd come in and bomb that target." The Air Force actually had a tank that would accompany 33rd Armored tank groups; this tank was equipped with special radio equipment and Air-force personnel, who had direct contact with P47, P38, and P51 fighter bombers. They would guide the pilots in to attack German tanks and gun emplacements.

German 88mm cannon captured by the 3rd Armored - Courtesy of University of Illinois Archives

German Tiger Tank (Mark VI) captured by the 3rd Armored - courtesy of University of Illinois Archives

German Panther Tank (Mark V) (3ad.com)

Destroyed Sherman (3ad.com)

As Louch stated, the Air Force support proved itself to be deadly accurate. Tankers like Louch considered them a heaven sent, "One time we got stopped by a hedgerow, and in the next field there was either a Mark V (Panther) or a Tiger. They were real close to us cause we was in one field and they [the Germans] was in the next one, and so they called for the Air Force and the P 51's came in and bombed that. And it just threw shrapnel on our tank. One of our colonel's, Colonel Roysden, was there right there by our tank."

Roysden, regimental commander, crouched down beside Sgt. Cady's tank as the P51 rolled in overhead. The target stood no more than thirty yards in front of their position. So as the bomber roared over them, they all began to fear that the P51 might mistakenly strike their tank instead. When the plane dropped the bomb, the angle of its decent seemed to be headed straight for them. As Louch proclaimed, "it was so close in fact, we thought he was gonna bomb us!" Shrapnel, dirt, and debris showered the tanks and the infantry. Black smoke quickly rose from the hulk of the destroyed German tank. The intensity of the explosion rocked the ground around them. Sgt. Cady who seemed unfettered, still stood with his head out of the turret and exclaimed, "Well, looks like they got him!' Roysden, climbed to his feet aside the tank, dusted himself off, and loudly groaned, "yea, but it is just too goddamn close, it's just too goddamn close!!!"

Colonel Roysden as Lou saw it, was a great combat commander and was always commanding in the thick of the fight, unlike The 33rd Armored's later Commanding Officer (CO) Colonel William Lovelady. Initially Roysden's men felt that he was soft, given his prim and proper appearance. This facade drastically changed however as he fought alongside his men in Normandy. Roysden suffered though the same combat and deprivations, day by day. In a short time, Roysden's once dandy façade was now filthy, disheveled, and unshaven. He could barely be distinguished from the lowliest infantry soldier fighting at his side.

"He was a good Colonel," Lou remarked, "he was right up front the biggest part of the time, he was quite a guy that Roysden." In fact, Roysden won acclaim after leading his taskforce on an attack on Haut Vents, helping holding back the elite SS Panzer Lehr Division. In a bloody firefight Roysden and his taskforce pushed back the battle hardened Panzer Lehr on the infamous Hill 91. Col. Lovelady later remembered that Roysden's actions at hill 91 astounded him. Roysden's courage and leadership reminded Lovelady of Teddy Roosevelt's famous charge up

San Juan Hill. With his tommy-gun waving, Roysden led the 33rd to victory at Hauts Vents and against one of Hitler's most feared divisions.

Louch recalled that Roysden was aggressive, but also an officer who bent the rules when he thought it might save lives. He was an outspoken critic of bad command decisions, and because of it he paid the price. Despite the respect his soldiers possessed for him, accusations arose that he continually failed to follow orders and push his men adequately. Consequently, division command removed Roysden from his position. Colonel Boudinot, then commander of Combat Command B, felt that Roysden hesitated when his taskforce battled a group of Germans dug in along a sunken railroad embankment. The incident occurred soon after General Rose took command of the division.

Roysden and the 33rd faced stiff resistance and had little means to push through. While Boudinot, who sat comfortably to the rear, radioed Roysden repeatedly to push forward and stated, "there is nothing in front of you but a thin line." Roysden returned, "it may be thin but its damn tough!"[12] Boudinot became immediately angry with Roysden's retort and perceived it to be an additional sign of ineffectiveness. As such, Colonel Boudinot reported the incident to General Rose, who having just taken command, more than likely chose to make a show of Roysden. Based entirely upon Colonel Boudinot's contention, Rose decided to remove Roysden from command. Colonel Dorrance Roysden now stripped of command, forcibly took a position at Supreme Headquarters Allied Expeditionary Forces (SHAEF). There, he served as a staff officer for the remainder of the war.

Louch understood that good commanders were scarce and many poor decisions on the part of the regimental and division command added to the already horrendous conditions faced by the taskforce's tank crews.

The 33rd Armored's command soon fell into the hands of Colonel William (Bill) Lovelady. Lovelady was just as much a stranger to the front as Boudinot. His taskforce (The Lovelady Taskforce) would push on through to Germany, and eventually take credit for all of Roysden's accomplishments up to August of 44. Lovelady was much less respected, and proved to be terribly scarce when the 33rd faced its worst combat. He was no Colonel Roysden.

Colonel Dorrance Roysden (3ad.com)

Despite some poor judgment, it must be said that there were capable and in some cases exceptional leaders in the 3rd Armored Division. In general, orders were rendered with exactness, respect, and without question. Subordinates held the highest regard for officers such as Colonel Roysden, and Captain Stallings. They were the kind of commanders who led from the front; they faced the same dangers as their men, day in and day out. They weighed their decisions on the real costs, in lives, as they were always with their men and trying to survive in the same storm of metal.

Yet orders given by some of the more inept immediate officers were not always followed to the letter when in combat. Even in the hedgerows, there were points of dissent. According to Grandpa, not all foolish commands were followed, and sometimes they were outright disobeyed. Such an act would have cost a man his stripes or initiated a court-martial, but as he stated, "When in combat, we didn't take nothing off of them officers."

"One time [while in the hedgerows] my tank commander, we came to a crossroads, ya know. My tank commander, he wanted to feel that out at the crossroads, cause it's usually zeroed in, or they had guns dug in most of the time. We was the lead tank. We stopped. He figured there was something dug in and we had the infantry with us. So, my tank commander told the infantry guys to scout up and see if there was any gun emplacement…" Cady sent out scouts to assess the situation because he had no intelligence as to what lay ahead and he knew all too well that the German's would target their guns on any crossroads. As they waited for the infantry to make a report, a jeep quickly pulled up aside their tank and screeched to a halt. Inside the jeep was a Major, Major Crosby, and he was particularly bothered by the now frozen column of vehicles before him. He stood up in the jeep, and quickly yelled at the commander of the lead tank, "Sergeant Cady, let's get moving, you got the whole column stopped up!! There ain't nothing up there, let's get going!!"

**Tank Commander Sgt. Joe Cady (left) and Lou Baczewski (right)
taken near St Lo. 1944**

Cady shook his head and replied, "There ain't nothing up there huh?" Crosby resented his insolence and he quickly became irate. He hollered again and assured Cady that there was nothing ahead of his tank. He blasted Cady, and screamed that the whole column was locked up due to Cady's order to send up infantry scouts. Cady grinned and replied to the major's prodding, "If you say there ain't nothing up there, then get your ass up there (he pointed to his tank) and we'll go. Get your ass up here on top, mount the infantry up and get your ass up here on this tank. If there ain't nothing up there then you can ride up here with us!"

Louch watched as the major quickly changed his tone of voice and demeanor. He shyly remarked, "Well, Sergeant Cady now don't be talking like that.' Cady replied, 'If there ain't nothing up there buddy then get your ass up here Major and we'll go. We'll take off!" Crosby quickly backed down from the argument. He reluctantly sat down in his jeep, and awaited the infantry scouts return. Soon afterwards, the infantrymen worked their way back and reported to Sgt. Cady. They had snuck in close

72

to the crossroads and discovered a fortified German position containing two 88mm guns. The Germans were dug in and waiting for the column to advance. If they had followed Crosby's orders they would have almost certainly lost their tank and more than likely been killed. Once the report came in however, the order came in to hold position and the colonel called for air support. Soon after, the P51's came rolling in and dropped their payload on anti-tank position. So as the smoke rolled out of the German fortification, the taskforce mounted up and pressed on.

In the harsh battle for the hedgerows, Cady was certainly not the only lead tanker to confront a commanding officer over an order to push forward. Baczewski recalled that, "In Sergeant Martin's tank, the driver got battle fatigue. You know, he started crying. He broke down. So, the captain called up and said, 'Sgt. Martin, get moving." Martin's tank was in the lead on that particular day and the entire column was held up due to the traumatized driver. Repeated calls came over the radio to Sgt. Martin commanding him to move. Before long, radio traffic went up the chain-of-command to Colonel Lovelady. Along the narrow French road, the entire taskforce sat idle.

Martin, hollered into the radio, "I've got a driver that's gone bad!" The colonel called and said, "I don't care what you have. Move!!!" Martin knowing full well that he was addressing the colonel himself exclaimed, "I wouldn't move this damn tank for you or General Eisenhower without a driver. I don't give a damn if you were Ike himself." Soon afterwards the colonel ordered the crew in the next tank to push around Martin's tank and take the lead. The whole column pushed past Sgt. Martin's crew. Louch remembered with astonishment that Martin received no disciplinary action after his refusal of the order, he said, "And ya know he never did get anything out of that, and he told them all!

Chapter 4
"Blue cats was mean"

"There are certain villages and towns, mountains and plains that, having seen them, walked in them, lived in them, even for a day, we keep forever in the mind's eye. They become indispensable to our well-being; they define us, and we say, I am who I am because I have been there. It is here that I can concentrate my mind upon the Remembered Earth. It is here that I am most conscious of being, here that wonder comes upon my blood, here I want to live forever; and it is no matter that I must die."
M. Scott Momaday

In the summer, the smells and sounds always take me back there. I think of it often. There in the late evening as the dark gathers, a small amount of anticipation and apprehension grows. The familiar sounds of the insects and frogs resound. The pinkish purple hues recede as the deep black abyss begins to take hold. On a moonless night only vague shapes in close proximity can be discerned. The warm glow of the fire or the lantern provides light around camp, but their reach is mere yards and beyond the warmth of the campfire, and the glow of the lantern, the deep dark engulfs us on all sides. The fire, if not tended with vigilance, will die down to mere sparkles of coals. Much the same, the lantern gas and mantles burn out unless tended and restored. And the dark waits.

It was always difficult to bring oneself to step away from a warm bright fire just to set out in the dark with just the mere chance of catching fish. The tough part was the knowledge that cold wet clothes and shoes full of sand awaited. The water even in August was cold to wade through, and there is no man alive that could hit waist deep water and not frantically gasp for air, even on a hot night. Upon every gleaming flashlight beam, swarms of bugs charged at us like Pickett's men. At times they would even envelope your face, especially with a head lamp on. You felt like a bee keeper without an outfit. Inevitably, the smallest bugs would shoot down your throat and up your nose, forcing you to snort and snarl like a water buffalo. In retrospect, late at night, there really wasn't anything worth going out there for, at least not for most people. But having seen at an early age the sight of a bankpole bobbing and dipping with the heaves of a fish, it tends to stick with someone. It is enough to draw even a slightly rational man away from the warm comforts of camp.

When Grandpa was a boy he, his brothers Ed and Joe, and friends; Dave Pagan, John Hustava, Stanley Cravens, Mel Weber, and Bill Kalous would spend perhaps a week or so fishing the creek. They would load down a two wheel cart with a live box, minnow seine, premade lines, pots and pans, bacon, flour, corn meal, bed rolls, 22 rifles, and whatever else they could fit. They would walk miles to a fishing spot. Once there, they would fish and hunt for days and days. They lived off the land and the creek. They never had a boat. My dad said that even up until his late 20's, that they still didn't have a boat, and they would walk the lines from the bank. Which if you have ever seen the steep clay banks of Shoal creek, you might ask how in the hell did they do did that? Well, it was a pain in the ass. I know. I have done it a few times. The tough part was that you would have to set your poles and run your lines and disturb the water as little as possible, which basically amounts to an act of redneck acrobatics. The best holes were next to steep cut clay banks or root wads, or monstrous log jams. I can't imagine how hard it was trying to climb around on a log jam while holding a lantern and land a 10 pound flathead without a net. Sometimes Grandpa and his friends would wear carbide miner's lamps to help them run the lines and keep their hands free to climb around the logs or steep banks. They would borrow the lamps from their fathers who worked in the Pocahontas coal mine.

Having little money for such trips, Grandpa and his friends would buy just a few cigarettes and bullets. Grandpa said, "they use to sell em loose. You could buy one bullet or one cigarette. Gun shells was three cents apiece, and cigarettes was three cents apiece." This was a lucky break for them, for Louch and his brothers and friends would only have a few cents between three or four boys. Even at the age of 12 or so, Louch and his friends could enjoy fishing, hogging logs, hunting squirrels, and basically living off the creek. They would raid local farmer's tomatoes, peppers, and corn, and cook up Grandpa's brand of goulash. He taught me how to make it one day when I was visiting, but that time he didn't steal the ingredients, and had long since quit stealing for both moral and practical reasons. On this occasion he just grabbed the ingredients from his vast garden.

He told me that sometimes he and his buddies Dave, John, and Stanley would sneak onto a farmers land and steal a chicken or two. Dave was good with a sling shot, and he was known to have shot down many a chicken. They would pluck it and fry it, right out there on the creek bank. They would cover the chicken in clay and bake it on the coals of the fire. Then they would break away the clay so that the feathers came off easily. They then fried it in some breading and bacon grease. Between Louch catching fish, and Dave snatching a chicken here and there, they always ate well on the creek.

Dave Pagan was famous not only for his chicken snatching skills, but also for being hard of hearing - even at an early age. Grandpa said that one time while fishing, he and his buddies asked Dave something about the live box (the handmade box they kept their fish in) and Dave thought they said that, "a squirrel ran up the bank with a live box on his back." Grandpa said, "Everybody started laughing, and I don't know how he got that outta what we said. Well, he was always like that. He was always hard of hearing. I don't know how he got in the service. He was in a field artillery outfit!"

Out of all the friends Louch fished the creek with, almost every one ended up fighting in the war - notably Dave Pagan, John Hustava, Stanley Cravens, and Mel Weber. Dave Pagan would later serve as an artilleryman, Stanley Cravens took the role of combat engineer, Mel Weber supported armored units as an armored infantryman, while John Hustava volunteered and became a parachute infantryman. Only one friend, Bill Kalous, ended up in the Navy, while all the rest strangely ended up in Europe serving in the US 1st Army. Even as these boys ran through the woods around Pocahontas Illinois and swam through the muddy water of Shoal Creek, a war was brewing in Europe. Little did they know what stood in their future. Yet war was something far from their concerns, as Grandpa and his friends just lived off of what they could, and made the best of their humble lives.

For Louch, "the best of it" was fishing the creek. It was during this boyhood time before the war, that Louch made a science out of fishing the Shoal. He fished with his friends and brothers for days on end, polishing his skills. I have never met anyone who could "read the water" like he could, as there were any number of factors that affected the placement of a bankline. He learned and studied the fishing subtleties of the creek as if it were a trade. He taught it to his sons and Grandsons as if it were an apprenticeship. Only a journeyman placed the poles, baited the lines, and netted the fish. Only a journeyman would man the bow of the boat.

Apprentices were there to assist. It took me many years before my grandfather, dad, or uncles felt that I had the adequate knowledge to man the bow. I felt as if it was an honorable rite of passage and I still hold my apprenticeship and eventual passage to journeyman sacred.

Some of Louch's friends from Pokey, standing on the Shoal Creek Bridge, circa 1939. (front) John Hustava, (middle, left to right) Louie Sandretto, Julius Weshinski, and Dave Pagan, (back) Stanley Cravens

The placement of the poles was not simple, and Grandpa growing up would even compete with his friends over who could do it the best. Other factors were always in play, but Grandpa always caught the most fish when he set the poles. There were many variables and considerations, and as with anything, experience was the best teacher. Then as now, you had to get out and check the depth, the change in depth, and the brush. Grandpa found that it was best to swim around the holes and through the log jams and test everything out many days prior to actually fishing, so as not to disturb the fish.

Even if your sets were good, and baited well, a bright or full moon would destroy or dampen any chance to get a good haul of fish. Weather and water level were always obvious factors as well. If the creek rose at a slow and steady rate and all the other cards were in place, you would have the best odds. On the contrary, if the water was going down, slowly or quickly, you were certain to do poorly. If the water came up too quickly after or during a storm, you might risk losing all of your gear and catching no fish on top of it. The odds for all these elements being correct were against us on every trip, but as Grandpa had always said, "it's all about persistence."

Then there were the differentials of depth, current, and cover, which in general dictated the types of catfish that could be caught depending on the setup and bait. The sleek grey channel cats prefer water with a bit of current. For the channel cat, the current needs to be moving, but not too swift as to make to the fish struggle to swim in the spot. A spot with good brush and adequate depth is no good if the current rushes through it. The water's pace has to be moderate, in order to make it fishable. Now, the flathead catfish on the other hand, with its spotty brown skin, flat wide brow, and stocky build is a consistent resident of the still and creepy depths of a log jam. A deep hole smothered in a convoluted maze of fallen trees and brush is always the best place to find a flathead. If the spot is topped with questionable looking tan colored foam, then this makes the hole even more promising. The dark and almost stagnant spots are the flatheads domain and despite being an ugly looking beast, the flatheads taste the best as they feed only on live bait.

Now, blue cats can and could be found in a variety of places. The blue cat is like an amalgam of the brown wide flathead and slender gray channel cat. The blue cat is rightly named, because its skin appears to have a bluish grey tint. They can be long like a channel cat, but simultaneously chunky like a flathead. Their head is thick and filled with rows of sharp sandpaper like teeth. They can bloody the hand of anyone foolish enough to try and grab them by the lips like a bass. In most cases, trying to lip a flathead or channel cat is easy, and not likely to tear up an appendage. Blue cats on the other hand, are a different story. Grandpa and his friends caught many blue-cats on their willow poles, but they would also "hog" them and any other catfish as well.

In many places it is called "noodling." The sport (if one can call it that) involves an in-depth knowledge of the subtleties of catfish spawning and nesting, and more importantly a complete disregard for self-preservation and a set of cojones the size of a refrigerator. Grandpa along with his buddy Stanley Cravens would catch catfish, some upwards of 40 or 50 pounds by swimming down in the dark brown water, grabbing them by the mouth and then pulling himself and the fish to the surface. No bait, no trap, no implements of any kind, just a man and a fish and a log.

The worst catfish to run into at this point was the blue-cat, because like an alligator, it would bite down and spin on the arm of anyone brave enough to stick his hand into a nesting spot. As Grandpa said in his own manner of speaking, "Blue cats was mean!" He had torn off the skin on his arms countless times wrestling blue cats, flatheads, and channel cats out of their nesting spots. He and his friends would swim the creek in search of a "good" log and as he stated, "Once ya found a log, well then, you hogged that log all the time and ya didn't tell nobody where it was. Ya just kept that to yourself… Well yea you just reach your hand in there. If it was a big log ya had to put your knees in there to make sure they didn't get out on you. And then if there was two openings in there, I generally carried a sack of weeds and you'd close that one hole with that sack of weeds. Then ya caught the fish from the other hole, ya know." He would have to reach in the log with his hand and let the fish bite down on his arm. The big ones, and especially the blue cats, would bloody up a hand or arm easily. As he stated, "Yea, you'd get all skinned up ya know if ya'd get a big flathead. And blue cats was mean and blue cats they'd bite ya know…"

Grandpa learned how to fish in many ways from Pocahontas locals, but mostly from what he figured out on his own. However, Louch's father Stanley Baczewski, my Great Grandfather, and a recent immigrant from Poland, taught him a thing or two as well. Great Grandpa would take Louch and his brothers fishing at places like Long Lake, Shoal Creek, and the smaller Beaver Creek. Mostly they would fish off the bank with a bit of line and a cane pole. Some of Great Grandpa's lessons on fishing were good, but others were obviously never attempted again. Of all lessons, Grandpa remembered one Polish fishing lesson of indelible glory. Lou fondly recalls a fishing, and or track and field lesson, that no one in their right mind would or could repeat. Grandpa said, "He took us fishing at Beaver creek, that's south of Pokey, and so we wanted to get across that creek. And he was about half tanked then. He was stewed. So he said, 'I'll show ya how they done it in Poland!!'"

Great-Grandpa grabbed a random piece of driftwood aside the creek bank and took a few paces back. To the amazement of his sons, he brought the limb low to his side and stepped agate in a drunken state of deep concentration. Then after a bit of studying his foreground, and with some matter of form and slurred knowledge of pole vaulting technique, Stanislaus drove forward with all of his might. He ran towards the creek

82

with his driftwood pole locked in the proper position. When he met the precipice, he drove his pole down into the mud of the creek and forced himself upright on the limb. For a brief moment, his sons stood in awe of his skill. Yet before he rose to full vault of the pole, the driftwood creaked and erupted into a variety of shrapnel like shards. Mean old Mr. Gravity quickly took hold, and poor Stanislaus plummeted into the muddy creek below. With a resounding slapping splatter, Stan hit the mud with all of his weight. When Grandpa, finished telling the story, he looked at me with a smile, shook his head, and stated, "well, never did forget that."

It seemed that great Grandpa was a bit of a track and field man back in Poland, and he obviously intended to show off his vaulting prowess on that particular day. No one was sure if he was any good at pole vaulting for certain, because he never attempted it again. One thing was certain though; his pole selection was certainly flawed. For years Great Grandpa would be pestered for that liquored up debacle. It seemed that every time the poor man would screw up, Great Grandma would always say in broken English, "is that how you done it in Poland." It was an incident that "lived in infamy" for Stanislaus Baczewski.

In truth, no one was quite sure how Great Grandpa "done it in Poland," and the exact reasons why my Great Grandfather and Grandmother had left Poland remains a bit of a mystery. Most contend that Great Grandpa left to avoid service in the Czar's army when the First World War broke out, but no one was certain about why they came here at all. Perhaps they were seeking the opportunities that so many others sought at that time. Grandpa and others felt that, Great Grandpa had most likely left Poland in order to dodge the draft and the utter carnage of the Great War. If that was indeed the case, I can't blame a guy for that. It seems that Stanislaws and Alexandria Baczewski moved initially to East

St Louis. At the time, it was a great town to live in, yet greed, corruption, and racial strife, have since turned this once "model city" and the surrounding areas into something resembling a post-apocalyptic war zone.

In East St Louis, Madison, Illinois, and North St Louis, Missouri, there once was a sizeable Polish population. Remnants of this community still exist today. There are clusters of elderly Polish Americans living around Madison still – some of our own extended family included. Madison still boasts a "Polish Hall" and almost directly across the Mississippi from Madison Illinois, is the notable Piekutowksi's butcher shop, which is very well known for its traditional sausage. In fact, the former Polish Pope John Paul even had requested sausage from this location when he visited St Louis in the late 1990's. My family still goes to this butcher shop and it seems as if it were an almost sacred rite, for we only go once a year before Christmas. To this day, I cannot eat Polish sausage or Krakow sausage, without thinking about Christmas Eve at my Grandparents.

Such places unfortunately are mere shadows of the ethnic enclave that once thrived in that area from the early to mid-20th century. Perhaps it was this grouping of Polish immigrants that brought Grandpa here. Indeed, he did have a brother who resided in Madison. According to Grandpa however, they were not close – or so it seemed to him. In truth, Grandpa knew little about his father's and mother's origins and it seems that his parents talked little about their past. What puzzled me the most was the fact that the family eventually moved to Pocahontas – a microscopic village about seventy miles from St Louis. However, the reason for this move was one Grandpa did know. The relocation it seems descended from a judicial order. The local constabulary and judiciary in Madison felt that Great Grandpa needed to move due to a "gambling and drinking problem" – the specifics of which are unknown. Pocahontas was not a mandatory destination, but I suppose it was somehow a logical choice at the time. Who knows? One does know however, that law enforcement officials indeed wanted my family out of Madison and for a variety of reasons. I could not be more proud.

So, while thousands of Eastern Europeans flocked to the major cities in search of work at the advent of the 20th century, my family headed into rural Illinois. Great Grandpa found a job in the Pocahontas coal mine, which bore the same name as the town. He worked as a timberman setting supports in the mine during the wintertime when coal was needed. In the warmer months, he did odd jobs for farmers, doing anything from clearing timber to building fences.

Here in Pokey, Great Grandpa and Grandma raised three boys who would reach manhood. They would also lose two children. One son perished in the flu epidemic, and their only daughter died after pulling a boiling pot of water off the stove. She was severely scalded and succumbed to her wounds some days later. Life in this time could be brutish and short, just as it was most certainly wrought with hardship. Money was scarce. Work was many times hard to find. Prohibition was in full swing and gangsters ran the area. According to Grandpa, times were rough, and trials constant, but they always had food on the table, and they always had some good times. Grandpa was the youngest of the three brothers. The other two have since passed on. Grandpa is the last remaining member of his immediate family. He looks back on these times with due fondness and with a visible sorrow for those loved and lost.

They lived in a primitive way by modern standards, residing in a house with no plumbing, no refrigeration, and only wood for heat. As boys, my grandfather and his brothers spent almost all of their summer cutting wood to heat for the winter. Although he worked in a coal mine during the winter, Great Grandpa could not afford coal most of the time and wood was their main fuel source. The family possessed an ice box, and by ice box, I literally mean a box which required a block of ice to cool it. Grandpa said, "it was about 25cents for a block of ice." But, this was a luxury, and ice could only be afforded on special occasions. An actual refrigerator was not to be seen in the house for a long time to come. Therefore, the family salted their meat and canned most of their food. They always had a big garden and raised a few animals.

As a freshman in high school, Grandpa would wake up at 5am and walk a few miles to a dairy where he milked 17 cows. When he was complete with this task, he would take the milk on a route through town and deliver it on the way to school. He did this all through high school. But despite all his work, as Grandpa said, "he [the farmer] didn't pay me nothing, the only thing I got was milk, butter, eggs, and every once in a while a chicken, but he never paid one cent of money. Or, if we went to the store he would say 'Louch you a want a soda' and he would buy me a soda, that was it." Everyone in Pokey called Grandpa "Louch" instead of Lou or Louis on account of Great Grandma's way of pronouncing his name. She spoke little English and had a very strong Polish accent, so Louis always came out as "Louch." He himself never learned to speak English until he started school in Pocahontas, and Polish was the only language that his parents fully understood. Neighbors and friends having heard the name Louch yelled more than once by his mother, started calling him Louch as well. Old friends like Dave Pagan, still call him Louch to this day.

In the Depression days of his youth, it was tough for Louch just to get a few cents together, but he found ways. He said that, "I done odd jobs and picked berries and stuff like that - I hunted junk too. I'd go through the alleys and try to find junk, like aluminum or iron." But the poor junk guy was not the sharpest fellow around because Grandpa said, "Whenever he wasn't looking, I sold him that junk two or three times. Then, when he would be doing something else, well heck I would cart some of it off, and then bring it back the next day and sell it again. We would try to scrounge enough junk to go to a movie, because your parents wouldn't give you ten cents. You would have to go and try to make it, or you sold berries, or mowed a lawn to get the money to go to the show. I worked for farmers too, like in the fall I shucked corn. You would work off a horse drawn wagon and shuck corn by hand. We were paid 25 cents a day and we got dinner."

"They had a show there in Pokey, they charged ya ten cents. Half the time, us kids didn't have the money to get in, so one guy would get in and he would sit by the side door. He'd open the door for them other ones and here while the show was going, kids was crawling in on their hands and knees, going underneath the seats and everything. People'd say 'what's going on; hey, what's going on there. Finally they got wise to that, and started locking the side doors."

In the depression things were desperate and as Grandpa stated, "things were really tight." Most people in Pokey according to Grandpa were on some form of aid throughout the depression, or they had to rely on some type of government work to get by. President Roosevelt's programs affected the family across the board, whether through aid, or work programs. My Great Grandfather Stanislaus, worked for the Works Progress Administration (WPA) on various projects as a laborer, doing road work for the city and county. Stanislaus helped built parts of the old route 66 or old route 40 which was one of the first highways in the country. While their father took a job for the WPA, Louch's older brother Ed joined and worked for the Civilian Conservation Corps (CCC) which had a camp in nearby Greenville.

Many times when I was growing up, if there was work to be done for someone in family, everyone would all get together and get it done. The jobs covered everything from pouring concrete, to building a shed or shingling a roof. The family showed up in force, hammers, and tool belts, and coolers of beer in hand. Everyone knew that their hard work would be rewarded by some home cooked food and even more cold beer. Grandpa would work as hard as anyone else, if not more, and if people were standing around he would say, "what is this a WPA job or something." He said that the old joke for the WPA (Works Projects Administration) was that it really stood for "We Piddle Around."

Grandpa said that back in the Depression, those in Pokey who weren't lucky enough to get a WPA job, "were put on relief." At the same time, the coal mine was shut down in town and there were not even jobs you could travel to in St Louis or East St Louis at the time. Everyone was hurting. Yet the aid and work programs enacted by Roosevelt, gave many the chance to have their basic needs met. As he stated, "they all thought a lot of him [Roosevelt] because he brought jobs back and everything. He helped the working people… The government gave out rations too, they gave out corn meal and stuff like that, and then they gave clothes for the kids like overalls and shoes and stuff like that."

As a child I believe most, if not all, of my deprivations were of merely luxuries. I might have complained or felt deprived if I did not receive the new GI Joe vehicle. Or, perhaps I was disgusted because I lacked the new Lego moon base set. My grandfather on the contrary, knew what it was to truly do without basic things that people take for

88

granted. My suburban upbringing most certainly lacked the grainy crudeness that painted a rural depression era childhood. In comparison to the hardships that my grandfather went through, my life has been nothing but gravy.

Despite this, I never once heard my grandfather complain about his youth, and the bulk of all of his stories were told because he looks upon his simple childhood with fondness. He has always talked about fishing the creek more than he ever spoke of hardships or bad times. The creek to him was a Mecca. It is a sacred place to him, and to all of us in the family as well. He had quite a boyhood there. To this day, he cannot talk about fishing the creek without developing an expansive grin.

When I was a boy, Grandpa would take my two cousins, Michael and Chris and myself to fish the creek for a few days at a time. Of all the grandsons, Michael and I loved the creek the most, and into adulthood would speak of it in hush and reverend tones. It was sacred to Grandpa, and so it became sacred to us. Many times, we would camp near the creek in a place owned by a local man named Cletus.

Cletus would come and fish with us sometimes. He was a Tasmanian devil when it came to collecting firewood – ya just didn't get in his way. Any normal man would step into the woods and come back with an armful of sticks or maybe a log or two. Cletus on the other hand, came back with arms full of limbs and logs and trees and stumps, while damn near dragging a sequoia behind him. He was a firewood force to be reckoned with – a damn campfire juggernaut.

At Cletus's place it was just Michael, Chris, Grandpa and I, and I don't know how he had the patience, but he did. He would set all the lines and we would help catch all the bait and together we would run the lines as best as we could. My cousins and I played in the water and on the sandbars and banks. We made mud slides on the steep bank sides and sloshed around in the shallow sandy pools during the days. Michael and I would go and explore the woods around our camp while Grandpa would keep fishing for bait or swim and find mussels while we played in the water. In the evening and after dark, we ran the lines and sat around the fire and listened to his stories. We would spend a few weekdays out on the creek since my cousins and I were on summer break and Grandpa was retired. My dad and my Uncles would come out once the weekend hit and many times all the men in the family were there, My dad, uncle John, uncle Dave, uncle Paul and uncle Charlie.

It was on the muddy banks of Shoal Creek that I learned not only how to camp and fish, but what it was to be a man. Everyone carried their weight. There was fun to be had, but tons of work to be done beforehand. We had to clear out a camp, gather the firewood, set up the stove, get the lantern ready, set up the sleeping stuff, and make a clothes line. Sometimes we would have to set up a tent or two, if we weren't camped under a bridge. Yet, most of the time we just slept like Grandpa had always done; on the ground under the stars.

Apart from arranging up the sleeping stuff, there was also the fishing set up, tending to the bait, moving around a car battery to run the aerators, helping set the poles, running the lines, paddling the john boat, pulling out the lines, helping the adults clean the fish. It never ended. When my cousins and I went on these trips with Grandpa, he didn't do things for us; he taught us how to do them ourselves. We were not spectators, we had plenty of jobs and errands to run, but we loved every minute of it. Nothing was easy, but we learned something from every step of the way, from every success and each mistake. From naming the trees, plants, animals and types of fish, to learning the best way to set a bait trap,

Grandpa, my dad, and my uncles taught us how to anticipate the next step, and work as hard as one could.

Many years later, I read an interview of a famous mountain climber and entrepreneur named Yvon Chouinard. He talked about CEO's climbing Mt Everest, and how they had Sherpas carry all their gear, paid huge sums for the best equipment and guides, and have everything done for them on the climb. They didn't have to understand the process; they only looked at the end result. All the tough steps and decisions along the way had been made for them, done for them; they were kids at summer camp led around by the counselors. They were oblivious to what really went on. Chouinard said that people like that really weren't climbers at all, and they might as well have the Sherpas put mints on their pillows on the way up the mountain. He said that basically they hadn't learned a thing. He stated that, "They were assholes when they started, and they were assholes when they were done."

I know fishing Shoal Creek was nothing like climbing a mountain, but some fundamentals were just the same. I felt just like Chouinard. If you didn't have to work hard for it, most things didn't teach you a damn thing. Any such trip was more mental than physical, and I have seen on many occasions that the seemingly toughest person in everyday life may well fold up like a lawn chair when faced with the grind of even a basic camping, hiking, climbing, or fishing trip. On every trip to the creek, I learned something, and not just about fishing. More importantly, I learned about myself and my family, and I learned that wisdom and process prevailed far more often than bravado and misguided brawn.

On the creek, I learned how to push myself and deal with tough situations, shrug off discomfort, and lend a hand. I felt that on the creek I learned what it was to be a conscious human being, to fail and learn from

91

failure, and understand that the steps in the process meant far more than the end result. I sat out in the john boat every night, under an endless expanse of stars and surrounded by an absurd universe, but I felt sustained and soothed by my minute and arduous task here on earth; or at least my task on Shoal Creek. With my grandfather, my Father, uncles, and cousins and in our crude battle to catch fish, there was order. There was stillness. And for the briefest of moments, things seemed to make sense, cause you just didn't care if they did or not. As each new day dawned on the creek, I walked in his shadow, and I hoped that someday I could be half as tough as my grandfather, in mind, body, and soul.

When I was in high school I would attempt to take my friends to fish the creek. I hoped to live up to the stories of Louch and his friends. Yet too few of my friends had ever done anything like fish the creek; even fewer could stand to get dirty or work hard enough to do what was necessary. On my first attempt to take friends to the creek, most of them were afraid to run the lines after dark. Coyotes howled off in the distance and they refused to leave the light of the campfire. I had to run the lines alone. I had to do everything myself. It was hard to imagine that my Grandpa and his friends were around the ages of ten and twelve when they had lived on the creek for weeks at a time. My high school friends could barely make it for a night.

On the next attempt, I tried to organize things better. I tried to split up the jobs among my friends and delegate a bit of responsibility. Along with other jobs given, like getting cooking stuff, or groceries, etc, I gave one buddy the job of getting the beer. It was a hot day in August. We were about half way out to the creek when I asked him for some ice to cool the bait fish. He replied, "what ice"? I looked at him quizzically, and said, "well the ice from the beer." He replied, "you told me to get beer, you didn't say anything about ice." He had two cases of hot beer sitting in the back of his hatchback cooking in the August sun. We had to drive a half hour back to town to get coolers and ice. To this day, I have never found good help when it came to bankline fishing, unless they were family or a very long time family friend.

Who makes it all easy finds it all hard,
therefore the sage makes everything hard,
he thus finds nothing hard
Lao Tzu

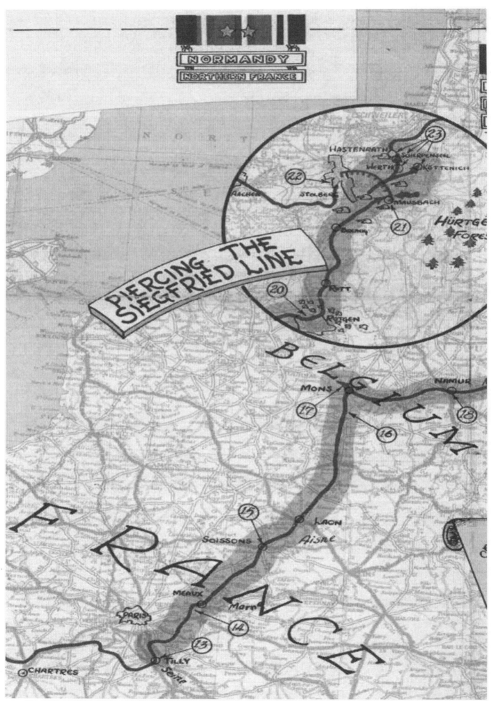

Detail of the Lovelady Taskforce Campaign Map – Central France Campaign
(#2 of 5 Campaign Stars)

94

Chapter 5
The Falaise Pocket

He is a lover of his country,
the one who rebukes and does not excuse its sins

Fredrick Douglas

While we sat at the basement dinner table of Grandpa's home, the subject of the Iraq war came up into conversation. At the time, there was a great deal of talk about France and how they were unsupportive of our war in Iraq, despite how we had aided them in WWII. For a time, French fries became freedom fries and a jingoistic banter held sway. To my grandfather however, the issue was fairly cut and dry. Despite having fought to aid the French, he himself disagreed in no way with their assessment of Iraq. As far as he saw it, the French had seen the face of war and the destruction and devastation that flowed with wars flood. To him, the French understood war in a way that few Americans ever could. He described the destruction of the French cities at the dinner table. Their homes and towns were piles of rubble. The people had to leave their homes and take only what they could carry. They were forced to either run and seek refuge in another town, or find some shelter underground deep in the rubble. This is how many of the French people lived and for a great deal of time. Many of them were half starved and on the run.

We in the US however, had been spared such destruction and had not known war in the same way as the French had. It was easy for people who had not seen war to wave the banner of violence for a cause. The average American has never seen wholesale death like my grandfather or other veterans have. Most Americans have never seen bloated bodies of soldiers, enemy and friend alike, civilians young and old, male and female, rotten cows, and decaying horses. They have never seen their towns occupied, their possessions destroyed or looted, their towns leveled. They have never smelt the stench of death with burning equipment and flesh. Such a stench had never escaped my grandfather. Throughout my life, Grandpa has always made it a point to remind us to be thankful for living in peace, while being equally skeptical of war and those who promote it. He was a shining example of the fact that it is truly possible to both be against a war and supportive of the troops. There never was a man more proud of his service or more sympathetic and respectful to the plight of fellow soldiers, but simultaneously he always questioned war and the purveyors of violence.

3rd AD Shermans rolling through a demolished town (3ad.com.)

Louch grimly recounted, "Going across France, well that was August and it was hot fightin all acrossed. All the way into Germany! It was real uncomfortable in that tank - all during the summer. Lotta cows and horses, they got killed, and bloated up and they'd stink! Man, they'd stink! Same way, if we'd hit a couple places where the front was stable and we wasn't moving, then we'd stop there and there'd be dead soldiers, ya know: Germans laying there. They'd just swell up and ya'd see them everywhere cause the Germans, they didn't pick em up, and our troops didn't pick em up right away either. Well heck, it wasn't long and they was swelled up and their eyes were sunk in."

The tank crews of Taskforce Lovelady, D Company, would see their fair share of blood and corpses in France. After operation Cobra, the 3rd Armored Division was able to make its way out of the hedgerows. The 3rd Armored, now under the command of General Rose, proved itself pivotal in the operation. Along with many other elements of the First Army 7th Corps, the 3rd Armored's mission was to help push the Western German Army into a trap. The massive Allied force of American, British, Polish, and Canadians, fought through the intense heat of July and early August, working to encircle the bulk of the western German panzer and infantry divisions. When they pushed the Germans into the region south of Falaise, a tremendous blood bath followed.

Upon touring the battlefield, Eisenhower described the destruction, "The battlefield of Falaise was unquestionably one of the greatest 'killing grounds' of any of the war areas. Roads, highways and fields were so choked with destroyed equipment and dead men and animals that passage through the area was extremely difficult. Forty-eight hours after the closing of the gap I was conducted through it on foot, to encounter scenes that could be described only by Dante. It was literally possible to walk for hundreds of yards at a time on nothing but dead and decaying flesh."[13]

The carnage that lay at Eisenhower's feet was the culmination of an Allied attack strategy which enclosed and a destroyed the bulk of the German Panzergruppe (Armored Force) West. Many historians see the victory as Pyrric, because many Panzer Corps leaders and troopers were allowed to escape, due to miscommunication and coordination among Allied units. This debate aside, no one can dispute the wholesale carnage and mechanical destruction that littered the narrow killing field.

Carnage within the Falaise Pocket

Carnage within the Falaise pocket - courtesy of University of Illinois

Many German grenadiers, officers, and panzer corpsmen managed to escape and fight in future campaigns, but the bulk of their equipment was totally destroyed. Were it not for the fumbling and arguing among the allies, more armored and infantry groups would have been captured or destroyed. The Allied failure to catch or immobilize the bulk of Panzergruppe West's experienced personnel, allowed the Germans to loosely restructure many of their panzer and infantry divisions, and thus propel the massive German counter offensive in December of 1944. This later drive would be known as the Battle of the Bulge; the largest and most destructive attack ever faced by US forces in Europe.

The reason why so many German groups did become trapped and ultimately destroyed was complex. The allied advance was stalled after the initial invasion, but once they had cleared the hedgerows, US forces broke through from the west and south. Simultaneously, the British, Canadians, and Poles pushed southeast. Hitler arrogantly ordered that the Allies be pushed back into the sea. However, his own decisions, and the misconceptions of his staff limited the already poorly equipped and undermanned western infantry and panzer groups. Were it not for the massive losses caused by the Russians on the eastern front, the Allied invasion of Normandy may well have been hurled into the English Channel. No panzer division was at full strength in the west and most had been placed in France to revamp their crippled divisions after facing the Russians. Luckily for the allies, the panzers were not only weakened, but they were held back from attacking the initial invasion in Normandy.

Hitler and the high command had sole control of the movement of the Panzer Corps, and they held many of them at Calais anticipating an invasion that never came. Calais stands as the shortest distance across the English Channel and was therefore a fortified location of massive proportions. There had been battlements set here long before WWII. In the days of Napoleon the proximity of the Calais coast to Great Britain was understood as a consummate threat. In fact, the German Reich built upon existing Napoleonic stonework and created a vast and impregnable set of pillboxes, bunkers, machine gun posts, and gigantic artillery emplacements. It was a very expensive and ultimately useless assemblage of armaments and resources.

Knowing the dangers of facing Calais head on, Allied intelligence created a clever ruse. A massive inflatable army was set across the pass of Calais on British soil. This army was only an army on paper, and of paper. Huge forces of inflatable tanks, jeeps, and equipment were planted, so that German aerial intelligence missions would easily see a colossal force standing ready to attack Calais. Allied bombardments and the strategic destruction of only certain radar stations strengthened the subterfuge.[14] As such, the invasion of Normandy was thought to be a "spoiling" mission and not the real invasion that was perceived to be coming to Calais. The German High command therefore did not want to immediately commit the bulk of their divisions in Normandy.

When the battle for Normandy increased in intensity, German forces were able to muster around 4,500 tanks to face the allies. In contrast, the allies' committed almost 1,500 tanks on D Day alone and by late July some 8,700 American, British, Polish, Canadian and Free French tanks would be deployed (the greatest majority of these tanks being Shermans).[15] The German failure to commit its tank forces early in the invasion enabled the allies to make a strong foothold and the allied armored divisions ultimately prevailed. Such events were due to the overwhelming numbers of tanks.

Despite the missing Panzer divisions, hedgerow country was no picnic for the American Forces and the 3rd Armored Division was still bogged down in hellish field to field combat by late July. Tank crew losses mounted and original tank crews began to split up more and more as tank crews were losing men. More experienced tankers moved up to take higher positions and replacements came in to take the assistant jobs. The demand for tankers remained so overwhelming, that completely untrained recruits were ending up being used in the absence of trained men. In one such case, a man was brought in to replace an assistant gunner in Private Baczewski's tank. Their experienced assistant gunner, Crosby, moved into another tank. At the time, Louch's tank crew consisted of Sgt Cady, (tank commander) Pat Gillespie, (gunner) and Virgil Decker (assistant driver).

"See our assistant gunner went in another tank as a gunner," Lou explained. This one time our gunner was Pat Gillespie… Pat burnt the barrel out of the 30 caliber so my tank commander, said to the assistant gunner you gotta replace that 30 caliber barrel and we just got this replacement, a guy by the name of Pitman." Pitman as it turned out did not even know how to change the barrel for the 30 caliber machine gun, and for a gunner, this should have been something learned very early in training. Pitman told Cady, "I never did change a barrel." So, Cady exploded, and ordered Lou over the radio to climb up into the turret. "Turn the turret up, crawl up here, and change that damn barrel!!" Cady yelled into his mic. "So, I had to crawl up there from the driver's seat, into the turret and change this other guy's barrel, because this kid didn't have training," Louch remembered with a hint of bitterness. "They were sending them guys over there with not much training because they had to replace these guys."

Eventually Pitman was moved out and replaced by another young man named Leslie Underwood. Grandpa described him as a "little bitty guy" who quickly became a good friend. All the members of his tank crew including Les would stay together as they fought from Normandy to the Battle of the Bulge. They all became very close.   Like Louch and the rest of the crew, Les had been drafted and sent to Fort Knox for tank training. He was not part of the initial group who headed across the channel in June. But he arrived in France soon after.

During his first night in France, Les quickly realized just how dangerous his situation was, and how randomly the hand of death was dealt. That night, he and other 3rd Armored men were camped near a roadside in Normandy. Les and another man were camped in a tent for the night, when a bomber dropped his load on a seven truck convoy parked aside the nearby roadway. The drivers were inside the trucks sleeping. The seven trucks were full of ammunition and every truck exploded with the force of the armaments contained in the trucks and from the TNT of the bombs. Les ran and jumped quickly into a bunker a few yards away. The explosions rocked the ground and trees all around them, sending shattered pieces of the trucks rifling through the air. The man who just minutes before lay sleeping nearby him was now dead and a greater part of his skull was blown apart by shrapnel. While he and others walked through the destruction left behind and searched for survivors, Les looked up to spy a haunting image. Hanging above him in the trees and fluttering in the wind like a flag, there was a set of shredded bloody pants. They more than likely belonged to one of the seven truck drivers who had just met their fate.

Shortly afterward, Les made his way up to the front line and joined D Company before the battle for St. Lo. He ended up in Louch's tank, as an assistant gunner. Les served as loader and radio operator. His job was a cramped, frantic, and deafening one man battle to load the heavy 76mm gun and keep up the rate of fire according to what was humanly possible. Les would remain a member of Louch's crew up until the Battle of the Bulge.

Once Les was brought onto Cady's tank, the crew and the remaining tanks of D Company worked their way through France. All the while, D Company switched the roll of lead tank day to day. Each crew knew that the head tank of the column would invariably take the bulk of enemy fire. As lead tank, each crew was lucky to survive the day. Les groaned, "I used to hate it when you'd be the fifth tank or something, and they'd say over the radio, 'number five take the lead." Louch had the same perception, with his head shaking he said, "Oh yea you hated it...cause it was always the first tank they'd pick off."

Leslie Underwood sitting on a Sherman tank (location unknown)

Each crew knew they were in an inferior tank, but when they were called to take the lead, they pulled ahead and drove into almost certain death - day after day. Understandably, not everyone could handle the pressure, and according to Lou and Les, many good men broke down due to the bitter carnage and overwhelming fear. At one point while fighting in Normandy, Les witnessed a tanker, racked with battle fatigue, jump out of another tank and run towards enemy fire in order to commit suicide. Such incidents were infrequent, but haunting enough.

To take the edge off their nerves, Louch's tank crew commandeered a case of cognac early on in France. When a day of fighting started, they would pass a bottle around the tank. Pvt Baczewski kept a bottle ready behind the driver's instrument panel. The crew would call to him over the radio to pass it around. Tank commander Sgt. Joe Cady, assistant gunner Les Underwood, gunner Pat Gillespie, assistant driver Virgil Decker, and driver Lou Baczewski would each day take a few swigs and say a few prayers. They knew that each day of combat could well be their last. No one ever got drunk, but as Les said, "at least it calmed everyone's nerves a bit."

For the crew, there was not just fear to contend with, but physical exhaustion to cope with as well. No one in the crew could ever get an entire night of sleep. There were guard duties and jobs to do around the clock. Louch exclaimed, "They'd bring the gas up at night in trucks. GI truckers would bring the gas up, then they left the gas by the tank and then you had to pour them five gallon tanks in – ONE AT A TIME! Heck! If you ran all night you might use forty or fifty gallon of gas."

The tank averaged about a half mile to mile per gallon, and the tank engines had to be operating all day. Louch recalled, "You never shut down the tank all day, you just kept it running, then heck, like in combat we didn't get no rest at all, because they'd bring up the gas after dark." Their orders were to perform all of the reloading and fueling, with no lights after nightfall, dependent on the amount of fuel and ammunition used, there may be close to 180 gallons of gas to re-supply and perhaps 90 rounds of heavy shells to load, machine gun ammo to load, and additional provisions as well. By the time all of these items were loaded it was often close to dawn. Louch groaned, "You'd pour the gas in there, but by the time you sat down and maybe get a little shut eye, here come the ammunition! By the time you got the ammunition in, well heck it was about time to shove off!"

A tired image of Lou Baczewski while at the controls of his Sherman - France 1944

On July 25th 1944, the 3rd Armored Division, and the rest of 1st Army VII Corps, spearheaded a massive coordinated attack designed to propel the Americans out of the hedgerows and into open country. On the dreary night prior, Colonel Boudinot showed up in the Combat Command B command post and proceeded to brief all the officers. Eaton Roberts looked on in astonishment as the colonel sauntered in an outfit that, "looked like a fisherman's rain suit." He accompanied the ensemble with a sleek horse riding crop, with which he pointed out the map objectives. Boudinot was considered to be a bit of a dandy already, but in this case he achieved new heights of "dapperness." Boudinot stood before his maps and blithely stated, "Gentleman, even though it is raining, we have a job to do. We're going to make a break out of this damned beachhead and it's got to be successful, even if it means the annihilation of CCB [Combat Command B]…This is Operation Cobra and it will be referred to by that code name from now on."[16] The officers were not encouraged by either his dress or caustic speech, but they checked their maps and headed out to inform their men. Ultimately, Omar Bradely's plan prevailed, as it hurled the 1st Army out into open country.

Operation Cobra began with a merciless aerial and artillery bombardment of the German defenders. Roberts knew that something was up, "No general announcement was needed…hoards of bombers flew over like a locust plague," Close to 3,500 planes were involved in the assault.[17] On the 25th, the skies filled with seemingly endless groups of B-17 flying fortresses, B24 Liberators, fighters of all types, and A 20 Havocs. The broad goal of the Cobra plan was to push the German Panzergruppe West into a trap. With 19 divisions, this force constituted the bulk of the Western German army or Wehrmacht. Although Operation Cobra initially stalled due to tough German resistance, within two days of heavy fighting almost all major organized opposition fell. The German lines crumbled. Panzergruppe West's divisions were numerous, but desperately short on materials and qualified manpower. They could not hold the Americans at bay. By August 6th the 33rd Armored Regiment had fought its way into open country and was finally poised to move into reserve and allow time for maintenance and rest.

Yet, just as soon as the 33rd pulled back for relief, the Germans mounted a counterattack in the towns of Mortain and Avranches. The 33rd quickly attached to the 30th Infantry Division jumped back into action. Initially, a force of crack Panzer troopers possessing superior numbers regained territory. Through the efforts of 3rd Armored the Panzer forces were eventually held from advancing. Yet the fight never stopped. Ceaseless waves of attacks hit the 33rd Regiment, only to be pushed back time and again for five days. Some forty-one vehicles were totally destroyed and sixty required major repairs due to the intensity of the combat.[18]

Louch's Tank - Central France 1944

Once relief finally came, Louch decided to take a look at the hull of a German tank which he and his platoon fired upon days before. In doing so, he discovered why American tanks were so extremely out-classed. "We knocked out this one Mark V [Panther]… The crew abandoned the tank. We seen em bail out. And so we went on, and we didn't know whether we hit it or what," he lamented. But then we got relieved and just from curiosity, we wasn't too far from there when we got relieved, I went to see where we knocked this Mark V out. I counted nineteen ricochets off of that thing, and one of them hit the gun port and went down through the top. And the other one, where the bottom of the tank and the rest of the tank came together there was a seam there, and it penetrated there. That was the only two. Outta, nineteen ricochets, there was only two holes in it!"

Despite the German's superior equipment and bitter efforts, the tankers of D Company pushed on. After their brief respite, they made their way towards Argentan; serving as one small part of a massive effort to encircle the Germans. To the north, the British, Canadian, and Free Polish

108

forces battled ferocious resistance and took heavy casualties in an effort to push the Germans out of Caen and south towards Falaise. The Poles, along with the American 90th Infantry Division, faced some of the most bitter fighting of the campaign, as they worked towards Chambois. The towns of Chambois and Trun served as the only significant escape routes for the German Panzer divisions. These towns possessed the only intact heavy bridges over the Dives River. Knowing this, the Germans threw their most fanatical Nazi SS (Schutzstaffel, or Protection Squadron) divisions toward the Polish 1st and 4th Armored Divisions.

The "Free Poles" fought with sublime resolve, after forcibly expatriated from their own country since 1939. During the 1939 German blitzkrieg invasion of Poland, the Poles were horribly outgunned. The country fell to the German onslaught in nearly a month's time. On many occasions, the Polish horse cavalry stood and fought as the only means to slow the juggernaut of German tank divisions. The greatest bulk of the Polish cavalry men were slaughtered. By 1944 however, the tides had turned and the Poles now stood at the forefront of the Allied battle to reclaim Europe. Although it was a step up from fighting on horseback, the Polish armored divisions now battled the German SS Panzers mounted on M4 Sherman tanks, and thus sustained a massive amount of casualties.

As the American 1st Army and 3rd Army pushed East and North, the British, Poles and Canadians combined to form a vast U shaped mass of men and armaments. At the center of the U sat the cities of Trun, Chambois, and Argentan and the bulk of the German forces. Understandably, the Germans fought desperately to hold these cities in order to maintain a lane of escape. Many historians and military scholars argue that the lane was left open and for far too long. This mistake allowed vast amounts of German commanders and soldiers to flee the encirclement.

As one would expect in August, fighting in the Falaise Campaign was unbearably hot, dusty, and miserable in general; especially for the tank crews. In the account of Eaton Roberts, temperatures inside of the Sherman's were reported to be 130 degrees Fahrenheit, in the shade! As the Allies continued to close in on the Germans, the intense heat accompanied by the lack of water, further tested the men's resolve and endurance. Adding to this extreme discomfort was the increasingly dense smell of rotting and bloated German corpses. Piles of German bodies quickly decomposed in the boiling heat. Their numerous corpses lined the roads and ditches. The Germans had been too overwhelmed to pick up their own dead soldiers.

Beginning On August 14th, the 3rd Armored faced some of the stiffest resistance they would endure in France as they drove towards Argentan and into some of Hitler's elite SS. One 3rd Armored Division taskforce found itself surrounded and the rest of the division worked feverishly to save them as well as maintain their own flanks. The fighting was again bitter on the 15th. Some men of the 3rd Armored's 703rd Tank Destroyer Battalion were captured by SS Panzer Grenadiers, only to be found soon afterward, unarmed and shot to death. Such incidents quickened the resolve of the 3rd Armored tankers and caused them to be increasingly callous and downright vindictive towards Nazi SS troopers.

On the 18th of August, the lead elements of the 3rd Armored Division made contact with British forces. The lead company that day was D Company of the 33rd Armored Regiment. According to Lou and Les, on the previous day, he and Sgt Cady's tank crew had been in the lead. Sgt Donald Ekdahl and his crew then took the lead the following day. They in turn met the British, and closed the VII Corps section of the Falaise Gap; making history. Scholars estimate that more than 1,200 German vehicles and tanks were destroyed at Falaise, while 10,000 German men were killed, and some 50,000 were taken prisoner.[19] According to Leslie Underwood, he respected the Germans for their fighting ability, but was astonished at how arrogant the captive soldiers were, especially the officers. As he stated, "Boy they [officers] were well dressed and cocky even after you captured them. They were good, but heck, they had been fighting six or seven years before we got there. Hell, all of us were new to war; we were green, and they couldn't take it that we beat em."

Falaise was an unquestionable Allied victory, but there was no glory in the rubble of men and material that lay in the farm fields of Falaise. Twenty years after the battle, Eisenhower would comment that, "no other battlefield presented such a horrible sight of death, hell, and total destruction." The hulls of German tanks, trucks, jeeps, and artillery lay strewn about for miles, burning and smoldering. Many of these charred vehicles were now tombs for their crews. Scores of horses used to draw artillery were blown to pieces and strewn about the smoking human and mechanized remains. The pungent stench of dead men and horses carried for miles in the hot August air. Into what had once been a peaceful countryside of rolling hills and farms, the Allies fired every ordinance they possessed. In the intense heat of late August 1944, artillery sent volley after volley of rounds, mortar crews launched a shower of shells, Sherman tanks fired their 75 mm guns, and infantrymen opened their machine guns into the narrow strip of thousands of trapped Germans. Allied fighters and fighter bombers strafed amid the merciless ground assault. In the narrow gap, the Allies put the German men and machines to a black and fiery death.

111

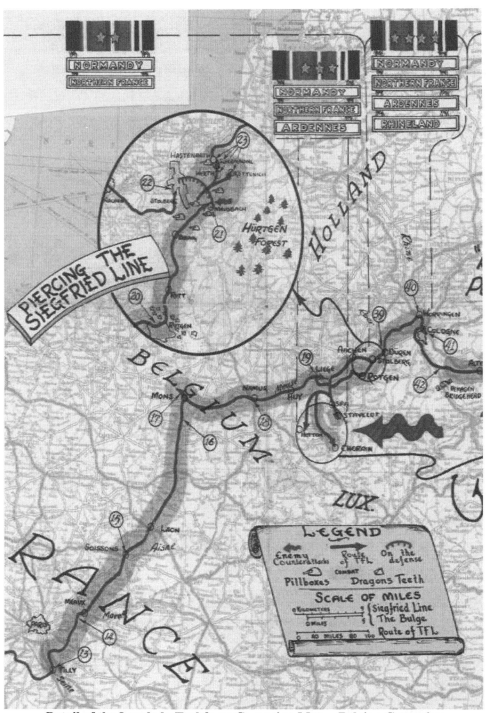

Detail of the Lovelady Taskforce Campaign Map – Belgian Campaign
(#3 of 5 Campaign Stars)

112

Chapter 6
Belgium
The Silver & Bronze Stars

The number of medals on an officer's breast varies in
inverse proportion to the square of the distance of
his duties from the front line.

Charles Edward Montague

I asked Grandpa if he saw a lot of Air Force action overhead throughout the war. He recalled times when there were so many planes that their squadrons seemed without end. Between the big bombing missions, dog fights, and their own calls for air-support against German Armor, he and his tank crew witnessed a great deal of activity above them. In combat, they were too busy to notice, but when relieved they stood in awe of the massive air traffic shooting back and forth above them. In the thick of the fight, the P51's and P47 fighter bombers were many times their angels in the skies, and they helped clear the way, especially once General Rose took over and began to coordinate Air-Force support. According to Tregaskis, General Rose was in fact one of the first American Commanders to perfect close air-support tactics.

When in France, the air support had helped the 3rd push past the German's superior tanks and equipment, due to the direct Air Force help via an Air Force tank equipped with special radio equipment. This tank had contact with the pilots as well as the tankers. The tankers themselves could listen to the communication with their eyes in the skies. Louch recalled on one occasion in France when a sniper's bullet struck an Air Force observer. Before D Company moved into a small town, the observer stepped outside of his tank as they assessed the situation. The bullet clipped the top of his scalp and cut off the better part of his ear. No one could locate the sniper. When the observer gathered himself together, he called over the radio to the Air Force. He was bleeding all over himself and understandably irate. Louch listened as the observer screamed into the radio for the Air Force to, "Take-out the whole damn town!!!" Louch said that in a few short minutes, "them P51's came in and they destroyed that town!" The planes swooped overhead and dropped everything they had in an attempt to get the sniper. Within seconds, they laid the whole town to waste.

With clear skies and air support, D Company "road marched" their way towards Mons, Belgium. During this particular drive, the 3rd Armored met only small pockets of resistance, as the Germans were pushed back. Throughout northern France and Belgium, the Air Force support had been invaluable and it helped make the push through Belgium easier on the 3rd Armored. The Air Force worked ahead of the column. They bombed and strafed the Germans, who after the defeat at Falaise were now retreating through the open ground.

The tankers had been trained to be able to spot particular planes. All American soldiers were supposed to be able to distinguish aircraft, friend or foe. Because of US air superiority, the Luftwaffe (German Air Force) only occasionally posed a direct threat to D Company throughout the war. It was rare to even spot a German aircraft. Yet at one point in Belgium, Sgt Cady's ability to distinguish German aircraft saved their lives. "In Belgium we got strafed one time." Louch recalled, "I had to go back to get a transmission worked on. We was all the way into Belgium and I couldn't hardly take both hands and shift that thing. So, they sent us back. We got relieved and they worked on that tank, and while we was there here come a bunch of planes." As maintenance worked on the tank, Louch and his tank crew flirted with some local Belgian girls. The girls and the tank crew stood around the tank while, maintenance inspected the transmission. Suddenly the hum of aircraft rolled overhead. As they looked up, "This one guy [maintenance soldier] says, 'look P51's!" Louch exclaimed.

"I looked up there and my tank commander looked up there, and he said, 'P51's your ass!!!' And we all dove underneath the tank ya know. And here they come, bop, bop, bop, bop, bop!!!!" The German planes strafed the ground all around the tank. Dirt flew up as the shells struck the earth in two paths of fire. Baczewski stated, "Nobody was killed and there was a woman there and she dove under there with us. Everybody was underneath the tank." The incident stood as one of only a handful of times when Cady's crew encountered an aerial attack.

Once the transmission was repaired, Louch's tank crew made its way down the open roads and fields of eastern Belgium and back to D Company. The 3rd Armored moved almost unabated until reaching the outskirts of Mons. Sitting 30 miles southwest of Brussels, Mons served as a vital artery of important roads. The city itself was not a stranger to war. Traditionally, a fortified town its origins reach far back to Roman times. There in the ancient city the fight stiffened. D Company soon threw itself back into bitter combat. On the edge of Mons, Cady's tank company met a firestorm of artillery. Louch recalled one night that was particularly bitter.

It was after dark and the tanks were all lined up along the road buttoned up tight. Small arms fire bounced off the tank, and artillery shells could be seen bursting in the trees all around them. Through their periscopes, they saw brilliant explosions and tracers blazing out of the darkness. There was a tank in front of them, a tank to their rear, and no order to move. Flaming shrapnel struck the rations and supplies strapped to the back of the tank and a fire broke out. Sgt Cady hollered to the crew that their gear was on fire. Yet, no one in the tank wanted to get out in the storm of metal raining outside. The tank crew yelled back and forth on their radios. They all knew that the fire might well spread to the two gas tanks and kill all of them, but no one wanted to leave the momentary safety of the tank.

Corporal Baczewski decided that the fire had to be put out. He knew that if the tank caught fire and if they were forced to bail out, the crew would then be completely exposed to the artillery barrage. He opened the hatch above the driver's seat and climbed out, exposing himself to open fire from all directions. Small arms and shrapnel pounded the tank as Baczewski scrambled to get to the burning supplies off the back. Artillery shells burst around the company in every direction while Baczewski frantically kicked off the flaming crates of 10-1 rations and infantry supplies. Once he pushed all of the burning contents off their Sherman, he crawled his way back toward the hatch, praying to dodge the intense explosions and bullets striking the tank all around him. Baczewski luckily made it back into his driver's seat unharmed. Company Commanding Officer (CO) Lieutenant Sally who witnessed the action through his periscope, promised to put Baczewski in for the Silver Star for his act of bravery.

3rd AD tankers outside Mons, Belgium 1944 (3ad.com)

In the days that followed, D Company and the rest of the 3rd Armored moved on Mons. The Germans at this point, stood scattered and disorganized as they scrambled to regroup and work their way to the Siegfried line. They were by no means finished however, and the fighting in Mons was chaotic and bitter. Lieutenant Sally did not make it through the battle for Mons. While standing partly exposed out of the turret, a shell burst nearby and his head was literally blown off. He did not survive long enough to tell Baczewski's story. According to Lou and Les, Sally was a great officer, but like so many others, he did not live long as the CO of D Company. According to Les Underwood, some D Company officers lasted merely minutes, and they had lost so many throughout the war, that there was never one consistent leader aside from Sgt. Joe Cady. There were times in fact that all the company officers were lost and Sgt. Cady was forced to become commander of D Company.

33rd Regt. Sherman's in Belgium (3ad.com)

Confusion and the loss of leadership were widespread in the battle for Mons, and there was essentially no clear front line or rear echelon. In early September of 1944, heavy fighting occurred everywhere around Mons, even the supply troops and cooks fought in heavy engagements. Fortunately for the Allies at the time, the skies were clear and the Air Force bombed and strafed huge columns of German equipment and supplies. Vast elements of the German 7th Army were engaged in the battle, but Allied airpower and the confusion on the ground kept the Germans disorganized. The carnage was wholesale. Like Falaise, huge trains of German equipment, horses, and men laid burning and mangled. By the 4th of September, a massive group of horse drawn artillery pieces were decimated and the corpses of hundreds of horses laid in streets and side roads. The roads around the city were crowded with burning equipment, horses, and human remains.

In more than one engagement, Louch watched through his periscope as Belgian civilians crawled from the crumbled shells of their former homes and buildings and made their way to the piles of dead horses in the streets. The fighting continued all around them. These residents of Mons carried burlap sacks, cleavers, and knives in their hands, and they crept through the mud and blood and filth filled streets. When they reached the mangled horse corpses they began to hack off the meat. They tossed it into their dirty burlap sacks while machine gun fire and rifle fire ripped through the air. They were starving.

Sgt Cady's Tank Crew receiving a toast from a thankful Belgian family
(Namur Belgium 1944)
(back row far left) Leslie Underwood
(standing to the right with his hand on the Belgian civilian) Lou Baczewski,
(kneeling up front to the right, with his hand on the Belgian girl) Sgt. Joe Cady

Namur 1944

3rd AD soldiers in Namur Belgium (3ad.com)

Louis "Louch" Baczewski with a Belgian Woman - Namur Belgium, 1944

With so many cities destroyed and looted by the Germans, the Belgian people were hanging on by a thread. Lou and Les marveled at how little they had in their homes and how scarce food was. "They hadn't had no meat, you'd go into their houses and they'd have potatoes or potato skins cooking and that's it. The German's just took everything from them. They were so happy that the Americans were there, that they offered us food anyway," Les remembered. Starving civilians even offered horsemeat in gratitude for pushing the Germans out of Mons. He recalled one man knowing little English, cutting horse meat in front of them and motioning to them, calling it "beef." Les said the Belgian stood with the bloody meat in his hands, excited as can be, saying over and over, "beef! beef!" He figured that the man just didn't know the right English word for meat.

In roughly three days, the battle for Mons was over. The 3rd Armored division captured some 10,000 German soldiers and the 1st Infantry Division captured some 17,000 more. The defeat was decisive, and the bulk of the German 7th Army was finished.[20] Three German

121

Generals found themselves captured at Mons, and Lt. General Rudiger von Heyking admitted that he had been taken totally by surprise. Many Germans surrendered without much of a fight, but the SS and the paratroopers present refused to back down. Many of the general Wehrmacht considered the war over, and hoped for its end. The fanatical Nazi SS however could not conceive of surrendering the "One Thousand Year Reich".

Consequently, patches of SS troopers refused to submit and as the 3rd Armored advanced past Mons, they were met by futile gestures and suicide missions perpetrated by SS soldiers. Baczewski recalled a peculiar incident involving an SS trooper which occurred on a road near Mons. At the time, Sgt Cady's tank crew lead the column. D Company was on a "road march," their hatches were open the infantry support mounted up on the tanks. No major opposition was being met, and nothing was expected. Suddenly, a lone SS soldier jumped out the ditch ahead of them, and fired a Panzerfaust (grenade launcher) right at their tank. The round bounced off the tank harmlessly. Sgt Cady yelled into his microphone, and ordered the tank to a screeching halt. Immediately, Cady jumped out of the turret in a rage. He leapt off the tank and ran towards the SS trooper. Before the trooper could get out of the foxhole, Cady quickly kicked him in the back with multiple blows. The trooper reeled from the strikes as he continued his futile struggle to climb out of the trench. Cady kept kicking him again and again. Cady screamed in rage, "I ought to kill you." Men of the 36th Infantry soon ran up and pulled the trooper away from Cady. They took the SS trooper prisoner and he was allowed to live. Louch was struck by the fact that the SS trooper despite having no chance of survival, still chose to fire that bazooka. Even if he had knocked out their tank, there was a whole column of tanks behind

122

them and they were loaded with men of 36th Armored Infantry Regiment. "That lone SS trooper, he didn't have a Chinaman's chance, but he still did it.[1] Oh Yea!!! They was die hard, they didn't care whether they got killed or not." Louch exclaimed with astonishment.

Throughout the war, when D Company encountered the SS, similar incidents of irrational bravery occurred. Members of the SS were determined fighters. They were so brainwashed and militant that they would always fight with extreme ferocity, even when there was no chance for success or survival. Members of the SS were not average German soldiers who were just caught up in the war much like any other Allied soldier. The SS were a different breed. In Normandy, the Falaise Gap, and Belgium, there were contingents of the Nazi SS met almost everywhere the 3rd Armored Division went.

The SS, (the Schutzstaffel) or Protection squadron, were a select group of soldiers. In the twisted minds of Himmler and other top Nazis, these soldiers represented the purest of "Aryan blood" and thus the best of the Third Reich. The SS was a construction of Reichsfuhrer Heinrich Himmler who was second only in rank to Hitler himself. Himmler desired the SS to be the, "the aristocracy that never grew old…the best physically, the most dependable, the most faithful men in the movement."[21] Each of

---

[1] (For clarity / apology sake, I wondered why in this case a "Chinaman" would have had less of a chance than anyone else, but I didn't ask him about that specifically. Being old-school, and unaware of certain conventions, I didn't think grandpa was aware that the, "preferred nomenclature," (as stated in the Big Lebowski) is Asian-American and that in general an Asian-American would mathematically have had the same chances as the German man mentioned. The point however of his statement was overall about the fanaticism of the SS and it had little at all to do with Asian-Americans.)

these SS men had been selected through rigorous laboratory examination and study over their Aryan features and familial backgrounds.

German prisoners taken near Mons, Belgium - Lou Baczewski's personal collection. Note: top row, far right sits a captured SS soldier with the distinctive SS markings on his collar.

The SS represented what the Nazis saw to be the Aryan Master Race, and they functioned beyond the trappings of the law. With the aid of the SS, Himmler orchestrated the death camps and helped drive the Third Reich through the "Final Solution." What guided his motives in all matters was a firm belief in Aryan superiority. This divine supremacy was bolstered and wound by a congealed "understanding" of occult mysticism, which can only be explained by the mentally divergent. The belief in mysticism, the concept of root races, clairvoyants, interpretation of archaic symbols, and the idea of "god men" all played a role. The SS troopers themselves were deeply driven by these mystical and racial concepts. These soldiers were not the everyday Germans who just hoped to survive the war; these troops were "Hitler's Own," the SS Leibstandarte (Protection Squadron). They were so furiously brainwashed in Nazi ideals that many lived for the fight itself, as one SS Leibstandarte Captain described fighting in Russia:

> It was in those defensive battles in Russia which I shall always remember for the sheer beauty of the fighting, rather than the victorious advances. Many of us died horribly, some even as cowards, but for those who lived, even for a short period out there, it was well worth all the dreadful suffering and danger. After a time we reached a point where we were not concerned for ourselves or even for Germany, but lived entirely for the next clash, the next engagement with the enemy. There was a tremendous sense of 'being', an exhilarating that every nerve in the body was alive to the fight.[22]

The great majority of SS soldiers fought with such ferocity that it made an indelible impact on the Allies on both European fronts. Why these men fought with such determination and cruelty is debatable, and such motives stemmed from a variety of factors and influences. Yet one undeniably paramount fixture of their mind set, derived from the Nazi belief systems and the subsequent Nazi propaganda monster. In fact, the ideological establishment of the Nazi SS was based on a farcical belief system centered upon the "Aryan god-man" and the runes of ancient Germany. All these concepts were very much promoted by Heinrich Himmler himself (Himmler served as the head of the SS and was second in command to Hitler alone. The Nazis themselves and the subsequent SS were born out of an archaic and cryptic system of belief, which stemmed from a bizarre ideology developed by German mystics - namely the "Ario-sophist" Guido von List. He and others claimed that by means of euphoric

125

trances, they could communicate and translate the symbols left by the "pure" ancient Germans. According to List, these ancients had lost their wings as god men, but only after when interbreeding with lesser races.[23]

These "Ariosophists," truly thought, that by purifying of the Aryan blood, the Nazi's could return to their former status as "god-men." Many of Hitler and Himmler's contemporaries and predecessors prescribed to such theories. In fact, the origins of Nazi beliefs derive from these same mystical perceptions which took hold in Germany and Austria in the late 19th and early 20th centuries. The Nazi party and some of its structural logic (If we can call it that) was built with these concepts in mind. Hitler was a pupil of the Thule society and of Karl Lueger, the anti-Semitic mayor of Vienna. In fact, Hitler lived in Vienna for a considerable time and spoke of Luger's influence on multiple occasions.[24] Many of the ideas expressed in Mein Kampf (My Struggle) Hitler's autobiography, were based on the Ariosophist concepts and Armanist ideas of Guido von List.[25] These concepts were elaborated upon, until the idea of Aryanism became the basis of medical, social, and societal logic in Nazi Germany, thus helping bolster the worst of the Nazi programs such as eugenics, racial cleansing, and eventual wholesale genocide. Sadly much of this has been forgotten and little is said about it in history, it should be of great interest and concern, because movements, the absolute worst of movements, grow from beliefs. Such beliefs, whether absurd or not, can be far more dangerous than any weapon in the long run.

Because members of the SS believed in their Aryan purity and god-man heritage, they were the most loyal and ruthless of all Nazi forces. According to both Lou and Les, it was rare that an SS trooper would surrender, most died fighting regardless of the odds. Throughout the war, the 3rd Armored Division would run into many fanatical members of the

SS. With their own eyes, the soldiers of D Company would see the cruelty, inhumanity, and wholesale murder perpetrated by the SS. Before the wars end, Les and Lou would witness countless atrocities committed in the name of Nazi ideology and Aryan belief. Eventually the 3rd Armored Division would discover for themselves that the SS in many cases were not just fanatical soldiers, but organized murderers and operators of the Nazi labor and death camps. The SS were faced in both France and Belgium by the 3rd Armored, but it was not until the Battle of the Bulge that the 3rd Armored would meet a massive unyielding attack of SS infantry and tank divisions.

Yet as for most of the Belgian campaign itself, and the events following Mons, fighting was scattered and chaotic. German forces could not form a coordinated counterattack of any significance, regardless of the presence of SS. For the 3rd Armored, the fight went on, town to town, house to house, until finally they stood at the door steps of Germany itself. In the battle for Belgium, elements of the SS fought to the end to hold the line, but the bulk of the German Army, began to fall back. Although the combat in Belgium was more sporadic and could be what some characterized as a route, it was still costly for the 1st Army. In general, losses were considerable for the Germans as well as in the Allied units.

In Belgium, D Company lost yet another good commanding officer after the death of Lt. Sally. Having perished, Lt Sally never turned in the necessary paperwork to give Grandpa the Silver Star. According to Lou and Les, many heroic efforts that merited medals, occurred without recognition in D Company. The commanding officers fell in staggering rates - some died within minutes of taking command and without the word of an officer, no medal could ever be awarded.

Cpl. Baczewski never received the Silver Star. Yet, when the end of the war finally came, Louch moved up to drive for another company Commanding Officer (CO). Knowing that Baczewski had seen so much action, the company CO, Lieutenant Alford, put him in for a Bronze Star. Despite the fact that the official citation was dated July 27th, 1945, Baczewski never received an actual Bronze Star from the Army either. In fact, it was not until the 4th of July 1998 that tank driver Louis Baczewski would actually grasp the Bronze star he earned fifty-three years previously for his role in five major campaigns. My Aunt Mary Kay had for the two previous years worked tirelessly to get Grandpa the medal he deserved. The bureaucratic holes were immense and the tangled red tape seemed to pull her down at each attempt.

Letters upon letters were sent to local officials. The VFW was consulted to no avail, and further complicating the situation, a disaster had struck the Veteran's Administration's records. The veteran's records archive in St Louis burned on July of 1973, destroying between sixteen and eighteen million Official Military Personnel Files.

In addition, millions of other files and documents were misplaced. In fact, hundreds of graduate students and history majors spent years searching through the remnants of the burned documents in an effort to reorganize after the fire. It was a massive undertaking and even in the 1990's the prospect of finding Grandpa's records was slim. According to my aunt, it was the uniqueness of Grandpa's last name that helped in finding his paperwork. Somehow despite the fire and towering tumult of remaining boxes and scattered documents, Louch's original (DD214) discharge papers were found. This was the first hurdle, the next dealt with the bureaucracy of the State of Illinois. Aunt Mary Kay's effort presented an Everest like climb, especially considering the reputation of the Illinois

Government. Efficiency and integrity have not always been the foremost attributes of Illinois officials, just ask Blagojevich, or any of the other Illinois governors who have ended up permanently dressed in orange jumpsuits.

With some luck however, Mary Kay was able to get in contact with Kitty Conner an assistant to US Senator Carol Mosely Braun. Conner was herself the daughter of a WWII veteran. Her father had passed away only recently. She was sympathetic to the situation and knew how to navigate the slip and slide of Illinois politics. In a short time after making contact with Kitty, Mary Kay was informed that her father would receive the official document for the bronze star and the medal itself, thanks to the efforts of Kitty Conner. Mary Kay set it up as a surprise. Grandpa had no idea what was going on. Mary Kay and Uncle Paul created a Fourth of July party and everyone besides Grandma and Grandpa knew what was to occur. Kitty Conner came down too from the State capitol in Springfield, and was present in Mary Kay's backyard for the event.

My cousin Michael was as always present and prepared to do whatever for the sake of a family event. Little did any of us know, but Michael and his friend Billy had something all planned out for Grandpa. My Aunt Mary Kay's son Michael was a tough, hard-working good old boy, and there was nothing more important to him than our Grandfather. In fact, Michael followed Grandpa's footsteps and joined the military right out of high school. He joined the Navy, and served on an aircraft carrier as a firefighter. Michael himself was decorated for fighting a fire on the USS John F. Kennedy. He received the highest non-war time medal possible, the Navy Achievement Award, after he was able to fight a fire unprotected, and long enough to suppress, and eventually squelch the

129

blaze. The fire engulfed an aircraft bay and threatened to spread to multiple aircraft. His actions saved numerous sailors' lives.

So, it was befitting that on the Fourth of July, Michael and his best friend Billy, a man who was presently serving as a sergeant in the Marine Corps, presented the Bronze Star to my grandfather, it was almost fifty-three years to the day when the award was finally handed to him. Bill and Michael walked out of the house in full dress, as the screen door screeched closed behind them. They walked in exact cadence.

If you counted civilian military personnel, all branches were represented around the pool that day, my Grandmother had worked for the Air Force for twenty-five years, my grandfather served in the Army, Michael served in the US Navy, and Billy was then enlisted in the US Marine Corps. To the recorded tune of *The Stars and Stripes*, Billy and Michael, marched slowly up the steps of the above ground pool deck and stood at attention before my grandfather. There was a pause among the family and a quiet stillness grew around us as we gazed at grandpa and the men in uniform.

The shade of the big maple trees scattered their dark spots about the crowd and deck. Sharp rays of July light pushed past the gaps in the leaves and illuminated random buttons and eye glasses and ice in the drinks. A slight breeze blew about and it shifted the leaf shaped patches of light and dark among all those standing there behind my Aunt and Uncle's home. As the gaps of bright sun washed across his polished Marine uniform, Billy broke the silence and called out, "Sgt. Baczewski! Ten Hut!" Sgt. Baczewski sharply popped up to attention as if he had never stepped out of his uniform. As the Marine in full dress saluted before him, Grandpa then saluted in return. His hand swept before him in a sharp, crisp, and proper manner. All the while, a confused and bewildered look grew across his face. It was obvious that he wondered what he was getting into. Billy had in his hands the full citation of Grandpa's Bronze Star Award. After a few coughs, Billy began to read the award aloud. Once Grandpa realized what was going on, tears began to well up in his eyes as he stood in the solid state of attention. He was not alone. Eyes were being wiped all around. On that hot Fourth of July day, the whole family looked upon Grandpa, as Billy read the following:

> As announced in section X, General Orders #64, this headquarters 18 May 1945, you have been awarded the Bronze Star Medal for meritorious service in support of combat operations against the enemy. The citation follows:
>
> Tec 4 Louis J. Baczewski 37417198, 33rd Armd Regiment, for meritorious service in support of combat operations against the enemy in France, Belgium, and Germany from June 24th 1944 to April 1945. Tec 4 Baczewski, as a tank driver, ably and aggressively carried out all driving missions given to him, exhibiting great coolness under enemy fire and contributed immeasurably to the successful combat operations of his company. His actions throughout the entire period reflect the greatest credit upon himself and are in keeping with the highest traditions of the military service.
>
> By Command of Brigadier General Hickey[26]

When Billy completed reading, Michael stepped forward with the Bronze Star in hand, to pin it on Grandpa's lapel. Michael was so nervous, that he dropped the medal and he fumbled around for it on the deck boards below him. Michael was never afraid of anything as long as I had known him, but you could see his nervousness. He and Billy had taken this all very seriously, they had spent weeks researching the proper ceremony, practicing their steps, and preparing themselves in general. It was obvious that emotion of the event overwhelmed him, and he became shaky. Grandpa was his biggest hero. Pinning the long deserved medal on his most revered and respected relative carried a heavy burden for Michael, and it showed. Eventually, Michael picked up the medal and righted himself, straightened out his uniform and looked back at Grandpa. Then, sadly he dropped it yet again, and went through the same cycle of movements and frantic searching. After another round of scrambling, he rose again. His big fingers struggled to hold, on as he finally pinned the medal on Grandpa's chest. Grandpa looked him in the eye and they shook hands. It had taken over fifty years, for the man to get what he deserved, who better to give it to him than his eldest grandson. The emotion was palpable, it was thick in the air like a cloud, and it gushed forth from all present. Everyone applauded with exuberance. Eventually, Grandpa sat back in his deck chair and wiped the tears from his eyes. Up until that point, I had never ever seen the man cry. He wore his bronze star the rest of the day, clasped to the blue and tan pocket of his short sleeve polo shirt.

Chapter 7
Skillets

Young people just now starting out in camping
probably have no idea that it wasn't but a couple of
decades ago that people went camping expecting to
be miserable. Half the fun of camping in those days
was looking forward to getting back home. When you
did get back home you prolonged the enjoyment of
your trip by telling all of your friends how miserable
you had been. The more you talked about the
miseries of life in the woods, the more you wanted to
get back out there and start suffering again.

Patrick McManus

It was Christmas of 2002. I was twenty-four and just home from
college. As always, the whole family was gathered together in the
basement of Grandpa and Grandma's home. The main room clamored
with all of the familiar sights, sounds and smells of the holiday. Every
present had been given out apart from a large box marked from Santa to
Stan, my dad. Like me, my father Stanley was named after his Grandfather
– Stanislaws Baczewski.

Dad grabbed hold of the box with his massive hands and placed it
on his lap. His paws were so big that I often joked that if he hit you square
in the face, he could give you two black eyes, a broken nose and a fat lip
all at once. Yet at this point, he was grinning with boyish glee, and was in
no way angry enough to strike blows with his mighty hands. Instead, he
was gazing upon his large box with a look of excitement and wonder.
Sadly, Dad was at that point thinking that he was actually getting
something worth a damn. He was wrong.

Once he ripped the wrapping paper, he had to pull out his pocket knife and cut the ridiculously thick tape from around the top of the box. His smile spread further across his face as the whole family watched. Once his hand reached inside, he initially found only newspaper, but as he reached deeper his hand came to rest on something metal. He lowered the box and pulled out the newspaper to get a better look. Eventually, his smile turned to a disgusted half grin as he said the words, "Son of a bitch! I told you to leave that damn thing at the bottom of the creek!!" The whole family broke out in laughter as he reached his hand into the box and drew forth the disappointing black contorted shape of an old skillet. Dad gazed on the battered and shameful example of cookery with a mixed look of laughter and disgust. As he glared at me roughly, I thought back to the fateful journey that had brought that skillet there on Christmas.

It was on a warm summer morning, five months prior to Christmas. I slid in and out of sleep as the sun began to shine brightly about the underside of the 140 Highway Bridge. Just like every trip, the stillness that so typified the creek was sporadically punctuated by the roaring hum of a semi racing over the 140 bridge. I awoke to the hollow resonance of the passing vehicle.

For most, a highway bridge might seem like the most unlikely place for a person to camp and feel at home. Yet strangely enough, I had always felt somewhat safe camped under a highway overpass. Because, I always thought that anybody who was going to rob us or kill us had to first question himself as to what kind of people would be camped under a highway overpass in the first place. Even a homicidal maniac might ask the question, "Are these really people I want to mess with? After all, they are camped out under a highway overpass and they might be just as crazy as I am." Such logic kept me sleeping like a baby on most trips.

In any event, as I said it was morning, and we were all waking up to the smell of the campfire and the occasional roar of a high speed vehicle. The harsh reality quickly sunk in, and I realized, that regardless of how hung over or tired I was, there was a lot of work to do. We needed to run the lines. Yet, my thought was that there may be some good fish on, and that was encouragement enough to get up from my sleeping bag. The morning was often the best time to run the lines, frequently the best fish were hooked at that time. The realization of this was fuel.

Dad as usual, had been up for some time. He was tending the fire and hanging wet clothes up on a makeshift line between the closest telephone pole and one of the bridge pillars. As I sat up in my sleeping bag, I struggled to make sense of my surroundings. Where were my shoes? Where was my hat? Why did it taste like a horse crapped in my mouth? Why did I purr like a cat when I breathed in and out? Lack of sleep, physical exhaustion, chemical withdrawal, and cigarettes had made me this way. It was not my fault.

Eventually I rose, bundled up my sleeping stuff, and grabbed something to drink out of one of the coolers. At the same time, Uncle Dave's stocky form was wandering about. Yet my brother Joe was still sound asleep. After a brief discussion between uncle Dave, my dad, and I, it was quickly decided that Dave and I would run the lines while Dad would start working on making an early lunch. David and I shuffled our way down the steep banks to the john boat and headed down to check the lines. We paddled downstream, landed a few fish, and baited up the lines as we went. The bright sun reminded us every second that we had drank too much the night before. Our movements were a bit slow and clouded, but we trudged on through the muddy water. After an hour or two of paddling and dragging over riffles, we returned to the bridge.

A steady stream of smoke drifted out along the pillars of the bridge marking our campsite. It was quiet, apart from the standard hum of bugs and occasional chatter of birds. Once we climbed the steep bank we saw that Dad was making up some beans over the campfire. In one skillet he was sautéing some bell peppers and onions. In another skillet he had a vast lump of beans. As it happened, we arrived just in time for a good old campfire cooking disaster. Cooking over a flimsy grill set over rocks on the top of a campfire never presents a picture of a cook at ease. On the contrary, camp cooking is its own form of art. From my perspective, camp cooking is a mix of both walking on hot coals and smoke-eating; all of this is simultaneously performed in painful yoga-like positions.

While slaving over the simmering fire you could see the frustration on Dad's face. With his body bent at 90 degrees in a cloud of smoke, there were moments when even Dad's sizable torso seemed to disappear. As he coughed and struggled to combine the onions and peppers and beans, the situation turned far worse for the now charbroiled cook. One might not think that combining such items a challenge, but because of my old burnt up camping skillet, it was a challenge indeed. The handle had long since burnt off, and a bolt now replaced it; if not held in just the right manner it would lose its threads and turn. Dad did not hold it right. As he attempted to lift the old skillet, the threads turned and an eruption of peppers and onions ensued. The shower of sauté was nowhere over the desired target. Precious onions and peppers fell at Dad's feet and into the flames. In strange karate like jabs and swings he frantically waved the spatula and spinning skillet hoping to slap the few remaining peppers and onions in the right direction. It was a desperate grunting scene that ended in failure and a short but exasperated slump of the poor camp cook.

It was at this exact point, that Dad, in his infinite patience had had enough. As the last of the onions and peppers fell to the sandy ground at his feet, he decided at that point, this very skillet with the trick handle was done. It should not be seen or endured by mankind any more. So, with all the might of a 270 pound construction worker and ex-college football player, the skillet was flung with all the force that Stan Baczewski could muster. A grunt ensued, and a bit of spittle slipped from the corner of his mouth as the skillet took to the air.

At that moment, it felt as if time slowed down. The skillet twirled, silhouetted in the sunlight for what seemed like a good ten minutes. Dad's speech followed the skillet with every bad remark he could muster. His own words intermingled into some unknown language of mixed cuss words and insults. No one knew quite what he was saying, but it was clear what he meant. Perhaps it was best for the skillet's sake that his language was so garbled. For the skillet must have felt rather bad about screwing up the only job it was made to do. Then having to be thrown into the air in a fit of rage; well, that must have just added insult to injury.

As the skillet swirled overhead and reached a height of what seemed to be at least 80 feet, Dad cursed it all the way. It was obviously cursing, but of the level akin to speaking in tongues. The sound, "Frat dit a ratta shift fratten son of a rat fratta ditta." and stuff like that, filled the air. We kept our distance and all looked on in silence and in awe. Eventually, the skillet returned to the earth. When it did so, it clanked, and gonged, and scrapped, as it struck the rip rap that lined creek bank before the bridge. My friend and camping companion for many years, was no more.

Instantly, I asked my dad, "What the hell ya do that for?" He replied, "You've had that piece of shit for years – bout time you get rid of

137

it." I replied, "but it works fine, you just gotta hold it right." He belted back, "I HELD IT RIGHT!!! Right inda that damn creek. Leave it down there!! That's the best place for it." Unfortunately for Dad, he would see the skillet once again despite his absolute disgust for it. When Dave fished it out of the creek it had so many dents in it that it looked like it had been shot with a twelve gauge shotgun at close range. It was then that Dave and I came up with a plan to wrap it up and give it to him on Christmas.

At Christmas, there was always a practical joke to pull, (or be pulled on you); it was as much of a tradition as fishing the creek. My dad saved the skillet and a few years later he wrapped it up and gave it to me on Christmas. I still have it; you just have to hold it right. Grandpa thoroughly enjoyed the whole affair, he had missed that particular trip to the creek, but he had heard all about what happened with Dad and the skillet. Dave and I told him what we planned to do before Christmas, and he was more than happy to be in on the surprise.

On that same Christmas, Grandpa told us a skillet story of his own, one that occurred during his boyhood on the creek many decades before. Louch and his buddy, Dave Pagan, along with Dave's old coon dog, had been camped out on the creek for a day or so. It was around lunch time, and they had killed a few squirrels earlier in the day. So, Louch fried them up in the cast iron skillet over the campfire. As soon as they were done eating, they decided to head out and check their lines and bait them up. Dave had lines upstream and Louch had his lines downstream, so they split up. After some time, Louch arrived back in camp with a few fish and decided to fry up some for dinner. He looked down on the fire grate to find the iron skillet clean and ready to go.

So, he started frying up a batch of fish. Before long Dave came back and they began to eat. As they were eating, Louch told Dave, "Hey, thanks for cleaning out that skillet and that mess from the squirrels." Dave replied, "Well, I didn't clean out that skillet." They looked at each other quizzically then it dawned on them both. Sitting on logs with their plates before them, and their mouths full of food, they simultaneously looked over at Dave's coon dog. The old dog had been nice enough to clean the skillet for the both of them.

Although nobody enjoyed doing the dishes, except perhaps for the dog, we always did cook and eat well on the creek, and at any family occasion for that matter. Grandpa was always a great cook. Because of him and my father, I was always raised knowing that there was no such thing as woman's work or men's work. Work was work, and everyone did their part, whether at home or on the creek. Men in our family always did household chores and especially cooked. Now Grandpa didn't just make toasted cheese or throw a piece of meat on the grill every once in a while. On the contrary, both my grandfather and father were excellent cooks as long as I had known them. They could make everything from blackberry cobbler to chicken and dumplings, and with hand rolled dumplings I might add.

In fact, Grandpa was the one who did most of the cooking for his tank crew in the army. When given the chance, he would scrounge whatever he could find to make up a good meal for his platoon or tank crew. He said they were not supposed to eat foreign food, but they were willing to risk getting into trouble, because eating rations was a battle of its own. Every few weeks unless they were deep in combat, they would be relieved and sent back from the front for some R&R. He said, "On my tank crew, I was the one that did most of the cooking - anything we could find. Once you was back, ya got relieved then you didn't have to always worry. All you had to do was worry about artillery coming in and stuff like that ya know. Other than that, it was kinda peaceful; ya'd only get a blast of artillery coming in every now and then." While on leave near Sherpenseel and Hastenrath during the Huertgen Campaign in Germany, Louch's tank crew killed a small cow: as it was cold, they hung it up and cut steaks for their crew and others in D Company. Lou, Les, Joe Cady, Pat Gillespie, and Virgil Decker were shacked up in a captured German house drinking cognac and eating steaks every night. Colonel Lovelady, (commander of the Lovelady Taskforce) caught word of the steaks, and even though consumption of foreign food was against regulations, he requested that some steaks be cut and sent up to headquarters. Louch and his crew quickly obliged him with a few prime cuts of meat.

Not all of Lou's stories of the war were of combat. Although it was rare, throughout France, Belgium, and Germany, he and his tank crew had some occasions to rest and goof around a bit. During combat operations they were in a state of constant exhaustion, since they could barely sleep between re-supplying the tank, pulling their guard shifts, and manning the next firefight. Les stated that most times when they were relieved and put into reserve they were so tired from combat that quite often all they did was rest.

Louis "Louch" Baczewski, Central France, 1944

In France, they did have a chance to take a break a few times. On one occasion, after the hedgerows, they were able to go see a movie, which had been set up in a French church. The Germans were however very close, and orders were to keep lights out and no smoking, so that the German forward observers could not see their position. The church windows were covered, so that no light escaped from the movie. Just as soon as they were able to relax and watch the movie, disaster struck. Les stated, "Someone outside lit a cigarette, and [German artillery spotters fixed on their position] they bombed, hit the theatre, and tore off part of the roof. We went back to our tanks. End of movie!"

D Company tank in Central France, 1944

When relieved, their only main concern was a burst of artillery coming in now and again. They had to be cautious, but they were able to relax a bit, especially when they were treated with the hospitality of the French and Belgian people. Throughout France and Belgium, almost every citizen they met was friendly. They met exalted praise and appreciation everywhere they went. Belgians invited them into their homes, and fed them. Even though food and luxuries like liquor were scarce, yet Belgian people still greeted D Company with such things on a frequent basis. The soldiers in D Company found themselves treated like honored guests wherever they went. When I jokingly asked Grandpa about the French and Belgian women and how friendly they were during an interview. He replied, "Well yea, there were a lot of good looking women and everything. But, I don't want to talk about that." As he stated this, a grin began to stretch so far across his face that I didn't know how it even fit on his head. He refused to say another word on the subject and we both began to laugh.

French Civilians meeting 3rd Armored soldiers (3ad.com)

However, not all the French and Belgians were pleased with the American presence. As Louch recalled, there were some French folks who were understandably aggravated with the Americans and specifically D Company of the 33rd Armored Regiment. Just as their Shermans had smashed many English cars as they trained on narrow roads of Salisbury, the French civilians lost their fair share of cars to the Lovelady Taskforce. Louch recalled one specific incident in France, where a French driver had parked too close to the road. A convoy of supplies was parked on the other side, in order to let the armored convoy pass around them. Thus the road was packed with GI trucks and tanks. "See there was a column of supplies parked on the road and them roads are narrow, ya know. We was doubling ahead of that column. And so, there was a car parked alongside the road [opposite the convoy]. So, we had to go by there and get by this truck convoy, so every tank would hit that car a little bit, and finally when the last tank came through that thing was smashed to the ground." The poor

Frenchman was out in the street waving his hands over his head screaming and trying to get the column off of his car, but to no avail, by the time the last tank in the column rode by, Louch said that the whole thing was as flat as a pancake.

On the narrow roads in France, there were constant traffic jams and logistical battles between the armored columns, supply trains of GI trucks, wrecked and damaged equipment, and civilian traffic and refugees. When they were sure no one would be hurt, it seemed like a tanker would take the opportunity to smash something out of his way as long as he could get away with it. Honestly can you imagine being 21 years of age and driving around in a 32 ton hunk of metal with a cannon on it, and not wanting to just smash stuff up just for laughs? I would figure that the desire to just tear up anything in your way was ever present. Louch recalled a few such occasions in France.

"One time we was going down there and we was the lead tank and here come a German motorcycle with a sidecar on it. And he come out of this side road and went right down in front of us. I was looking through the periscope and I hollered… I said, 'Pat there's a motorcycle!!!' Here he pulls out right in front of us and Pat Gillespie was our gunner; he shot that thing, and that sidecar went this way and the motorcycle went that way, split it right in half with the main gun!!"

In fact, D Company destroyed the greater part of a town or more in the effort to get at just one motorcycle and kill one German motorcycle messenger. As far as they could tell, the civilians had evacuated the town and only spotty German resistance remained. The German motorcycle driver had somehow become caught up between D Company's roadblocks, and was driving up and down the grid of streets searching for an escape. As he passed each tank they would fire off their main gun.

144

"That was France, we was parked by the street…and that guy on that motorcycle just kept running back and forth and there's buildings against the street, and every time that motorcycle would come across there. Well our gunner would fire and the motorcycle driver he'd go back down that way, and then we heard other tanks firing, and here he come back. D Company's tanks had every road closed off, so the motorcycle driver kept riding from road to road searching for a means of escape, all the while the tanks were firing their main guns, taking pot shots at the driver. The town itself was being leveled by the rounds, in the effort to kill just one motorcycle driver. Louch recalled, "there was stores and everything, and all them 75mm's was hitting all them stores and tearing everything up. Sometimes, ya didn't care where it landed."

Shortly afterwards, on the 25th of August, the 3rd Armored crossed the Seine River in Tilly, France. The division's heavy equipment and tanks crossed a US made pontoon bridge. As Louch stated, the floating bridge, "came up in front of ya like a wave, it was kinda shaky going across the Seine river… It [the river] was vast, oh yea, it was wide as the Mississippi. Well we didn't get much fire going across there; just a few infantry was all. Stanley Cravens, his outfit was there at the Seine River, cause see he was in the 7th Armored Division, and I knew he was in I think the 33rd Engineers…"

3ʳᵈAD Crossing the Seine River (3ad.com)

In fact, Louch's boyhood friend and Shoal Creek fishing buddy was part of the 33ʳᵈ Armored Engineer Battalion. Under heavy fire, the members of the 33ʳᵈ Engineers constructed that very bridge. Stanley's MOS (Military Occupational Specialty) was listed as that of a "Rigger," similar to an ironworker. Little did Louch know that Stanley Cravens and the men of his outfit had literally paved their way. According to the After Combat Reports of the 33ʳᵈ Engineer Battalion, they not only constructed that bridge, but they also dynamited or compromised every nearby bridge on the river. Most importantly, the 33ʳᵈ destroyed all the bridges that connected to the nearby city of Corbeil. This village contained a force of 3000 German soldiers and 14 Tiger tanks.[27] The reason why Louch's Regiment took little fire and easily crossed the pontoon bridge was due to the efforts of the 33ʳᵈ Engineer Regiment. Had the 3ʳᵈ Armored Division met that German force by the bridgehead in Tilly, France, history may have been far different. More than likely, no such crossing would have been possible; at least not without the loss of many lives and tanks.

Two young men from Pocahontas, Illinois, (which had a population of 800) had somehow ended up in the same battle, for the same bridgehead, and on the other side of the world. It was an amazing coincidence. Stanley and my grandfather had been very close friends since childhood. They were neighbors. Louch and Stanley had fished Shoal Creek together during their youth, and were good friends all throughout grade school and high school. They would both do a lot of hogging (noodling) together on the creek, catching flatheads, bluecats, and channels with their bare hands. Sometimes they would catch fish weighing up to 40 pounds or more. In the spring time, they would also search for arrowheads together. They found different Native American artifacts in the freshly tilled fields all around town. As Louch stated, "Stanley, he used to go scout them fields after farmers plowed, he was real interested in that, he was looking for arrowheads all the time. He had arrowheads and tomahawks and everything, he found all kind of relics, he had walls full of em."

So when Louch crossed the Seine and saw vehicles marked 7th Armored Division 33rd Armored Engineer Battalion, he tried to look for Stanley there. "The 7th Armored Engineers and their vehicles was around that pontoon bridge and when we stopped there I started asking around... I thought well, maybe I'll see him. I kept asking them guys if they knew Stanley Cravens, but none of em knew him, so we had to move on, but that was his outfit, cause I wrote to him."

"Ya know, he got killed. He never survived." In less than a month, Stanley Cravens was killed in action as his battalion tried to hold yet another bridgehead in Sillengy, France. They were working in support of

Operation Market Garden, which was a British plan to secure bridges throughout Holland for a major offensive and eventual thrust into Germany. The mission of crossing, holding, and constructing a bridge over the Seille River fell into the hands of 33rd Engineer Battalion. Despite ceaseless heavy artillery fire, major construction went on throughout the 18th of September.[28] The engineers reverted to "infantry tactics" due to the artillery and German ground attacks.

On the 19th of September, Stanley Cravens was killed. The German artillery eventually rendered bridge construction "impracticable" according to the after action report of September 20th 1944, and the mission was called off. The 33rd Armored Engineers were eventually retreated due to a significant German counterattack. After losing his life there, in the fighting for Sillengy, PFC Stanley Cravens was eventually laid to rest in a US Cemetery outside St. Avold, France. He is buried there along with more than 10,000 other Americans. He was nineteen years old.

Although Louch didn't know it at the time, he was surrounded by his boyhood friends from Pokey throughout the war. Almost all of his friends from the creek ended up in US 1st Army and four out of five were in 7th Corps. John Hustava, like Stanley Cravens, was involved in Operation Market Garden, as he was a paratrooper in the 82nd Airborne. About the same time Stanley was killed, John was dropped in to help take the bridge at Nijmegen. Dave Pagan was nearby as well, driving an M5 tractor, and pulling artillery pieces for the 78th "Lightning" Division. As for Mel Weber, his story was the most surprising, because he was actually fighting right alongside Louch throughout the war. Mel was an infantryman in the 36th Armored Infantry Regiment and part of the 3rd Armored Division.

When I was younger, Grandpa would tell lighthearted stories about the war while we sat around the fire and waited to run the lines on the creek. He would talk about hunting for food or running over cars with his tank and such. He would also tell tales about his boyhood friends. Even though these stories about Pokey seemed so far apart from the war then, the truth was that his friends had been with him all the way, from the creek through the war. While at the creek, Grandpa would almost never speak of the darker aspects of the war, or the combat he had seen. It wasn't until I started researching and asking more exact questions that he began to tell me more. When I found his after combat reports he began to read through them almost daily, and a lot of things came back to him about the war. I think he was beginning to realize that he may not be around for too much longer. More and more, it became apparent that he wanted, and in a sense needed to tell this story.

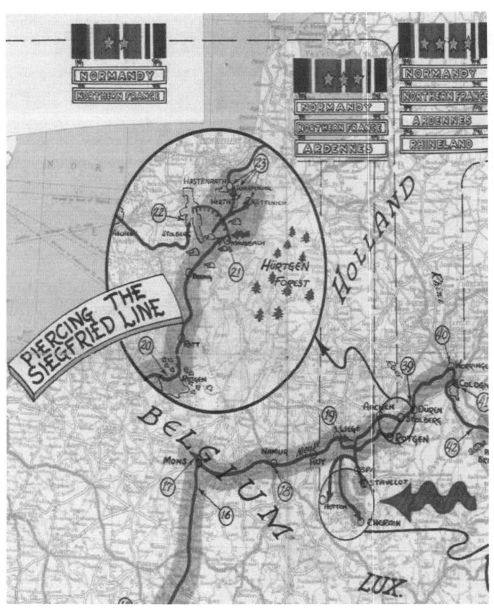

Detail of the Lovelady Taskforce Campaign Map – Rhineland Campaign
(#4 of 5 Campaign Stars)

Chapter 8
The Siegfried Line
& The Huertgen Forest Campaign

In the Huertgen Forest proper, our gains came inch by inch and foot by foot, delivered by men with rifles — bayonets on one end and grim resolute courage on the other. There was no battle of Europe more devastating, frustrating or gory.

Major General William G. Weaver
8th Infantry Division

In the waiting room, my grandfather and family were treated to snacks and refreshments and the infinite courtesy of the members of the Washington High School Student Council. My grandfather and father commented on how nice the students were and how respectful they were to all in attendance. I sarcastically told them, "I don't know any of these kids, I teach shop, I don't deal with the good ones. Half of my kids are probably hiding somewhere finishing off a pint of whiskey before school starts." Grandpa and Dad looked at me and laughed. It was funny because it was true, they knew that from experience.

It was the morning of the high school's yearly assembly to honor Veterans. I had to trick Grandpa into coming, but he came. There were roughly 1,500 people in attendance between the students, staff, local Veterans, American Legion color guard, school board members, and various community members. Even the mayor was there. My father, stepmother, fiancé, uncle, and Grandfather, followed in a processional to the recorded tune of "Amazing Grace" played on bagpipes. The whole student body stood in recognition as we were seated.

151

For the past few weeks I was having trouble getting to sleep, because I thought about the speech all the time. I read and proofread and rewrote and reread my speech, over and over again. I had given speeches in front of groups before, but never one this large. I was scared for days. My hands shake now even as I think about it. Yet when I stood up and was asked to approach the microphone, my fear left me. I knew in my heart that I was going to tell everyone in attendance an important story. For far too long, it belonged to our family alone. Colleagues later commented that I looked completely relaxed. I almost felt like I was, because I was telling everyone a true story, and there was nothing to be afraid of. It was Veteran's day of 2009 in the Blue Jay gym of Washington, High School, in Washington Missouri.

In hindsight, I probably should have had a haircut before the speech. I am sure that as I approached the podium, plenty of the vets there were looking at me and wondering what this long haired hippie had to say about veterans. I had some long wavy locks of hair at the time. The speaker before me was a young student who recognized all the women who had served in our armed forces, I remember wondering how a high school student was able to become so skilled at speaking in front of such large crowds. I hoped to do half as well in presenting what I had to say. After her speech was complete, I was called to the podium to speak. A young girl from student council called my name and then extended the menacing looking microphone in my direction. It was my turn.

My dress shoes slapped on the maple basketball court and my tie flapped about as I stepped up to grab the microphone. I was surrounded by the creak of bleachers and the faded whispers of an entire high school. I cleared my throat and set the speech on the podium. I did my best to compose myself and looked out into the crowd of 1,500. My speech was as follows:

I stand before you today, on this honored day, to tell the story of one specific soldier (my grandfather), and in doing so to tell the shared story of so many other men and women who served and now serve in our armed forces. Sgt Louis J. Baczewski was a poor young man and 1st generation Polish American from Pocahontas, Illinois. In 1944 he was sent half way around the world to fight in Europe where his parents had previously fled to avoid the First Great War. He served as a tank driver for the 3rd Armored Division, 33rd Armored Regiment, 2nd Battalion, D Company. He was part of the Lovelady Taskforce, a regiment of the aptly named "Spearhead" Division of First Army.

He was one of only eighteen men out of 152 in his regiment to make it through the war and home without a scratch. He was the only combat tank driver in his company to make it through the entire war, most of the eighteen who were not

153

killed or wounded were non–combat troops. He lost a tank commander, a driver, and a lieutenant in his tank alone. He went through many replacements and saw the bulk of his entire company killed in the Battle of the Bulge; even his commanding general was killed in action. He received a Bronze Star for his combat record, and was to be put in for a Silver Star, but the officer who witnessed the action was killed before he could complete the paperwork. Sgt Baczewski's Combat command was responsible for the destruction of more German tanks, captured soldiers, and enemy losses than any other armored combat command in WWII. The costs of this were however terribly high: Sgt. Baczewski's combat command sustained a staggering amount of casualties and the highest tank losses of any American Armored Regiment in the war. The Lovelady Taskforce was also the first American Regiment to fight its way across the German border. The 33rd Armored Regiment also gained the grim distinction of concentration camp liberator, once it took the town of Nordhousen, Germany. My grandfather stated that "it wasn't a pretty sight" as people who were merely skeletons attempted to clap when liberated, but lacked the strength to even make a sound when their hands met.

The Sherman tank Sgt. Baczewski drove from Omaha Beach to the heart of Germany was horribly outgunned by German (Panzer) armor and it is and was widely considered a death trap. Sherman tank armor was comparably thin, the guns were of low velocity and diameter, and the gasoline tanks sat on both sides of the personnel compartment – when hit, they would explode and incinerate the men inside. Tank crews gave it the name "Ronson Can" after Ronson lighter fluid, because it always lit on the first strike.

The following is a first-hand account of the harsh combat he experienced. At the time, his regiment was on a "road march" a term for when the column was moving forward at a fast pace loaded down with men and equipment. Supplies and soldiers were piled on the backs of the tanks and armored vehicles and openly exposed to enemy fire as the regiment moved forward. The Germans commonly set ambushes in areas to await such columns, as American tank tactics proved horridly predictable. The German's were typically equipped with 88mm artillery, which was capable of knocking out a Sherman tank in one shot. What follows is an account in his own words:

"We were in Germany, we were just rolling along pretty good wasn't hitting any resistance or anything at high speed when we went over a crest. Then all of a sudden it dropped down ya know. Infantry was loaded on the tanks and we were moving fast. Then all of a sudden the first four tanks got knocked out. They [Germans] had 2 self propelled 88's dug in and when we went over the crest, I was the fifth tank that went over the crest. They knocked out four tanks ahead of us and the infantry was riding on the back. They slaughtered the infantry. I remember this one infantry guy running and screaming – he had his arm blown off. And he was just running alongside of the tank screaming. And so my tank commander said "Lou, put it in reverse, back up. He kept hollering – 'backup, backup, backup!!!! We wanted to get back over the crest of that hill. So, reverse you have to push a button on your gear shift and bring it over and then back. I saw them tanks burning ahead of me and everything. I was so scared that I kept putting it into first gear instead of reverse, ya know. Finally, Joe Cady kept hollering, 'Lou get that thing in reverse!!!' And I kept lunging that thing forward. He said, put that thing in reverse!!!! I finally got it in reverse and backed over the knoll. They had to call the Air Force in and the P51s to bomb those gun emplacements before we could move on.

"When we were on a road march like that, the infantry climbed on the back of the tanks. That was one heck of a deal, he hollered at me three times to put that thing in reverse. I finally got it in reverse. They talk about people that don't get scared when they are in combat – they are crazy. Whenever your life is at stake, it is just like those guys in Iraq now; you can say everything you want about patriotism and everything else like that, but boy when your life is at stake you think about your life. And these soldiers that got killed, don't think that they weren't scared or if they worried about their own lives. Whenever your life is at stake it is a whole different thing.

My grandfather still carries his tank driver's license in his wallet even to the present day and the memories of his experiences and of his fellow soldiers still live with him in clarity. A few years ago when my family was going to rent some vans to drive to Dallas to see my sister's wedding, my Grandmother protested. She didn't like the idea of grandpa driving such a large van and stated to my grandfather, "you don't know how to drive a van like that." My dad countered and said, "Mom, he drove a tank all the way through Europe in the middle of a war, he ought to be able to drive a darn van."

In closing, such stories should not be told in an effort to honor war, but to give homage to those who were called to fight and serve. There is no glory in war, and Veterans Day was not made to commemorate destruction, but instead the end of bloodshed and the service of those loved and lost. This day was made to mark the end of the first Great War and the Armistice, the time when the guns ceased. Throughout history and on to the present, it is the service of those men and women in uniform that allows us to sit here today

in safety, whether in war, or in the
protection of peace, so lest we forget.

The toughest part of the speech was, when it was over, I had to look directly at him and say, "Sergeant Baczewski, will you please stand." My voice quivered, and tears welled up in my eyes. I looked out into the crowd of young women and men and saw their red eyes and the wiping of tears. I then had to try and choke back my emotions enough to say, "I ask the student body, the staff, and all those in attendance to please stand and recognize Sgt. Baczewski for his distinguished service to our country." The gymnasium lifted with uproarious applause. Then, my grandfather, 87 years old at the time, with tears in his eyes walked up in front of all of those people and gave me a hug. Grandpa wasn't big on hugging all the time, once you became a young man it was handshake time. Yet on that occasion, a hand shake just didn't suffice for him.

When he sat back down, I improvised a few things to say to all the students. I was surprised I did this, but I felt invigorated and thankful that I was able to share his story with so many. I told the students, "This is not like TV, this is not "Call of Duty" the video game. These are real people who served their country and they deserve your thanks and praise." I wanted these kids to see that they needed to listen to these men and women and understand what war and sacrifice was really all about. I felt one of those fleeting magical moments of teaching where… damn-it they were really listening. The bulk of them heard every damn word, and many students would comment about that speech for years to come.

The first-hand account I had included in the speech had come from Grandpa's recollection of the 3rd Armored's advance into what the American's called "The Huertgen Forest." The only part that had to be changed was a bit of the cussing. In truth, Cady had yelled at Lou using quite a few expletives. I couldn't exactly yell cuss words in front of an entire high school, so I cut those out, and Grandpa noticed. He later told me I left out a few God-damn-its in that speech. Sgt Cady was screaming at Lou, because it was a matter of life and death, and despite all of the lunges forward, their tank did not get hit by the dug-in anti-tank guns. The heated incident included in the speech occurred a few days after Louch and Task Force Lovelady crossed the German border and the Siegfried Line.

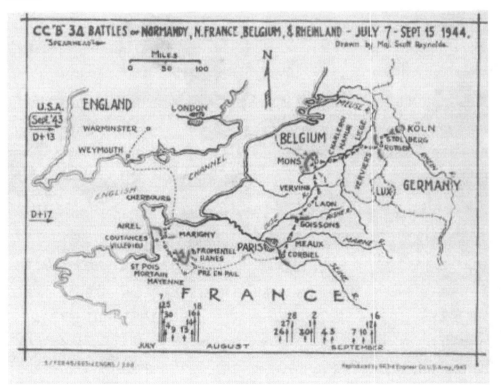

After making their way through Belgium, the First Army was the first to cross the "Westwall." The 3rd Armored's Combat Command B was the first Combat Command to cross the German border in force. According to Louch, when he and the rest of D Company initially crossed the first barriers of the Siegfried line, "We didn't hit much resistance at all, we just more or less rolled in there and rolled through it. Well, cause the war was about over, except that they had most of their soldiers going for that push in Belgium [the subsequent Battle of the Bulge]. Our outfit was the first ones inda Germany." At 4:51 PM, on the 12th of September, 1944, the Lovelady Taskforce entered Roetgen Germany. It was the first German town to be captured and occupied by Allied soldiers. According to Eaton Roberts, some correspondents were there to see the landmark event, notably Dick Tregaskis, author of *The Guadalcanal Diary* and affiliates of NBC. There were other small army groups that had crossed the border previously, but Taskforce Lovelady was the first in force, and certainly the first to capture a German village. The 3rd Armored Division was the first major force to enter Germany (or what was then Prussia) since the invasion of Napoleon in 1810.

3rd AD Tankers crossing the Siegfried Line (3ad.com)

161

Although much more is said about General Patton and the 3rd Army, it was in fact the 1st Army with its many divisions such as the 3rd Armored, which made the first foothold in Germany, covered the most ground, destroyed the most German tanks, and captured the most German soldiers. First Army Commander General Hodges was a quiet man, and not fond of publicity. However, Patton had a famously large mouth, and sadly in history, that takes precedence. Additionally, Patton as head of the 3rd Army received a good deal of undue credit because of the 3rd Armored Division's accomplishments and the perception that 3rd Army and 3rd Armored meant the same thing. Honestly, it should not matter who conquered what, but that the job was done and the Nazis destroyed. Yet to this day, it is a discredit to all the men in the 1st Army that they should have to hear Patton's name brandished as if he were the soul conqueror of the Third Reich.

In truth, it was Patton's poor conception of tank strategy which helped bring about the deaths of so many US tank crews. Because as stated before he pressed to make sure that the Sherman was chosen as the main battle tank for the US Army. Before Normandy, the M26 Pershing was available, but ignored due to Patton's insistence. The Pershing had a 90 millimeter cannon, better armor, better traction, and speed. Patton felt that because the M4 tank was lighter and required less fuel than "the M26 [Pershing], it would be faster and better equipped to perform the mission of the armored divisions." According to Patton, "tanks of an armored division were not supposed to fight other tanks, but bypass them if possible and attack enemy objectives to the rear."

Mass production of the Sherman occurred, despite the possibilities of the Pershing. Few Pershing tanks deployed, even by war's end. In this vein alone, it is a travesty that we as a nation hold George Patton to such high esteem, especially when considering divisions like the 3rd experienced a tank replacement rate of roughly 6 to 1. It is such a tragic and bitter irony that Patton is in the minds of the everyday American, the greatest tank tactician of World War Two. In truth, the man's tank tactics and decisions were languid at best and costly at least.

When the 33rd as part of Combat Command B (CCB) crossed the Siegfried Line at Roetgen, resistance proved to be minimal, at least initially. Yet the battle stiffened quickly in a push towards Stolberg, and the 3rd Armored became bogged down and slowed by destroyed or blocked roadways, pillboxes, and anti-tank (AT) guns. Even though the dragon's teeth and massive rows of concrete barricades on the edge of the Siegfried Line had been crossed, the formidable barrier of the thick forests, concrete encased pillboxes, and dug in emplacements began to take their toll. Despite the perception that the Siegfried area was manned by poorly trained boys and old men of the "home-guard," Lightning Joe Collin's 7th Corps faced a formidable challenge. This was in great part due to the terrain and structures and the overall lack of skillful strategy and intelligence.

A short time after losing four tanks due to the German ambush, D Company tanks rolled into a muddy mine field. Among so many other shortcomings, the Sherman's traction proved dreadfully poor in deep mud. Consequently, the crew had to bail out as soon as the tank became stuck. Under a hail of small arms fire, the crew ran along the path of their tracks and back towards a nearby house. Somewhere along the way, Les Underwood became separated due to the small arms fire. As Lou, Sgt. Cady, Virgil Decker, and Pat Gillespie ran into one abandoned German house, Les ran into another. When Les opened the basement door, the basement was full of German soldiers. He quickly slammed the door and ran off. Les claimed that his ability to survive the war was directly due to his skill at running away – fast.

Later, Les was able to find the rest of his crew, but not before a lot of frantic running and searching. According to Lou and Les, the Germans occupied most of the town near the mine field. The town was a mish-mash of German and Allied controlled homes. Battle lines were cloudy at best. Between the mud and murky battle lines, chaos reigned for D Company tankers, as the bulk of the tankers were forced to dismount their tanks under fire. Their Shermans bogged down in the mud and became impossible to free from the quagmire. According to Les, as the men climbed out of their tanks the new CO (who had been in charge for roughly 15 minutes) took a direct hit, right in the head. He fell dead immediately.

3rd AD recovery vehicle (3ad.com)

Many D Company tank crews held up in abandoned German houses for days, as they waited for retrieval crews to arrive. Once hauled out and back on the roads, D Company's tanks moved deeper into Germany. In the days that followed, they ran into scattered but increasing resistance and obstacles. Anticipating their steps, the Germans set numerous traps before them. In the Huertgen Forest, the Germans not only set many traps, but they also used their artillery in such a way as to enlist the forest itself as a weapon. As most German artillery shells went off on contact, they would contact the treetops first; this sent not only shrapnel, but tree bark and chunks of wood in all directions. Troops normally trained to hit the deck and lay prone in an artillery attack found themselves horribly exposed to the "tree-burst." If the terrain, structures and tree-bursts were not enough, there were additional problems facing the campaign. The cloudy autumn sky hindered most help from air support, which was already slimmed due to missions north and south of the Huertgen Campaign. The British Market Garden Operation continued simultaneously in Holland to the north, while Patton's men trudged and tripped their way slowly through France to the south.

This lack of aerial aid left the Sherman tank crews alone to face superior German armor throughout much of the Huertgen Campaign. The whole mission was a gamble. Even at its onset, with air support diverted and supply lines strained, the German defenses thickened with each American step into German territory. Despite the fact that the main outer defenses of the Siegfried line fell easily, the inner pillboxes and gun emplacements would exact a heavy toll. In many cases these fortifications held fast, impervious even to flame throwers or air attack.[29]

Additionally, units such as Task Force Lovelady had been pushed feverishly for two months and had little or no respite. Collins's units

165

striking into Germany were in many cases under equipped, and undermanned due to the hard battles they had fought to make the border. The Lovelady Taskforce had taken immense losses in that time. According to the 33rd Armored's After Combat Report of September 26, 1944, the task force had lost a total of 133 medium tanks (Shermans) to enemy action since entering combat in July. With it now being September, they were tired, worn, and needed rest. Their clothes were literally falling apart on them; their bodies and the inside of their vehicles were dank and filthy. According to Louch, "Well you know you don't get to wash, you just have to wear them stinking clothes, for quite a while. Well heck sometimes a month and longer than that. Sometimes you didn't get relieved right away. Normally ya took [the front] for a couple weeks and then ya got relieved. Sometimes you didn't get relieved, so ya just kept going, kept pushing, and fightin, and that was it. Sometime if you had to go to the bathroom you went right in the tank."

"Would there be no respite? Especially infantrymen, but tankers too, were physically exhausted to the near breaking point," Surgeon Eaton Roberts lamented. "They were tired, cold, wet, and dirty. Their uniforms were worn and actually rotting, many hanging practically in shreds. Eyes were blood shot, cheeks hollowed, shoulders bent forward, and what few grim smiles were encountered showed stained and lusterless teeth framed in drab, cadaverous faces."

From the day they crossed the German border, to the 25th of September, Taskforce Lovelady fought in various attacks and defended against armored and infantry counterattacks. Nine such attacks occurred in one day on the 19th of September.

Finally, when they approached Stolberg, D Company received some well-deserved R&R. After a short bit of rest, and finally a chance to change clothes and get a shower, the tank crews and infantry were returned to the front lines. It was not long after returning to the lines that Sgt Cady was again smarting off to an officer for making a foolish order. "Before we got to Stolberg, we ran into a Tiger and we ran into this infantry colonel by the name of Yeoman." Lou recalled. "He motioned us. This colonel told my tank commander, 'there's a Tiger over there, go on over there and slug it out with him. And my tank commander said, 'you just blow it out your ass, we ain't gonna attack no Tiger.' He said we'll take turret defilade."

Turret defilade was a term for a tank tactic, in which the tank crew would use a hill or other defensive position to fire from. Then, after they had fired a few rounds, they would quickly move to a different defensive position and fire again. In this way, the other tank would have trouble zeroing in on other tank's position. On this occasion, Cady followed this procedure and it forced the Tiger tank crew to abandon the tank. They were never sure if they truly knocked it out, but the German crew disappeared, leaving the tank in the field. In any event, Cady smarted off to the Colonel, because he knew that they could not take a Tiger head on.

When Cady and his crew pulled back from the front, soon afterwards, Captian Stallings, came to speak with Cady. It seemed that Col. Yeoman had contacted Stallings, and was by no means happy with how Cady addressed him. When Stallings asked Cady for his side of the story, Cady coldly retorted, "By God, I told him to blow it out his ass. I can't tackle a Tiger. I wasn't gonna slug it out with a Tiger." Stallings, ever understanding the difficulty Cady's job, merely returned, "Sgt Cady, you shouldn't talk to an officer like that. Colonel Yeoman don't understand tank tactics. That was as far as the situation went and Stallings let it drop, knowing all too well, what tangling with that tiger tank would have meant for his men.

Abandoned (Mark VI) Tiger tank, Germany 1944
- courtesy of University of Illinois Archives

According to Baczewski, Captain Stallings was a great commander and he understood exactly what his men were going through. He himself lost a tank in the hedgerows. Stallings and his fellow tankers became riddled with burns when a flamethrower struck their Sherman. The damage was so severe, that the tank could not be moved. His crew, just like Cady's, bailed out under fire. Stallings and the others scrambled into hiding places in the hedges, as the rest of D Company retreated from the

Germans. Once night fell, Stallings and his stranded comrades were able to sneak back through enemy lines and rejoin the company.

Captain Stallings was soft on Cady and his big mouth, but only because he knew damn well what he and his men went through each and every day. Cady was never officially reprimanded for the incident. Captain Stallings understood that taking a Tiger tank head on with a Sherman would have been certain death. Cady was just telling it how it was. According to Baczewski, such incidents were commonplace. Good sergeants were too important to be court-martialed or removed from the front. Officers who were not doing the fighting themselves were often quick to put men into terrible situations that could be avoided, but Stallings was not one of those officers. As time went on, Louch said he and other men with combat experience were less and less apt to put themselves in bad situations for no good reason. Their job was too difficult as it was, and it was too hard to stay alive, even for experienced men.

Task Force Lovelady fought its way through to Mausbach on the initial penetration into Germany, and eventually served as the main thrust in the capture of the industrial town of Stolberg. The 3rd Armored Division flanked by the 1st Infantry Division in the north and the 9th Division to the south, held the area surrounding Stolberg until relieved on September 27th. On the outskirts of the city, Les recalled that Colonel Lovelady himself ordered their company to take an area on the high ground near the city. There was an apple orchard on top of a hill, and Colonel Lovelady assured them that there weren't any Germans there anyway.

Despite their misgivings, D Company headed up the hill to take the orchard; once they crested the hill they found the situation was altogether different from Lovelady's description. "Colonel Lovelady sent us in and said, 'there ain't nothing up there.' But, heck, there was the whole German army up there, infantry all over the place," Les angrily recalled. "We had to pull back, and Lou ran a bunch of em over. Machine gun bullets was bouncing off the tank, they sounded like someone throwing peas on the side of a can. They only had infantry, but they were swarming all around us." Their company of Shermans turned and ran, as the German infantry soldiers hurled themselves at the tanks. The German soldiers frantically tried to climb aboard the tanks in order to grenade the crew members inside. Many fell before the tank tracks and were crushed as D Company pulled back to escape. The actions around Stolberg were chaotic to say the least and incidents such as these were a standard for the campaign.

During the assault on Stolberg, the mud and difficult terrain once again stymied the advance and added additional burdens and issues. Artillery support occasionally fired on friendly forces. The gun stabilizers sank into the mud during initial volleys and sent further rounds in short of their targets, right down on their own men. The fight for Stolberg was a muddy slog of bitter house to house, and building to building combat. Numerous German counterattacks were sent in to push back the allied advance, but the 3rd Armored along with the 1st and 9th Infantry Divisions held firm, until eventually the town was secure.

In the last stages of the battle for Stolberg, Lou seized a chance to explore the wreckage of the city. The fighting had died down and any time there was a break in the fighting, one of the tank crew would usually explore around the rubble of the cities and villages. They would justify this by calling it a "G2" mission (a mission to "gather intelligence"). In truth, it was a way to find souvenirs or cognac. "I did a lot of G2'n." Louch recalled. When he did so in Stolberg, he stumbled onto a manufacturing facility, with smoke still pouring out the stacks. He walked through the factory alone with a Thompson machine gun in hand.

"There was a plant there that was making tanks ya know, and we took that plant over and they had tanks half assembled and that, inside that plant. And there was bomb craters all around that plant, but none of em hit the plant. And I thought, why in the hell didn't they bomb that plant, there's craters big as my basement. Craters all around it ya know. The biggest part of the buildings and everything around there were bombed but that plant, wasn't bombed. Well anyway, things died down and I went and took a walk in that plant there. I was what they called G2'n. I was looking through these desks and everything, and there was a bunch of these pencils, an ever-sharp pencil. I picked one of them up, and it said Ford Motor Company USA." He still has one of these pencils in his box of miscellaneous souvenirs from the war. In fact, throughout the offices in the plant, the desks were full of pencils and pens and stationary, all marked Ford Motor Company.

Ford had a German subsidiary company named Ford-Werke which started operating out of Germany years before the onset of the war. Although the average person in the United States is unaware, previous to and during the war, Ford Motor Company possessed German factories in Hamburg and Cologne as well. Ford did in fact build vehicles for Nazi Germany throughout the war, and Ford was sued in various cases for using slave labor to provide manpower. The debate continues as to the level of control Ford's Dearborn Headquarters had during the war. Ford itself, has maintained that they lost contact with their Ford-Werke subsidiary around 1941. After the BBC produced a special on Ford's involvement with the Nazi regime, Ford hired research historians in an effort to debunk any claims of direct involvement between Ford and the Nazi government.

Additionally, it is difficult to ascertain how much actual profit Ford made during this period, due to the Nazi nationalization of all German industries. Yet despite a lack of clarity in regards to the logistical specifics of the time, Ford's relationship with the Nazi's was undeniably frightening.

What cannot be disputed is the fact that Ford himself published an anti-Semitic pamphlet, titled the, *International Jew, The World's Foremost Problem.* Henry Ford was without a doubt a fan of the Nazi Regime. This adoration was mutual and prior to the onset of the war; the Nazi Government issued Henry Ford the highest of civilian awards. According to a *New York Times* article dated December 20, 1922, Hitler's office contained stacks of books written by Henry Ford, as well as a "prominently placed" photograph of the man himself. A 1998 article from the *Washington Post* stated that Ford and GM support of the Nazis was more helpful than any collusion between the Reich and Swiss bankers.[30] Sadly, few Americans are aware of the depth of corporate involvement that played out during the war. Ford and GM were not alone, as other American companies, notably IBM and Coca-Cola also played similar roles in Nazi Germany. As Gore Vidal once ruefully stated, "We live in the United States of Amnesia."

Such details along with the facts of the Huertgen Forest Campaign seem to fall through the cracks and some get lost to obscurity. Similarly, the Huertgen campaign was no stranger to American forgetfulness. Thus, many authors have called the Huertgen Forest a forgotten campaign. In truth, the entire Huertgen Offensive was a debacle at best, and most historians consider it to be a waste in lives and resources. "Lightning Joe" Collins, the commander of the Huertgen Offensive, later commented, "if we could break it [the Siegfried line], then we were that much to the good;

if we didn't then we could be none the worse."[31] In a statement only a cold and myopic man could make, Collins seemed to flat out ignore the carnage and costly battle that went on from September 1944 to January of 1945. The mission had been to probe the defenses and see how far a "reconnaissance in force" could march into Germany. But with supplies and air support being diverted, the Huertgen campaign was hindered at its onset. The infantry divisions and armored infantry support troops fared the worst. It was a ghastly reminder of WWI trench warfare. The bodies stacked up. According to Baczewski, the carnage was wholesale and the line shot back and forth, day in and day out

"One time, the front was stable at Sherpenseel and Hastenrath. Well guys was laying there and the front was stable there." He grimly recalled. "They just didn't pick them dead people up. You'd go up and hold and then you got relieved. You'd be there a week or two and then another outfit would pull in there. When you'd go back again, why them soldiers would still be lying there, just rotted and the meat was off of their face and everything. They just didn't have a chance to pick them bodies up. It wasn't at all pleasant to see."

Throughout October and November Combat Command B, moved slowly through dogged defenses and counterattacks taking the cities of Werth, Kottenich, Hastenrath and Sherpenseel. Day to day the front line ebbed and flowed, so quickly that it was confusing to both sides. No one seemed to know who held what ground. Assault after assault, counterattack after counterattack, the line ripped back and forth like a saws-all. Les recalled that for weeks upon weeks, they dug in and held on, then they pull back again for relief, gaining little to no ground in the area of Hastenrath and Sherpenseel. All the while, the weather began to turn colder and colder as the reciprocating battle continued. Both Les and Lou commented that it was always hard to tell where the lines were. Germans and Americans were scattered around each other, sometimes in houses right next door to one another.

On one occasion, Les walked a short distance away from where the tank was dug in. He headed towards a house to find a place to go to the bathroom. When he stepped into the door of the house (which sat only yards from where the tank had been parked for days) he found two German infantry men. They were sitting at the kitchen table eating. Their rifles sat idly leaned up on a wall only few feet from them. They quickly raised their hands to surrender. Les, who wasn't expecting to run into anyone in the house, didn't even have a weapon drawn. Like a fumbling western showdown, he struggled to get his 45 caliber pistol from its holster. Luckily for him, he grabbed his gun reasonably quickly, and just fast enough to keep them from reaching for their rifles. He took them both prisoner and marched them back to the company Command Post (CP). The problem was; he still needed to go to the bathroom. I never asked how he resolved that dilemma.

The next day, Les was a bit jumpy given the events of the previous day. So, he cautiously hung by the tank in the tree cover. Late in the day as he was standing aside the tank, he heard a rustle in front of him in the brush. He quickly assumed that a German soldier was approaching his position. Sticks snapped and the noise came closer and closer. He stiffened, and he reached for a grenade. He was almost ready to pull the pin and throw it, when a house cat jumped out of the tree in front of him and right at his face. He struggled with the growling cat until he tossed it away. Once the cat righted himself on the ground, it snarled at him and ran off. He wasn't sure who won the fight, he or the cat. Despite all that he had gone through to this point, he said that the damn cat had provided him with one of the most frightening incidents of the whole war. It must have been a scary revelation; even the German cats were on Hitler's side.

(left to right) Virgil Decker, Louis Baczewski, Les Underwood –
taken near Hastenrath and Sherpenseel during the Huertgen Forest Campaign, 1944

As the days dragged on, they found themselves still jammed up near Sherpenseel and Hastenrath. Soon, the snow and ice began to take its own toll in October and November and the worst winter in 100 years started creeping up on the allied advance. Lou said that the rubber tracks on the Shermans were not the best in the snow. They were even worse on ice. In many incidents in the Huertgen, he recalled that the tank would slide uncontrollably even despite its weight of 32 tons.

The taskforce would stay in the Hastenrath Sherpenseel area and hold the seesawing front from October to the 19th of December. The loss of men and material was staggering. While accompanying a shattered unit in the Huertgen, Ernest Hemingway, christened it "Paschendale with trees."[32] What was supposed to be a swift blow to finish the Third Reich (according to the plans of Collins and Omar Bradley) turned out to be a long and merciless meat grinder campaign. There were some 24,000 US casualties incurred during the advance, and as the cold weather began to take its toll, more than 9,000 troops suffered from frostbite and other weather related ailments.[33] Unlike all the other campaigns on the Western Front, the Huertgen resulted in more US wounded and dead than German. Prior to the "Bulge," the campaign ran to a standstill for the 3rd Armored Division in the German area near Sheerpenseel and Hastenrath. At this point, the casualties had taken their toll on the 33rd Armored, and D Company was once again replacing their CO. "We was holding right around the town of Sherpenseel… but see, we'd go up and hold. We was waiting for supplies to come up, we was so far ahead of supplies." The company was preparing to move back into combat, when a new lieutenant arrived, to replace yet another commanding officer who had been killed. As Baczewski stated, "we just got a new officer, cause our officers was getting killed left and right. They just shipped him in."

**Assistant driver Virgil Decker (left) Gunner Pat Gillespie (right) -
taken during a lull in the fighting near Hastenrath and Sherpenseel, 1944**

It was only a short time before the new commanding officer and Cady were at odds. D Company was set to move back up to the line and relieve another outfit. When Lt Burns briefed his men, it became quickly apparent to all the seasoned men that this commander did not have a clue what was going on. He directed the men to push forward through open land and back into a wooded position. Based on the map, he thought that the forest was too wooded for tanks to maneuver. The seasoned men knew that pushing into the open would certainly draw fire and perhaps wipe them out.

Immediately, Sgt. Cady told Lieutenant Burns that he thought they should move through the woods and into position. Baczewski knew that the Lieutenant resented the dissent, and Burns quickly replied, "Now see this is a wooded area up here, and it's too wooded for tanks! We're gonna have to go out in front of that wooded area, and then back into position!" And Joe Cady, he looked at him and said, "Well I'll tell you lieutenant. You don't know your ass from a hole in the ground. We been run out of there twice already. They counterattacked, and we been run out of there twice! We'll go in from the back end of the woods." After Cady smarted off yet again, it was not too long before Captain Stallings was back again to have a talk with him. Once again he could have lost his stripes, but Stallings as ever supported his men, and reprimanded him in the softest way. As Louch stated, Captain Stallings he said, "Sgt Cady I know that the new officers don't understand anything just coming up here, but you really shouldn't talk to that lieutenant like that. I know that he don't know what's going on."

Stallings was a respected officer, and would soon be promoted to Major. Grandpa could barely speak of him without getting a little choked up. Orders from Stallings were followed without question, because unlike Colonel Lovelady, Stallings was always up front and always well aware of the situation and its gravity. Les couldn't remember seeing Lovelady in the front very much. Lou as well complained, "I didn't see him up front one damn time." It was obvious that neither one of them had any respect for Colonel Lovelady, but they most certainly held the highest regard for Captain Stallings.

Years later, when I reviewed my interview tapes and listened to my grandfather's stories about the Huertgen Campaign, I discovered that in one case, I had left the tape recorder running and long after our conversation had turned away from the war. When I listened to the recording, I recalled that Grandpa and I had been sitting at the table in the basement. Each of us was drinking a glass of his homemade wine. I listened to the sounds of the room as Grandma came in and sat with us as well.

Even though we had changed the subject, she worried that Grandpa would not sleep well that night, and he would dream of the war. We spoke on and through two or more glasses of persimmon wine. We discussed everything from catfish breading to the garden and as always, the weather outside. When I listened to the tape again, I realized just how damn lucky I was to have been able to sit and have a glass of homemade wine. I was lucky to sit and talk with my grandfather and grandmother and talk about whatever came to mind. You just do not realize how important such moments are until those opportunities are gone.

After the Veteran's Day speech in 2009, a student named Matt, came up to me and asked, "Why didn't you follow your Grandpa and become a tanker like him?" I felt he had the wrong idea about why I presented the speech, so I told him, "I'd rather follow my Grandpa and become a better fisherman, make good wine, and grow a bigger garden, but like him if I had to go I would do what I had to." Strangely enough, the closest thing to combat I had ever faced was dealing with Matt's brother and other rare students like him. We were in the woodshop and the

178

bastard threw a board right at my head, he just about started a fist fight between the both of us. Even with such incidents, I still consider myself very lucky to have had the chance to stick to fishing and battling high school kids, instead of driving a tank.

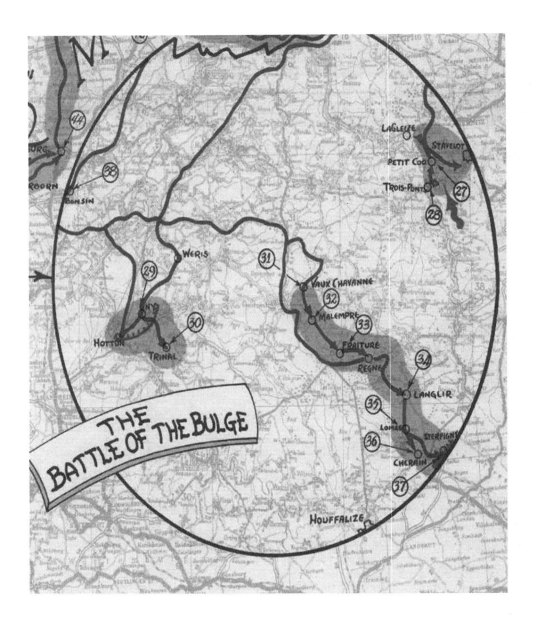

Detail of the Lovelady Taskforce Campaign Map – Battle of the Bulge Region, where the 3rd Swept south to cut off the 1st SS Panzer Division from its supply lines in the winter of 1944.

Chapter 9
Christmas Eve 1944

LOG BOOK OF SECOND BATALLION 2190-G

21 Dec 44 – Advance held up at 678992 D Co.sent out from point 682007 to advance and secure Staevlot, got as far as Porfondroy 706006. Encountered German infantry in large numbers, killed many captured few, mostly SS and paratroopers. Found many civilians killed by Germans. Quite heavy mortar fire and light artillery fire toward CP at 579996. Contacted F.O. from 82nd Airborne Art. Support which was needed.

22 Dec 44 – Our column cut by enemy infantry in great strength at 68006 just south of of Pt. Coo. First half of column isolated. Held off German attack by SA fire and very close artillery support. Germans wearing our equipment; Germans captured our aid stations plus vehicles.

23 Dec 44 – Attempt made to regain contact with our forces. Attack started at 0900, got little or no place, due to strong resistance, doughs and artillery fire. Lost two light tanks, took three prisoners. Many enemy doughs killed by SA and artillery fire.

24 Dec 44 – Attempt made to regain contact, contact made at 1100 after stiff fighting. Many enemy doughs killed our losses very small. Units alerted to move after relief by 30th infantry division. Relief completed about 2300, still on road moving at 2400.

I guess it is Pavlovian or something, but I always equate the smell of Piekutowski's Polish sausage boiled in barbeque sauce with Christmas Eve. I could be on Jupiter, but if someone is cooking Polish sausage in barbeque sauce, I instantly transcend time and space and sit down at one of the tables in my Grandparents basement. I will be seated at a table covered in a polyvinyl table cloth in equally displaced squares of red and green. The top of this table, and all the other tables in the room, constructed from a cheap cannibalized hollow core door. I settle myself in for the best meal I will eat all year, on a smooth finished concrete floor in the basement backroom of my Grandparent's home.

I remember how the room rustled and clamored with the sounds of old voices, dead voices, and voices long removed. The festively colored Styrofoam plates creaked and groaned with the weight of their burden as ham, Great Uncle Joe's recipe stuffing, Piekutowski's sausage, and a heavy helping of Aunt Mary Kay's potato salad was applied. Meat was then piled on top of meat, and then mixed with meat and vegetables with meat, so that the few vegetables tasted more like meat. There was no vegan alternative for sure, and, even the few vegetables available seemed to be made of meat. Perhaps a bowl of chicken and dumplings adorned the mix, and a cacophony of random jokes, laughter, conversation, and the din of eating ensued. After dinner, all the kids ran towards the overly decorated tree to await their assured bounty.

Year after year of traffic led to marked paths worn in the brown and orange shag carpeting. The thinly padded carpet floors of the main basement room told their own story. The walls were constructed of tan paneling and adorned with pictures found at any given yard sale. There were prints of paintings of ships at sea, Jesus, photographs of deer, sixties era knickknacks of Christmas, and brilliant garland and such pasted about the basement. The live tree was always surrounded by huge masses of gifts, bags upon bags and boxes upon boxes.

In my youth, there were an abundance of grandchildren as there are now. We would be so excited that we were just about to burst. After we opened our presents, we would run around and play until our little bodies reached the point of exhaustion. Grandpa would have the fireplace blazing hot and the basement air would become thick with the heat of the fire and the over exuberance of seven wired children.

Then as now, there were no petty rivalries. There were no strange awkward moments between aunts and uncles and grandparents. Sure there were some foolish disagreements, but never arguments, never condescension. To this day, I feel it is my favorite day of the year and perhaps the most important. Everyone just had a great time and they still do. Sure, Aunt Roseann always brought that dip ball which after one bite tasted something akin to shoving a raw 5lb bag of onions in your mouth. Or, there were all those years when Uncle Dave's weird ex-wife kept making these strange taco dips that tasted like taking a bite out of a junior high school locker room. You had to eat a bit just to be nice, yet it was like giving yourself stitches – you just had to do it. But damn! It hurt even the people watching. Every time I saw it happen, I just imagined that scene in Rambo "First Blood," when he had to perform minor surgery on himself with his oversized survival knife, but in this case you couldn't even cry out in pain.

There was also that bag of farts joke that just kept going, year after year. All it took was a paper bag and a naïve kid searching for that last gift under the tree. The gag went back to Great Aunt Gurtie, my Great Uncle Joe's wife. She would take a paper bag, write "Santa Farts" on it and hide it behind the tree. The youngest kid in the family would always get roped into the con. Somebody would always tell them that there was one more present just for them and "it was behind the tree." There, despite all their exuberance and expectations, they would find behind the tree only an empty paper bag, marked "Santa Farts."

There was also the constant pressing of Grandma for all of us to sing or play her worn out 70's version of the game *Password*. Everyone

183

tried to avoid direct eye contact with her when she started pushing for it. She knew all the game cards and would administer a severe gangster beat-down to anyone foolish enough to take her up on an invite to play. It was demoralizing. Everyone knew to avoid *Password* at all costs. That was about the worst of it. The only bad memories are not really bad memories at all, but just dumb funny stuff that happened. Like one year, Uncle Paul got locked outside in a snow storm and we were all down in the basement and couldn't hear him. The sad thing was that nobody knew he was gone, and he had to walk to the neighbors and call us on the phone before we let him back in.

Such is my memory of Christmas. It is an amalgam of a lifetime of Christmases lived in that very basement, a basement which sits dark and dormant for all year: all year apart from that very day. In my grandfather's case, Christmases weren't always the same, and the Christmas spent in 1944 was the antithesis of the savored ideal of Christmas. It was recorded as one of the worst winters in decades, before or since, and on Christmas Eve 1944 and days preceding, my grandfather and his entire company were surrounded by German infantry. Crammed into the hull of a poorly constructed frozen block of steel, surrounded by shrapnel, small arms fire, and two giant 90 gallon tanks of gasoline on either side of the frigid personnel compartment, there he sat celebrating Christmas.

On the 16th of December, my grandfather and his platoon prepared to enjoy the holiday. He and his tank crew requisitioned a house, and "G2'd" around enough to find plenty of cognac, mattresses, and luxuries of all kinds. They gathered enough dishes that when they dirtied a dish, they would just throw it out the window and grab another. "Doing the dishes" took on a new meaning. They had been moved back from the front and placed in reserve. The entire division was disengaged and effectively reorganizing, maintaining equipment and supplies, and receiving some R&R. The collective thought was that they would be able to celebrate Christmas in relative safety and a good distance from the front. All around the Allied front, there was a perception that the war might be all over by Christmas. There was an overwhelming opinion that the German's had neither the material ability, nor the initiative to continue the war, much less the drive for a full counteroffensive in the dead of winter. Yet, this was exactly what the German's did.

Entirely conceived by Hitler himself, the plan seemed destined to fail and none of his veteran commanders apart from Jodl thought it remotely practicable.[34] Yet in the early hours of the 16th of December 1944 a massive Blitzkrieg began, over 250,000 German troops, accompanied by 970 tanks of assorted types, and 1,900 artillery pieces deployed.[35] The whole buildup of men and material was done entirely in secret and no allied intelligence source indicated that such an attack was even feasible, much less eminent. Reports from front line soldiers in the Ardennes told of the sound of equipment mobilizing and captured German soldiers warning of a full Panzer onslaught: all of which was ignored by command. The Allies made a calculated mistake. The front line guarding the bulk of the Ardennes stood loosely guarded and manned by forces composed of green troops; worn down battle riddled divisions, outfits short on rest, undermanned platoons, and sparsely connected infantry regiments. Strangely, no one thought that the Germans would ever attack through the mountainous Belgian wooded corridor of the Ardennes, despite the fact that historically the Germans had marched massive invasions through this forest and on three separate occasions. Who said no one ever learns anything from history?

The attack was merciless, and it took the American forces entirely by surprise. The massive Blitzkrieg attack smashed through the Ardennes as the brave defenders were crushed or captured in the blood wake. Many of Hitler's crack infantry and tank divisions deployed. Paratroopers dropped in and counter insurgents led by the infamous Otto Skorzeny (the man who orchestrated the rescue of Mussolini) dressed in American uniforms and infiltrated behind the lines to misdirect traffic and sabotage movements of supplies and reinforcements. The fear of Skorzeny's infiltration was ultimately more effective that the practical exploits of his men, but damage was done in so far as the fear of spies spread throughout the ranks. Rumors and fears slowed the reinforcements and ultimately created distrust among fellow US soldiers.

The bulk of general issue German paratroopers were also more effective in spreading fear than in actual seizure of ground. Many paratroopers were dropped haphazardly and far from their intended targets. Most of the paratroopers themselves were new to combat and had been rushed through training. Additionally, poor weather and the depleted resources of the Luftwaffe hampered air support and precise air-drops of men and supplies. The resources and efforts thrown into this attack were foolhardy in some cases, but overall it showed that the German's (notably Hitler) were desperate for a break out, and were willing to throw every last resource into this drive. Hitler himself saw this attack as his last hope for his 1000 year Reich. In the days to come, the attack brought about the largest mass surrender of American troops in history. Far too many Americans had no choice. They were cut off and running out of ammunition.

On the 19th of December, Taskforce Lovelady mounted up and dropped their plans for Christmas in order to drive to a location 2 ½ miles outside of Spa Belgium. Spa, formerly the headquarters of the First Army was evacuated by headquarters, in fear of the closing German armored attack. First Army Commander Courtney Hodges and his staff fled the advancing 1st SS Panzer Division as it battled towards the Meuse River.

Meanwhile, within twenty-four hours of the attack, General Rose had performed an amazing feat, by pushing part of his division seventy miles from the Aachen-Stolberg area to meet the Germans in the gap between Hotton and Manhay. The 3rd cut the German assault force from its support and supplies. The Germans were completely surprised by the maneuver and the logistical prowess of the 3rd Armored.[36] On the 20th, Task Force Lovelady attacked and pushed their way toward the town of Stavelot and into "Hitler's Own Division," the 1st SS Panzer Division.

The 3rd Armored Division taskforces split in various ways to join up with the 82nd Airborne Division and the 30th Infantry Division. Combat Command A (CC-A) became attached with the 82nd and (CC-B) was attached with the 30th Infantry. The goal was to stem the tide of the relentless coordinated attack which had progressed more than 20 miles from its breakthrough in the Losheim Gap only 3 days prior. The battle lines blurred, and for the first nine days of the Battle of Bulge, the tide was in the hands of the German Army and cold cloudy chaos.

On the 21st of December, Taskforce "M" (McGeorge) headed for Le Gleize, TF "J" (Jordan) headed to Stoumont, TF "H" Hogan worked toward Hotton, while TF "L" (Lovelady) made its way to Parfondruy. In all cases, the 3rd Armored was meeting the ranks of SS and the bayonet end of the 1st SS Panzer Division, Kampfgruppe Peiper (KGP), led by the legendary Nazi tank commander Lieutenant Colonel Jochen Peiper. Luckily for Jochen, his admittance to the hospital for a small injury in early August of 1944 coincided with the encirclement at Falaise. Because of his experience as a tank commander and the fact that he had survived Falaise unlike so many others, he was tasked with leading the spearhead of the SS Panzer Corps to the Meuse River. Peiper was a member of Adolph Hitler's personal bodyguard (the SS Leibstandarte), a close associate of Heinrich Himmler, decorated Panzergruppe leader in the French and Russian campaigns, and a German national hero.

Peiper was such an iconic figure, that in the 1965 movie "The Battle of the Bulge," Robert Shaw played a fictionalized version of Peiper. Despite some interesting roles and big name actors, (namely Charles Bronson, Telly Savalas, and Henry Fonda) the movie contained a plethora of historical inaccuracies and downright farcical depictions of tank warfare. Many veterans including my grandfather forcefully derided the movie for its inaccuracies. In fact it was so unrealistic, that the battle scenes lacked the correct uniforms, equipment, and terrain, and showed the Germans driving 60's era American battle tanks. The painful Battle of the Bulge factors of cold, snow, and realistic forest landscape were also absent. The Ardennes and especially the areas towards the German border were densely wooded with deep valleys and scattered hamlets connected by windy narrow roads. The terrain was difficult for infantry soldiers let alone tanks, and no such terrain was shown in the 1965 film.

According to my grandfather, the harsh conditions, terrain, and tank combat faced in the Battle of the Bulge was absolutely nothing like the movie depiction. As they approached Parfondruy on the 21st of December 1944, Lou and the members of 3rd Armored Division Combat Command B would soon meet the fringes of the real 1st SS Panzer Corps, as well as difficult Belgian terrain, and severe cold and snow. Amidst the rough geographical and weather borne difficulties; they would also soon find the carnage left along Peiper's path.

Despite certain logistical problems and shortages of Panther and Mark IV tanks (due to Falaise), Peiper's KG was a significant force and whatever tank shortages were supplemented by an addition of 45 Royal Tiger tanks. The Royal Tiger (or Tiger II) was an awesome weapon, its hull structure surpassed the original Tiger design, giving it roughly seven inches of frontal armor (as compared to the Sherman's 2 inches). The Royal tiger also possessed a high velocity 88mm cannon, and despite weighing roughly 76 tons, the top speed was around 25 miles per hour. Peiper's force was arguably the most significant armored attack force in the Ardennes offensive and its infantry support was provided by the 2nd SS Panzer Grenadier Regiment, which included the elite 3rd and 9th companies of SS Pioneers, and the artillery support of the 13th SS Panzer Heavy Infantry Gun Company.

Peiper also had the accompaniment of the 10th Panzer Anti-Aircraft Company and the 84th Luftwaffe Flak Battalion. Peiper's force was the spearhead for the 1st SS Panzer Corps which was commanded by General Wilhelm Mohnke. Monke's command included not only Peiper's but further Kampfgruppes (KG) and an additional KG of similar strength. The second most powerful KG commanded by Lieutenant Colonel Max Hansen included the 1st SS Panzer Grenadiers. They soon met D Company in Parfondruy. Hansen's force was tasked with finding another means across the Ambleve River, after Peiper's column became stalled after pushing past Stavelot.

Regardless of the strength of the immense Royal Tigers possessed by Peiper's contingent, the 1st SS Leibstandarte Adolf Hitler Panzer Division, was short on gas. And one of the objectives of Peiper's force was to secure a fuel dump just north of Stavelot. In initial attempts to take the fuel depot, Peiper's head elements ran into road blocks set up by the

30th Infantry Division. While unsure of the defensive strength of what stood in front of them, Peiper's group stalled. Had they understood that all of the defensive positions were made up of ramshackle groups setting isolated roadblocks, they may well have pushed through to the fuel. As Peiper's group assessed the situation however, American units frantically tried to haul away all the fuel. The massive assemblage of fuel had taken 1st Army more than two months to acquire and store, but miraculously it took only twenty-four hours for the Quartermasters to get it safely away from the Germans.[37] Most of these Quartermaster troops were African-American soldiers. They had been the supply and support soldiers who helped the 3rd Armored and all other combat units stay a few steps ahead of the Germans. They are some of the many unsung heroes of the war, without them, combat units like the 3rd Armored would have never been able to keep up the fight.

On Thursday, December 21st, the Lovelady Taskforce held back the SS onslaught in the areas around Stavelot and was encountering stiff resistance from Kampfgruppe Hansen - which was attempting (to no avail) to cross the Ambleve River. Taskforce lovelady had successfully cut off Peiper's supply train and support from KG Hansen. Meanwhile, Task force McGeorge Combat Command A was engaged with Peiper's force in La Gleize, northwest of Stavelot. The SS Panzer Corps frantically tried to find a way to link with Peiper's force. Few bridges remained across the Ambleve, and even fewer that could support armored columns thanks to the efforts of many American Combat Engineers. The inability to cross the river and move out of the Ambleve gorge slowed progress and ultimately cost the 1st SS dearly. While E company commanded by Major Stallings engaged tanks and SS infantry in Stavelot, Lovelady ordered D Company, (then commanded by Lt Richard Edmark) to move through the town of

Petit Coo, and into the small hamlet of Parfondruy in order to flank the SS forces in Stavelot and acquire the high ground.

As D Company approached the city, they encountered stiff resistance from the SS. After a bitter fight through Thursday, and with the help of the 117th Infantry, by midmorning on Friday December 22nd D Company entered the small city of Parfondruy. Corporal Baczewski and the rest of his tank crew quickly became curious as to why the town was so quiet. D Company had been accustomed to meeting exaltation and revelry when liberating Belgian cities, but such adulation was now strangely nonexistent. Only the sounds of distant guns in Stavelot and the far off crack of small arms could be heard. The town itself was eerily silent. No folks waving flags; no cheerful greetings or gifts from grateful civilians. After stepping out of the tank, Corporal Baczewski wandered down the deserted street. With his 45 caliber pistol drawn, he walked towards a home and tapped on the door. He heard no answer. He cracked open the door and peered into the small Belgian home. There he quickly found the reason for the silence, a whole family was laying before him, dead. The adults were shot, and their children bludgeoned to death presumably to save ammunition. I asked him if he stepped into more homes or buildings, and he stated, "No, that was enough for me."

In the wake of the 1st SS Panzer Corps, the men of Taskforce Lovelady would find the remains of a multitude of murdered civilians. All across the small Belgian town, men of the 3rd Armored were discovering similar macabre scenes. The bodies of women, children, babies, and old men laid strewn about the town. The SS gunned down entire families in their own homes. One old man was found lying in bed, shot in the throat multiple times. Only a few living civilians remained. They huddled into cellars, in fear of a similar fate.

Elements of 1st SS Panzer Division were also responsible for the "Malmedy Massacre" of Seventy-one American POW's and the murder of civilians in the Belgian cities of Trois Ponts, Baugnez, Ligneuville, Renardmont, and Stavelot as well. Reports of such atrocities can be found in the After Action Reports of the 3rd Armored as well as those of the 117th Infantry. Gruesome scenes were found from town to town and house to house. The SS troopers left indelible marks everywhere they went. The SS gunned down one hundred and twenty-five civilians in Stavelot alone.

Anger and frustration with such atrocities unfortunately bred similar responses toward German prisoners. During the Battle of the Bulge, cold calculated murder took place on both sides. Following Parfondruy, D company captured a group of SS soldiers on the city's outskirts. Soon afterwards, Headquarters ordered that the prisoners be walked to the Headquarters (HQ) for interrogation. The guard marched towards the HQ and off into the woods. Not long after he passed beyond a tree line, the rattle of his Thompson machine gun was heard. When he returned, he told Lou and his tank crew that, "Oh, them Heinies tried to run off." According to Baczewski, everyone in D Company knew that the prisoners had not tried to run off. The infantry man had just gunned them all down in cold blood. Yet, after seeing all that they had witnessed, most turned a blind eye to such actions, especially when it came to the SS. Colonel Lovelady himself later admitted that such incidents did in fact occur.

The victims of such actions were most often members of the SS. However, few members of the SS allowed themselves to be captured in the first place, because of how desperately they fought and how bitterly they were despised. Even when I asked Lou and Les about the SS years later, Les seemed to talk about their deaths in a very cold and calculated manner. He stated that, "They died like any other private, I guess we put a few of them in their place, and the ones we didn't shoot, Lou ran em over." Although he and les never harmed a prisoner, Louch admitted that he ran over his fair share of soldiers while driving his tank from France to Germany. When he told me this, his face dropped. He starred down towards the floor in a blank stare, and just kept nodding. It seemed to me the first time throughout all of my interviews, and questions, that Grandpa told me in his own way that he himself had killed many German soldiers. Who knows how many? I never asked, and never will.

Shermans in the snow (3ad.com)

On the 22nd of December, the 2nd SS Panzer-Grenadier Division struck hard at D Company. The German infantry attack split the taskforce in two. The 10th SS Panzer-Grenadier Company moved towards the Lovelady Command Post (CP) by an unsuspected route, scaling the cliffs to the north of Petit Coo. When they surmounted their obstacle, they slowly and carefully approached the CP and aid station. Surgeon Eaton Roberts recalled that the aid station radio was at the time out of commission, had it been working he would have heard the anxious calls from Major Stallings warning them to move back immediately. Stallings radio messages went unheeded as the men in the CP and the aid station watched a group of infantry men slowly approach. "There were about fifty of them," Robert's determined initially, "but more and more came over the crest of the hill until eighty were counted." The light tanks (Stuarts) of E Company opened up when the infantry came within fifty yards, dropping many with the 37 mm cannon rounds and 50 caliber fire. Although many fell according to Roberts in the initial onslaught, the SS Grenadiers kept coming, as more and more flowed over the hill. They soon took out the light tanks with bazookas and began to bombard the aid station and CP with mortar fire. Roberts and others scrambled out of their posts as they quickly "became completely untenable."

Eventually, the Germans overran and captured the command post, aid station, and many vehicles. D and E companies were now entirely cut off. They were surrounded by the best SS infantrymen. D Company's infantry support had been decimated and literally none remained. The situation looked bleak. North in Le Gleize the 82nd Airborne and Taskforce McGeorge engaged Peiper's immense Tiger II's and the bulk of his remaining force. They were cut off. Taskforce Hogan of the 33rd also ended up completely surrounded. Eventually Taskforce Hogan destroyed their own equipment and snuck back toward the American lines. Rose was by no means pleased, and he accused Hogan of dereliction of duty.

Air support was impossible during these days before Christmas, and the dense cloud cover, deep snow, and bitter cold all added to the utter misery of the situation. In all, the future did not look promising for the

194

men of Taskforce Lovelady, as tank losses mounted and infantry support became nonexistent. All around Stavelot, and the surrounding hamlets, the men of the 30th Infantry Division, the 82nd Airborne Division and the 3rd Armored Division, battled against what the Nazi's considered the absolute best of Adolph Hitler's soldiers and equipment.

From the 22nd to the 24th of December, the Lovelady Taskforce found itself surrounded and fighting for its life. On Christmas Eve the men of D Company fought off wave after wave of infantry attacks. Corporal Baczewski stated, "Well, we didn't have no infantry, we was surrounded there. Come nighttime, we didn't have no infantry to alert us. We had wire in the tank, and so what we did, well, we spread wire all around our tank and put it through the pins on the grenades. So, if anybody hit the wire it would pull them pins. It was nighttime, and all of a sudden. Bang! Bang! They started going off. The hand grenades was going off! Well, we thought here they come!"

Lou and the rest of D Company expected that this might be it; they would die on Christmas Eve. Louch felt that it would be it for all of them. They would be overrun and with no infantry to slow down the attack, they would more than likely be trapped in their tanks and slaughtered. They feared that in the dark, they might not be able to see clearly enough to repel a significant attack. Then the attack came, and the blasts of the grenades surrounded them. In their periscopes, silhouetted in the flash of explosions they witnessed a surprise attack. The attack came from a herd of cows running towards D Company through the deep snow. Louch stated, "It was a cow attack!" Unfortunately for the cows, the attack was a failure. For the men of D Company however, it was a sigh of relief. They laughed a bit, and they thought for a brief moment that they might actually live to see another Christmas.

Chapter 10
"Colonel, this is D Company!!!"

Never give in –
never, never, never, never,
in nothing great or small, large or petty,
never give in except to
convictions of honor or good sense.
Never yield to force; never yield to
apparently overwhelming might of the enemy.

Winston Churchill

I have seen some fiery speeches on film and some in person. I have listened to the speakers weave tapestries of fervor and emotions. Yet no such speech stands out more as a testament to a man's personal frustrations then the flaming oration uttered before me one evening many years ago. I was at the time 18, and therefore ignorant of basically all matters of substance. On this particular occasion it was my lack of understanding of protein diets and the cost of oversized cans of mixed nuts that brought about a brief but memorable lecture.

I was just out of high school and living with my father. At the time, Dad had transformed the Atkins diet into his own "Stan Baczewski" version. For a period of six months to a year, he subsisted almost strictly on a pork steaks and nuts. There was nothing in the house, but pork steaks and nuts. Everywhere you looked there were generic mixed nuts. All around the kitchen, throughout the living room, and so on, there were bright white economy sized cans of mixed nuts. There were also some pork steaks in the fridge if you wanted something a bit different.

My freeloading friends and my freeloading self would content ourselves to sit around, watch TV, and eat each and every one of the good nuts out of all the cans. Soon, there were ten or twenty gallon size cans of dried out peanuts accompanied only with a brazil nut or two, or perhaps mere shards of the once abundant cashews, pecans, and almonds. Poor Stan Baczewski would come home from a hard day of working construction to finally sit down to relax and reach for a giant can of mixed nuts. There he would only find the remnants of the once diverse nuts his hard earned money had paid for. For some time, he had casually mentioned that there were too few good nuts left in the cans. Yet one day, the situation came to a head. Against all odds, he sought to preserve what few luxuries he had afforded himself on his all protein diet.

On that fateful day, my buddy Keith and I were sitting around watching a movie, when my father's large biboveralled form sauntered in from another day at work. He wandered about the kitchen and gathered all the necessary items and tools for the consumption of pork and nuts. He gathered up his utensils and heated up his pork. He then began to search for a well-stocked can of nuts. With every burp of the plastic lid on each and every can of mixed nuts, he found the same story. He walked about from living room, to den, to kitchen, finding only dust and peanuts in each and every can. We knew what was going on, but we kept watching the movie and tried to ignore the growing frustration. It started with a low grumble as he began to lament about the lack of quality nuts in each can he inspected. Soon the grumble grew into a roar as the search through can after can yielded the same results. Foolishly, we began to chuckle under our breath. The situation was quickly escalated due to our sophomoric behavior and we provoked an all-out attack.

Silhouetted by the kitchen light, amidst our laughter, we suddenly saw a half empty can of nuts hurling towards us at incredible speed. We went into evasive maneuvers. Keith dove right. I went left. The mostly cardboard nut can crashed into the couch barely missing us both. It bounced off the cushion and landed on the floor with a hollow rumble. Before we could even assess the situation, my father had moved with ninja like speed to stand before us; face red, eyes ablaze. His knees were bent and his back arched ready to pounce. He stood there like a gunslinger all awash in the hazy light of the flickering TV. He was through runnin.

Instead of beating us down (like he easily could have done) he preceded to chew us out. Simultaneously, he demonstrated and explained how to properly eat mixed nuts. He grabbed the can of nuts now resting on the floor and while his hands played out the proper movements, he loudly exclaimed the following: "Quit eating all the good nuts, Goddammit. You reach in there and you take a handful!! And you take what you get! There's no…no… reachin in there and pickin out the good ones!!! Damnit you just reach in there and ya take what ya get!!! Ya just take what ya get!!!"

This wasn't just about nuts; it was a metaphor for life. As humans, we all have to reach in, take a handful, and take what we get. At the time, I didn't see it for what it was. Sure perhaps it was simple, and it was by no means a Churchill speech, but it was damn funny and a reminder to me of just how easy I have had it in my life. What was flabbergasting, was that he really wasn't even mad about us eating the nuts, he was angry that we didn't appreciate what we were given. He was mad that I was not even considerate enough to take a free meal in the right way. I didn't know enough then to think about the person giving me a handout.

When I started to learn more about my grandfather in the process of researching this book, it made me think about how easy my life has been, and how a person should appreciate getting some free mixed nuts now and again. Throughout my whole life, I had been given so many things that I didn't appreciate until I grew older. I always had a warm place to call home, food on my plate, and lived my whole life completely removed from war. Despite all of his lifelong hardships, Grandpa never complained about his life, but he was quite certain that some of the worst days he ever lived were during the Battle of the Bulge. When it was cold outside and he heard us complain about it, he would sometimes remind us that it was not as cold as it was in the "Bulge," and no one was shooting at us either. More than a million soldiers found themselves wrapped up in the battle. As the scale of the battle encompassed far more area than that of even the battle of Stalingrad, Sgt. Cady's tank crew made up a mere speck in the massive conflict. The battle lines were on a vast ring stretching roughly north and south from the Ruhr region in Germany to Luxembourg, and bulging west almost to the Meuse River. All along this massive front, thousands of American soldiers were overrun, thousands surrendered, and thousands stood and fought. The scope of the initial attack and the subsequent bulge in the American lines was of almost unimaginable breath and carnage.

While split up and in some cases cut off, in late December of 1944, General Rose's 3rd Armored Division barely held on. The men of Task Force Lovelady battled "Hitler's Own" 1st SS Panzer Division, while far below them to the south, General Anthony McAuliffe and the 101st Airborne sat trapped and freezing in the small Belgian crossroad town of Bastogne. Surrounded by German panzer and infantry divisions they quickly began to run out of supplies. When asked to surrender,

McAualiffe's sent a succinctly worded response. It was quite possibly the most profoundly confusing one word slap in the face ever stated on a battlefield. The reply merely stated this single word, "Nuts." The note was more than likely not discussing the "anyone for nuts" type of nuts, which had brought my father to extreme emotion in the late 1990's. The Germans didn't get it. They actually requested clarification, to no avail. Most historians still don't know for certain what General McAuliffe meant by stating "Nuts," I do not know if anyone knows the true meaning for certain. Maybe he felt that the German's (who were mostly SS) were a few nuts shy of a can of mixed nuts. Perhaps he was saying that the German's were nuts for asking him to surrender. Or, perhaps he was saying he and the men of the 101st Airborne were nuts for not giving up. Maybe he was just saying "aw, nuts." Whatever the case, he and so many other men in the US Army now faced the largest battle ever fought by US soldiers.

I joke about my dad's own speech about "nuts" because in contrast to my grandfather's life, my life has been beset by comparatively trivial turmoil, just like most Americans. I didn't realize how easy I had it until later in life. I just did not understand all the handouts and luxuries I was given by my mother and father and grandparents throughout my youth. I often try and think about just how damn easy we have had it in contrast. I find it hard to believe how the bulk of my generation seems completely unaware of this. Sadly when I talk to people of my generation, or the students I now teach, too few know anything about their own family history.

In researching my grandfather's life alone, I have learned volumes, and now have a greater appreciation for how good I really have it. As the Roman orator Cicero once said, "To not know your past is to forever be a child." My generation is a generation of mainly children, and we have proven this time and again. While my grandfather is part of what Tom Brokaw termed the "Greatest Generation," I am sadly part of something between Generation X and what Mark Bauerlein called the "Dumbest Generation." Sometimes I feel like so many of us have no sense of history and therefore no clear picture of our future. After years of research, I now have a huge appreciation on how difficult my parents and grandparents daily lives were. I have an understanding of how many luxuries we really have in contrast. In regards to the war, I know that I would not be here at all, if Grandpa had not survived the horror of the Battle of the Bulge. Far too many good people did not. I now have an understanding of how close I came to not existing at all. To both my grandfather and Les Underwood, The Battle of the Bulge was the worst thing they had ever lived through. They barely lived through it, and very few members of D Company would.

When orders came to move out from the Huertgen Campaign on the 19th of December, Sgt. Cady's tank crew ran out of luck. Since the hedgerows of Normandy, they had driven in the same tank and unlike so many other crews they had not been knocked out or split up. They also were lucky enough to have had a Sherman with a high velocity 76mm cannon, which unlike the standard issue 75mm short barrel, it had significant penetrating power. One 33rd Armored regimental colonel, for reasons no one understood, decided that all the firepower should be moved to one tank company. So, he took Sgt. Cady's tank away from him. Colonel Lovelady came to Joe Cady in person to take the tank. Joe Cady told Colonel Lovelady to his face, "We brought this tank all the way here, damn-it, we're gonna keep it," Lou recalled. Yet Colonel Lovelady, neither cared nor truly listened, to Cady's appeal. Lovelady coldly replied that it didn't matter what Cady said, the tank was no longer his to command.

The poor displacement of tank destroyers and tanks able to combat heavy armor had been a problem throughout the war, but for some reason, Lovelady decided to make the change. As Les stated, "they had some guys that they made officers that should never have been in command." Especially when crews were out gunned already, decisions such as these struck men like Sgt. Cady at their core. After they took their tank away, Lou saw a change in Joe Cady. As they headed into the Bulge, Cady's normally courageous and strong demeanor began to change. Eventually as they worked their way towards Stavelot, Cady confided in Lou. He felt deep down that he was not going to survive the coming battle. "My tank commander said, 'Lou, this is my last trip. They took our tank away. This is my last trip.' And I said oh, Joe we went all this way we are going all the way. We are going back to the States. I said Joe don't talk that way. And sure enough he got killed in the Battle of the Bulge. He had a premonition. Something was telling him that he wasn't gonna make it."

Shortly after Christmas, and after they had escaped the SS encirclement near Parfondruy, an artillery burst went off in the trees around the tank (tree burst). Cady's head was exposed out of the turret. A huge piece of shrapnel ripped through his heavy helmet and his tanker helmet. Les said, "the shell took half of his head off, and his brains was on his back."

"Cady got killed by a tree burst. Artillery killed him. He had one of them tank hats on and then he had a tank helmet on, with earphones on, and then he had a steel helmet on and a piece of shrapnel about that big." Lou then held up his hand with his fingers fully outstretched. He continued, "It went right through that steel helmet, and right there, he just slumped down in the turret. He was dead. He got killed instantly."

The man they fought for many long months with, and one of their best friends, fell dead before them. His lifeless body slipped through the hatch and fell to the floor in the turret of the tank. As they were in combat and on the move, they were forced to remove him from the tank. There was no time to mourn their friend. There was no time to say goodbye. Under heavy fire, Cady's tank crew laid their friend and leader in snow. The snow grew red with his life's blood. Even as their comrade lay before them and the bitter cold ripped through their thin tanker's coveralls, they had to press on and continue the fight. Their leader and the man who had challenged every ignorant order put to them from the hedgerows to the Bulge was now gone.

Years later, Grandpa would read the after combat reports and find that at the end of December 1944, Joe Cady was listed as MIA (missing in action). He never learned if his family truly knew what became of him. For a short time after Cady's death, Les Underwood assumed the job of tank commander, but eventually the tank crew was split up. Les went into another tank, and Lieutenant Burns took over as tank commander. Virgil Decker remained assistant driver, and Pat Gillespie stayed in as gunner.

While taking heavy losses of vehicles and irreplaceable men, the likes of Sgt. Joe Cady, Taskforce Lovelady had played a major role in holding back the best of Hitler's SS. Peiper and his KG ran out of gas and supplies, and were now unable to cross the Ambleve River in mass. This was all due to the tough resistance the SS met from the 30th Infantry Division, the 82nd Airborne Division, and the 3rd Armored Division. The Americans had held back the spearhead of "Hitler's Own" and squelched his plan to reach the Meuse River. However Aryan and god-like they imagined themselves to be, the 1st SS Panzer Division was done. Peiper and his remaining men abandoned their vehicles and walked back towards Germany.

Although it is unclear if Peiper ever had a direct role in the killings of civilians in various cities, and American soldiers at Malmedy, men under his command had committed these acts, and it seems improbable that all of the incidents would have gone unnoticed. All evidence against him was circumstantial, but the 1st SS Panzer Division was not new to accusations of war crimes. In both the Russian and French campaigns, there had been questionable incidents. The search for real justice in regards to the atrocities at Malmedy bred a vindictive fervor and the initial post-war trial at Dachau was a mockery. Forty-three of the accused were very quickly sentenced to death by hanging, Peiper among them. The remainder of the seventy-four SS men accused were sentenced to twenty years imprisonment. Given that the sentencing took less than three minutes per defendant on average, many argued that impartial jurisprudence was lacking.[38] The trial that took place was an injustice to both those accused and the victims in Belgium. Eventually the courts overturned many of the previous decisions and Peiper himself served 10 years imprisonment. Afterwards, he became a car salesman – which to me, there's not much of a stretch between SS officer and car salesman, so I suppose it was a good fit. On Bastille Day of 1976 someone took matters into their own hands, and Peiper was burned in his own home thanks to the three Molotov cocktails that magically ended up there. Although it was murder, it is hard to sympathize with a man who was a close associate of both Hitler and Himmler. Peiper was in fact a favorite of Himmler's.[39] There is even documented proof that he toured Auschwitz in the summer of 1941 in the company of Reichsfuhrer Himmler himself. He was by no means ignorant of the motives, ideals, and exploits of the SS.

In any event, even though Lou and Les had survived the initial battle with Jochen Peiper's SS, the Battle of the Bulge was far from over for the both of them. While Peiper walked East through the ice and snow, the men of D Company regrouped and ordered to send a "reconnaissance in force" to the city of Trinal. According to Eaton Roberts, "D Company performed their mission, losing only one tank to a mine. Retribution was more than equal, for they killed a hundred enemy soldiers, in addition to knocking out a self-propelled and an anti-tank gun." Despite Robert's jovial account, Les Underwood had an altogether different perspective on that mission, as his tank was the one who hit a Teller mine. Les stated that, "I swear I felt that tank come off the ground."

All 32 tons of the Sherman went up in the air, when the pieces of it landed, everyone in the tank except Les was dead. He gathered himself together. Totally disoriented, his head swam from the pounding concussion of the blast. He searched in the hopes of finding another living crew member in the smoky haze. Unfortunately, he soon found that all four crew members had been utterly destroyed. Miraculously, he lacked even a scratch. Eventually, he climbed out of the turret and while under fire, he ran through the deep snow and back towards the American lines. He soon joined another D Company tank crew.

As December ended and January began, Colonel Lovelady fell sick and Major Stallings temporarily assumed command of the 33rd Armored Regiment 2nd Battalion. For the next fifteen days the Lovelady Taskforce would face their worst engagements of the war. By the 15th of January, the taskforce would be totally decimated, until only three light tanks and two tank destroyers remained fully functional in the entire Regiment.[40] When they set off southeast from the Belgian city of Vaux Chavanne, the taskforce hit town after town of heavy resistance, artillery, and mortar fire. They were on a path to take the vital crossroad town of Cherain.

3rd AD Shermans in the snow (3ad.com)

A seeming endless stream of screaming rockets and artillery pounded their force as they pushed in to the city of Malempre on the 4th and 5th of January. Huge V1 and V2 buzz bombs could be heard roaring above them. Louch recalled, "hell you could hear em, and you was hoping that they didn't drop there. Whenever they got silent and dropped, that's when you had to worry about it." Les recalled that the flames from the rockets seemed almost endless as they roared overhead in a tremendous clamor. Between the rockets, and the buzz bombs, and the artillery, the area was awash in carnage and flame. Eaton Roberts reported that an estimated 3000 rounds of artillery hit their area around Malempre in only one day.

Hundreds of wounded swamped the aid station and the bitter conditions increased the frequency of frostbite and trench-foot. This was the absolute worst drive they had ever been on. The combat was just as bitter as the increasing cold and snow. The air outside and inside the tank sank below zero. The Sherman, along with all its other shortcomings, lacked any kind of heater. Les Underwood maintained that the best way to understand how cold it was in the tank was to, "Just wait until it is around zero outside, and then crawl into a 50 gallon steel drum and see how that feels. That's about how it felt in that tank. I am surprised none of us got trench-foot or frostbite."

The dogged battle to take Malempre continued through January 5th. On the 6th, the taskforce attacked and pushed its way into the next town of Fraiture. On the same day, the taskforce took 287 prisoners and destroyed a great deal of enemy equipment. On the 7th of January the 2nd Battalion reached the outskirts of Regne. While leading a group of foot soldiers, Stallings and his infantrymen met a dense battery of small arms fire. Surgeon Eaton Roberts reported that, "a burp gun bullet hit him in the back, breaking ribs and opening his chest in a great sucking wound that threatened him with suffocation. Blue and breathless he was brought to the aid station by Lt. Columella in a reconnaissance jeep." Upon hearing of Stalling's injury, Lovelady soon returned and assumed command of the taskforce.

Between the 7th and the 14th of January, the bitter fighting continued through the towns of Langlir and Lomre. The painful cold and the trench-foot continued as well, and slowly Taskforce Lovelady's men, equipment, and supplies dwindled. Only a handful of tanks remained and few infantry troops were left to support them. The aid station flooded with dead and dying tankers and infantry men alike, but ahead of the Taskforce laid the town of Cherain, their ultimate objective. They had to push on.

On the 14th and 15th of January, the taskforce badly outnumbered and outgunned, tried in vain to take the city of Cherain. The city stood as a major highway impasse for German supplies between the cities of Houffalise and St. Vith. The goal was to cut this vital artery. On the first attack, the task force lost two tanks and with little in the way of accomplishment. On the following day, the ten remaining tanks in the taskforce moved in again to take the town. It was a day that my grandfather and Les Underwood would never forget. They both agreed that it was the worst day of their lives. Heavily fortified, the town contained five Panther tanks, one Mark IV, and a large mass of infantry and anti-tank guns. Lt Alford headed up the attack. He and his tank crew knocked out a Mark IV tank, but not long before their Sherman hit a mine and became disabled. The Panther tanks and dug in 88 mm anti-tank guns opened up on the Shermans. The Sherman's 75 mm rounds ricocheted off the Panthers while one American tank after another took direct hits and burst into flames.

Lou's tank was towards the rear in the engagement, because of his new tank commander Lt Burns. Burn's did not impress Baczewski, according to him, "He wasn't worth a shit. He was scared to death, wouldn't look for targets, or for any acquisition or anything. He was just scared to death. Well, when we got engaged there in Cherain, we lost almost all the tanks. It was me and the field artillery observer's tank that was left."

3rdAD tanker on foot after losing his tank (3ad.com)

Every tank in front of Baczewski's had been hit and knocked out. The few surviving crewmembers were abandoning the tanks as they burned. Some crews never left their tanks at all; their Sherman's became their tombs. Les Underwood's tank was among those hit. Les's tank was commanded by Sgt Humphries, and they were engaged with a Panther. Les quickly shot off five rounds hitting the vehicle point blank. Each round bounced off harmlessly. When the Panther returned fire, Humphries tank was penetrated and the front hull and turret exploded from the impact. Lou's tank was hit in the track as well.

He stated, "I didn't have a chance. So there we was all by ourselves. Them 88's was splitting them trees in front of us and I started backing up. Burns wouldn't do anything. [Assistant gunner] Decker yelled at him, 'damnit get up there in the turret and see what's firing at us." Burns was curled up in the fetal position and refused to do his job. Lou continued, "So we went on and headed back. And this Lieutenant was down with his head down and not doing anything, I had to turn the tank

210

around… I back tracked. He was supposed to stick his head out and guide the tank but he didn't."

They pushed back through the snow about a mile or so and the field artillery tank followed. Eventually, Lou stopped the tank and climbed out to inspect the tracks, they had been hit earlier in the firefight, but the hull had not been penetrated. As he inspected the tank for damage, the fighting still continued in Cherain, small arms were still cracking and poping, and the smoke rose from the hulks of D Company's tanks. Eventually he discovered that they had been hit in the track and that a bogey wheel had been blown off. While Sgt. Baczewski inspected the damage. Lt. Burns was still down in the turret. He was balled up in the fetal position shaking in fear. In a short time Sgt. Baczewski heard men approaching to his rear. He watched as a group of American infantry men immerged from a bunker. It was soon apparent that there was a colonel among them, and he walked towards the disabled tank.

Baczewski, stepped up from the track and watched the colonel approach, "There was a pillbox there, and out walked an infantry colonel, and he said, 'Sergeant! Who is your tank commander?' I said, Lt Burns he's up there in the turret." Baczewski pointed towards the tank. After a few hollers from the colonel, Burns slowly began to climb out of the tank. The colonel stood stiffly before him and watched him with disgust as he crept down from the commander's hatch. Louch recalled, "That lieutenant couldn't even talk, he was so scared. The colonel said, "Lieutenant what are you doing back here? You should have stayed up there and fought it out."

The colonel soon stood face to face with Burns, who was still shaking with fear. The colonel screamed into his face for backing off of the fight. Up on the hill behind them, the bulk of the 33rd Armored

211

Regiment's tankers were dead or dying, and this colonel had the nerve to call the lieutenant and everyone else in the tank crew cowards. Baczewski stood there before the colonel and listened to his rant. Lou thought about all the men he had served with in combat since Normandy as this colonel called them cowards. All the while D Company's men lay burning in their tanks above on the hill. Baczewski's lieutenant couldn't speak, but Sgt. Baczewski, now enraged stepped forward and spoke up to the colonel. Sgt. Baczewski drew the colonel's attention and motioned to one remaining, but damaged tank in the regiment. He yelled, "Colonel, this is D Company right here!!!!"

Standing before this colonel was a disabled tank, a shattered lieutenant, and his tank crew. They made up D Company and what remained of Taskforce Lovelady's attack force. What was once a company of seventeen tanks each accompanied by a squadron of infantry support, now stood as one tank and literally no infantry. All of their infantry support was dead or wounded. Nearly one hundred infantry soldiers had been lost in the engagement.[41]   Baczewski looked at the colonel in the eye and said it again, "Colonel this is D Company right here! This is all that's left!" The colonel looked away. He walked off back through the snow towards his bunker and seemingly ignored his comment. Nothing more was said. Lou couldn't believe that as he stood next to the only remaining tank in his company, that this colonel would have the nerve to tell them that they should have stayed up there and died. "We lost all of our infantry and we lost our tanks and he told that Lieutenant, 'you should have stayed there and fought it out." Lou said he was consumed with hatred for the colonel. After all, the bulk of his entire regiment, and many of his friends were up on the top of that hill burning. He said he really thought about shooting the colonel. He really thought about killing him right then and there. Assistant driver Decker even started to pull his pistol, but Lou stopped him. He said he really would have done it, but there were too many people around.

Earlier during the firefight in Cherain, the tank directly in front of him was hit and immediately started to burn. The tank was commanded by Sgt. King and, "No one got out of that tank." After the war, Sgt. King's father wrote to Baczewski hoping to find out what had happened to his son. He had received conflicting reports from the government. "He got confused over the War Department." Lou recalled. "He got a notice that his son was killed then another that his son was missing. He was from New York. So, he wanted to know, and so he wrote everybody who survived. I wrote him back and said, I didn't see anybody get out of the tank." His father later sent him a thank you, along with a picture and prayer handed out at the final service held for Sgt. Francis A. King.

The bulk of taskforce tankers met their fate on the 15th of January 1945. Yet on the same day, Cpl. Les Underwood, found himself in an altogether different predicament. The driver and assistant driver were killed instantly after taking a direct hit to the front hull. They were both obliterated. The members of turret crew, the commander Sgt. Humphries, the assistant gunner Octaviano Carrion, and Les scrambled to abandon the tank. Small arms fire and artillery bounced off the tank all around them. Humphries and Carrion, managed to run in the right direction and find a place out of sight. Les dove into the snow and played dead, as German troopers quickly overran the area around the tank. A mortar shell burst right near Les, it was so close in fact, that his jacket caught fire from the heat of the blast. After discretely patting out the flames, Les did his best to lie motionless. He knew that surrendering might well cost him his life. Once the Germans approached him, he lied as still and quiet as possible.

They kicked him hard in the ribs to see if he was alive. One big German even lifted him up off the ground, shook him a bit and said, "Kaput," as he threw him back down in the deep snow.

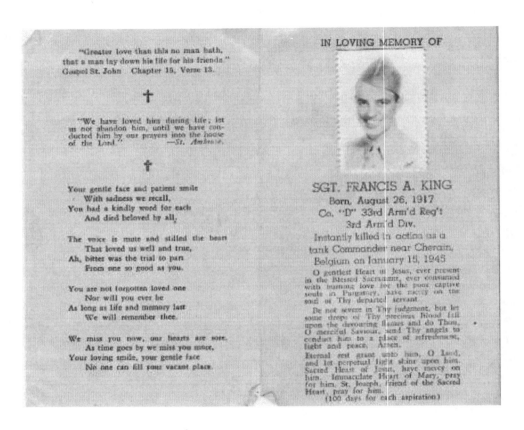

After corresponding with him in regard to the events surrounding Sgt. King's death, Sgt. King's father mailed this prayer card to Louis J. Baczewski. Francis King died along with the bulk of D Company's tankers and infantry support on January 15th 1945, just outside the city of Cherain, Belgium.

Les said that it was the longest day of his life. All day he played dead as small arms racked the ground and cut through the cold air around him. The bitter cold tore through his body, but he couldn't even allow himself to shiver. All day long, he had to somehow keep still regardless of how cold he was. I cannot imagine how hard it must have been, to refuse the overwhelming desire to curl up from the cold, to chatter his teeth, to allow his muscles to twitch. It was an unfathomable feat of self-discipline, of stoicism, to lie still in a pallid subzero shroud of agonizing cold.

Once nightfall finally came, Les began to crawl his way back to the American lines. He made his way into a ditch and snuck past two more German sentries. Simultaneously, Sgt Humphries and Cpl. Carrion were making their return as well, carrying a wounded infantryman they had found along the way. Eventually they were all able to make it back to safety. Les Underwood would later receive the La Croix De Guerre medal from the Belgian Government, for his actions that day in January of 1945.

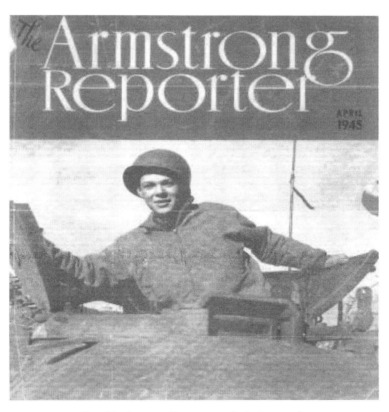

Les Underwood's personal photograph
was pasted on the front page of a local news magazine
in April of 1944, the article enclosed discussed his harrowing experience.

On the following day, Taskforce Lovelady received 17 Shermans and 10 light tanks from maintenance. Regardless of the events of the previous day, the remaining tankers of the Lovelady Taskforce attacked Cherain yet again, now under cover of darkness. Despite all of the carnage of the day before, despite all that they had lost and endured, the very next day, the men of D Company took that town. With the help of an infantry regiment from the 84th Division, Taskforce Lovelady pushed their way into Cherain, knocking out five Panther tanks and a battery of 170mm artillery pieces. The fight was bitter. Even after seizing the village, the taskforce became pinned down by constant artillery and mortar fire which fell throughout the night. In spite of all the horrors that befell them, they had accomplished their mission, and on the 17th of January, 3rd Armored command relieved Taskforce Lovelady from its duties at the front. For the few remaining men of the 33rd Armored Regiment, the Battle of the Bulge was finally at an end.

As the spearhead of the First Army in all these major operations, the 3rd Armored Division destroyed more German tanks, inflicted greater enemy losses, and participated in the capture of more prisoners than any other American armored division. In accomplishing this distinction the 3rd Armored Division lost more American tanks than any other armored division. Of the three combat commands in the 3rd Armored Division, Combat Command B [Lovelady Task Force], destroyed more German tanks and lost more American tanks than any other combat command.[42]

Belton Cooper
3rd Armored Division Ordinance Officer

Chapter 11
Dora-Mittelbau & Nordhousen
Liberated April 11th 1945

   <u>After Action Report 33rd Armored Regiment</u>
   <u>11 April</u> 1st Bn Attacked to seize Northern half of
NORDHAUSEN while 2nd Bn attacked southern half.
Town was secured by 1100. At 1500, a force was sent
to HIBDER-SACHSWERFEW to establish roadblocks and
investigate reports of a V-2 factory there. The road
blocks were successfully installed and the V-2 factory
captured while still in operation. One enemy MK 3
tank destroyed.
   2nd battalion occupied its sector of NORDHAUSEN
and also SUNDHAUSEN. A labor camp with hundreds of
sick, dying, and dead inmates was liberated. Medical
care was given. One US secret agent was freed, and
sent through channels to higher headquarters.[43]

Everyone knows the name of Auschwitz. Many know the names
Dachau, Buchenwald, Sobibor, Treblinka, and Sachsenhausen. These
names invoke horror and confusion as to how human beings could be
capable of such calculated gore. Yet the name Dora-Mittelbau evokes no
such response, because this place was left purposely misnamed and
ignored despite it being comparable in size to camps such as Auschwitz or
Sobibor. Both the American and Soviet governments wanted the name of
Dora lost to obscurity, and so it was.

Unlike Auschwitz, or Dachau, Dora did not possess a death camp,
with the strict purpose of wholesale extermination. Dora on the other
hand, was a factory of hellish conditions and productions, and although
different in design, it shelled out death and misery on a massive scale. The

name Nordhausen became associated with the camp in spite of the true name of Dora Mittelbau. This discrepancy was due to the American 3rd Armored Division's discovery of an indescribable barracks in the town of Nordhausen, Germany on the 11th of April 1945. This barracks contained scenes one would only imagine to encounter in the deepest corners of hell.

When Eisenhower saw the camps for himself he was confronted by the horrid absurdity and inhumanity. He worried that because the brutality of the camps was so indescribable, that people may doubt that such a thing could actually occur - after all it was undeniably and inhumanly absurd. He therefore required American troops to walk through the camps to view them. He also mandated that the German's themselves be responsible for disposing of the countless corpses. Eisenhower stated the following after a visit to Dachau on April 12 of 1945:

> I have never felt able to describe my emotional reaction when I first came face to face with indisputable evidence of Nazi brutality and ruthless disregard of every shred of decency...I visited every nook and cranny of the camp because I felt it my duty to be in a position from then on to testify at first-hand about these things in case there ever grew up at home the belief or assumption that "the stories of Nazi brutality were just propaganda"...I sent communications to both Washington and London urging the two governments to send instantly to Germany a random group of newspaper editors and representative groups from the national legislatures.[44]

General Dwight D. Eisenhower,

Supreme Commander, Allied Forces Europe

There was no collective US effort to shroud what was done by the SS in the Nazi death and work camps. Yet in the specific case of Dora, US disclosure became shrouded in subterfuge, due to the desire to keep German rocket technology in US hands and away from the Soviets. The collusion that would eventually unfold between former Nazis and the US government also required a cloud of deception. The Dora factory and labor camp, remained purposely out of the limelight because the Americans and Soviets found a veritable gold mine of unknown technology as well as knowledgeable SS personnel. Once Germany fell, the former SS administrators of the Dora facility were now more than willing to show both the US and also the Soviets how their rocket technology worked, thus keeping their necks out of the noose.

Regardless of all the horrors witnessed throughout their campaign, the men of the 3rd Armored Division, 33rd Armored Regiment, 2nd Battalion, could not bear the sight of the barracks they found in the city of Nordhausen, Germany. Surgeon Eaton Roberts refused to even directly comment on what he experienced in his memoir, despite all he had seen in the war up to that point. Les Underwood stated, "My god you never seen anything like that in your life, all these people were piled up everywhere. The ones that were living you could see every rib in their body."

Lou reluctantly added, "Well in Nordhausen we liberated that concentration camp, Nordhausen. And man, they was stacking bodies! We stayed there overnight; almost two days we stayed there in the town." I asked him if he could smell the camp in the town and he replied, "Oh yea you could smell it!! Ain't no way that the local people didn't know it was going on. Them prisoners who were still alive were hanging on the fence, ya know. They was nothing but skin and bones. Some of em was trying to clap ya know, because we liberated them." They were so week that when their hands met to clap, they failed to make the slightest sound.

"It was a bad sight. To see something like that, it it…" Again, as he spoke to me, he paused, and he lost his speech. Even though it had been so long ago, it brought him to such emotion to speak of what he saw there. It was quite painful for him to talk about, and for myself it was quite horrible to watch him struggle to recall it. Eventually, he continued once more, "Boy, them people was so glad to see us. It was a pitiful sight really, all them people dead and everything. And people that were living were nothing but skin and bones - nothing to them. I mean it made ya sick just to see it!! And the smell!" He paused yet again and began to shake his head. He lost his speech for a second time; and he just sat there, just shaking his head. He looked down at the ground as his right hand rubbed his forehead. He just kept saying, again and again. "It was a bad sight, it was a bad sight. It was something terrible."

3ʳᵈ AD Tankers in Blocke Kaserne, Nordhousen Germany (3ad.com)

220

**Blocke Kaserne, Nordhausen Germany part of the Dora Mittlebau complex –
courtesy of University of Illinois Archives**

Nordhausen Barracks, Dora Mittelbau – courtesy of University of Illinois Archives

In the 3rd Armored Division's official history, "Spearhead in the West," the barracks is described in haunting detail:

> Although the taking of Nordhausen did not constitute the heaviest fighting of April 11th, that city will live forever in the memories of the 3rd Armored soldiers as a place of horror. The Americans couldn't believe their eyes...no written word can properly convey the atmosphere of such a charnel house, the unbearable stench of decomposing bodies, the sight of live human beings starved to pallid skeletons, lying cheek by jowl of ten–day dead...Hundreds of corpses lay over the acres of the big compound. More hundreds filled the great barracks. They lay in contorted heaps, half stripped, mouths gaping in the dirt and straw: or they were piled naked like cordwood in the corners and under the stairways. Everywhere among the dead were the living – emaciated, ragged shapes whose fever bright eyes waited passively for the release of death. Over all the area clung the terrible odor of decomposition and like a dirge of forlorn hope the combined cries of these unfortunates rose and fell in weak undulations. It was a fabric of moans and whimpers of delirium and outright madness, here and there a single shape tottered about, walking slowly, like a man dreaming. There was no hope for many of the prisoners in this place...

What Lou Baczewski and the other members of Taskforce Lovelady discovered was Boelcke Kaserne. This barracks was only a small section of a much larger complex, which made up the Dora-

Mittelbau camp. The true name of the camp was a nonsensical name made up by the SS to remove any hint of the camp's location or significance.[45] The barracks that Combat Command B discovered in Nordhausen was a dumping ground for the SS. Prisoners sent to the Nordhousen barracks, were there because they proved unfit to perform the necessary jobs at the Dora rocket complex. As the Allies closed in, the SS dumped a great deal more of sick, dead, and dying in the Nordhausen camp. The true work camp and factory itself fell to Combat Command A, the 32rd Armored Regiment of the 3rd Armored Division. There, they encountered the massive Dora rocket complex and the adjacent work camp and SS barracks.

3rd Armored ordinance officer Belton Cooper witnessed that, "The factory was staffed by slave workers, primarily from Eastern Europe. They lived in wire enclosed concentration camps, and survived under the most primitive conditions. Those who were recalcitrant or failed to do their masters' bidding were transferred to another enclosure, where they were slowly and deliberately starved to death." Upon touring the factory, Cooper was astonished by the conditions in which the workers toiled as they constructed the V2 missiles. He was also in awe of the German assembly plant and organization which, "was a lot more extensive than we had thought. Not only were some of these tunnels more than two miles long, but they extended in layers some 600 feet below the surface, completely impervious to bombing."

In fact, it was British bombing which had brought the entire facility to the Harz Mountains in the first place. The German Baltic Sea island of Usedom housed the original V1 & V2 missile factory called Peenemunde. After a series of strategic bombings organized by years of British intelligence work and orchestrated by the RAF (British Royal Air

Force) in April of 1943, Nazi high command ordered the entire factory complex uprooted to insure safety from Allied raids.

The "buzz" bombs that had soared overhead of the 3rd Armored during the Battle of the Bulge (although fired from various launch pads), had all originated from this factory. These "buzz" bombs were in fact the first ballistic missiles in existence. Neither the Americans, nor the Soviets possessed such technology at the time. There was a definite desire amongst both the Americans and the Soviets to grab as much of this technology as they could, and before the other side had a chance to do so.

Back in August of 1943, the first prisoners transferred from Buchenwald in order to start the necessary preparations for the building of a new V1 and V2 rocket factory. The existing V1 and V2 missile base and manufacturing facility built in the island village of Peenemunde had been heavily bombed by the British in June 1943, thus disabling a great deal of their manufacturing capability. For the new missile site, the SS selected a group of tunnels which had been previously dug into the granite core of the Harz Mountains. Originally started as a means to protect fuel from Allied bombing, the tunnels now became the new factory site for Hitler's "Vengeance" (V) weapons. Shipped by train from the remains of Peenemunde, the missile parts and personnel found their way to the rugged region of Thuringia.

In a tale that seems more like a James Bond movie than a true historical event, the Nazis worked to create a huge missile factory in the depths of a mountain side. It was a Herculean effort in both material and money and its ultimate construction was only practical due to the Nazis use of slave labor. The whole undertaking was unfathomably gargantuan. In fact, the internal factory was so vast, that the fully assembled V2 rockets measuring 14 meters (roughly 46 feet), could be stood completely upright for final inspection. The factory consisted of two main tunnels running parallel to each other, and each tunnel had perpendicular galleries at specific intervals. The two main tunnels were over a mile long, and each gallery off the main shaft was 490 feet in length.[46]

3rd AD soldier inspecting a V2 rocket (3ad.com)

In the summer of 1943, the construction of the missile factory, the work camp, and the SS Barracks went on simultaneously. Slave laborers performed the greater part of the project.. These laborers were a mixed bag of common criminals, suspected resistance fighters, Jews, gypsies, political prisoners, and so on. The Germans incarcerated the bulk of these prisoners based on flimsy evidence and mere accusation. The inmates came from every region in Europe, and basically every piece of land that the German war machine had rolled through. Inside the factory, there were men from France, Russia, Poland, Ukraine, Serbia, Slovenia, Croatia, Italy, and on and on. German political prisoners and criminals were also present and they typically held the higher posts or served as "kapos" or guards. Many of these inmates turned guards would later be put on trial with the SS for their murderousness and brutality. "…Dora was one of the first and ultimately, the largest concentration camp founded with the exclusive goal of exploiting the labor potential of its inmates."[47] Dora was not a death camp, it was hell's own production facility and its "corporate externalities" necessitated a crematorium just the same. The workers were pushed at breakneck speed. With scarce food, no sanitation, and horribly dangerous working conditions, the workers died in droves. As such, the Dora crematorium ran constantly, disposing of the workers who fell each day either from starvation, disease, accidents, or brutality of various forms.

Andre Sellier first arrived in Buchenwald and was then shipped to Dora along with his father. They were both held under suspicion of aiding the French Maquis (resistance fighters). Later in his life, he published a full history of the camp in which he described the logistical and physical development of the complex, as well as the day to day functions of the factory. He worked tirelessly to include vast amounts of personal accounts of the inmates who survived Dora. In grave detail, Sellier described the treatment of prisoners and the deplorable squalid conditions in which each inmate tried to survive. The lack of humanity in his account is strikingly unfathomable. The reality in which these men toiled day to day was unimaginably horrible. The SS concerned itself with production and not lives. To the SS, these men became units, they were numbers on a paper, and as soon as a number was crossed off, all that was required was to send for more "units" from Buchenwald. In a time frame of roughly twenty months alone, the death toll for inmates stood at an estimated 26,500 victims.[48] The construction phase proved indescribably costly in human lives, despite the short lived construction and operation of the factory itself, from only August of 1943 to April of 1945. This death toll does not however include all of the fatalities additionally administered by the missiles constructed in the factory itself. "The total number of people killed by V1's and V2's was 8,938 in England... and 6448 in Belgium."[49]

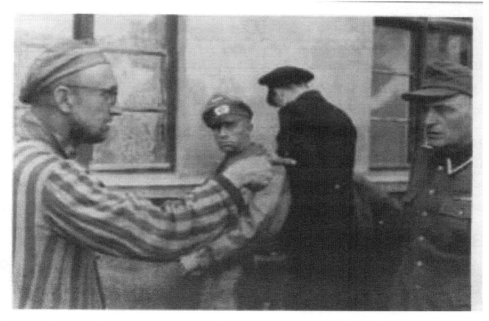

Dora prisoner points out a camp guard - courtesy of University of Illinois Archives

Dora's ends and its means were death. It is an injustice to all that suffered there that the general public still knows little to nothing about its existence. One of the main reasons for such secrecy and subterfuge was because the administrator of both Peenemunde and Dora was Werner Von Braun. Many Americans should recall his name in regard to NASA and

227

the US Saturn missions. In the 1950's and 60's, Von Braun became known as the foremost expert in rocketry in the US, and arguably the world. Von Braun followed a very puzzling path out of post-war Germany. He avoided the noose for his role in Dora and somehow checked himself in as a bona fide US citizen. In fact, he was not the only SS officer from Dora to later find himself in the US living as a free citizen.

Upon hearing of Hitler's death on a radio broadcast on the 2nd of May 1945, Von Braun contacted the first available Americans he could find. In a short time, he obtained safe-conduct papers for seven of his collaborators. They had hidden the bulk of documents related to the V2 missile production in an abandoned mine at Dornten. A board of technicians administered by Dr. Richard Porter of General Electric quickly questioned Von Braun. The GE executive arrived in Germany with the expressed purpose of digging into the V2 rocketry program.[50] There was a rush to gather all possible resources related to the rocket program before it fell in the hands of the Soviets.

In the days and weeks that followed, a massive effort was put underway to procure all possible hardware and intelligence from the Dora facility and from the mine in Dornten. Sellier describes the effort as follows:

> ...the fourteen tons of documents were transferred by trucks to Nordhausen on May 27th, then to Paris, and then shipped to Abberdeen, Maryland – under heavy guard all the way...Colonel Trichel had asked to have a hundred or so V2's delivered for trials at White Sands [New Mexico]...The corresponding pieces for the quantity of units had to be gathered together in the Dora factory, packed up, and loaded...All in all the operation involved

340 freight cars carrying 450 tons of
material...The convoys arrived in Antwerp
and the cases were loaded onto sixteen
liberty ships after the most fragile pieces
had been repacked. The cases were
unloaded in New Orleans at the end of
June, then shipped by railroad to the White
Sands base, where they awaited assembly...[51]

Von Braun and other German rocketry specialists assembled the V2's at White Sands and instructed American technicians as to the proper procedures. In the spring of 1946, seventy rockets were assembled and fired. Many launch attempts failed and some obvious telemetry issues resulted in one missile landing in a graveyard in Juarez, Mexico. Despite some failures in the firing of the V2's, Von Braun and some of his colleagues were living in the graces of the American government, specifically the intelligence services. Approved on July 6th of 1945, Operation Overcast established an expressed mission to recruit German rocketry technicians. Von Braun and his comrades escaped Germany with their families, and found themselves removed from any accountability for their crimes against humanity. Rationalization for such actions at the time was based on the threat of ongoing war with Japan, and the need for additional military technology. The American rocketry program and Werner Von Braun became one and one. Von Braun received full US citizenship in 1955. Showered with awards and accolades throughout his life, Von Braun drew plenty of justifiable disdain from Dora survivors.

Ironically, the Soviets were able to build their missile program out of the ashes of Dora as well. While the US had Von Braun, the Soviets were able to secure the service of Helmut Grottrup, a former assistant to Von Braun. Grottrup and a team of minor German technicians helped assemble captured V2 missiles and organize their launches in the Soviet Union. The German technicians and the presence of the V2 technology played a distinct role in shaping the Soviet rocketry program. The Soviet expert Serge Korolev oversaw all of these launches, and it was Korolev who eventually orchestrated the launch of Sputnik as well as the initial Soviet ICBM (Inter-continental Ballistic Missile) program.

When the men of the 3rd Armored took the city of Nordhausen and witnessed the atrocities in Boelcke Kaserne, and the Dora factory itself, little did they know how huge a role all this would play in global politics for years to come. The sad thing was, that ultimately the desire for the rocket technology would trump the quest for justice, despite the fact that more than 26,500 people died as a result of Dora. The tens of thousands of Dora survivors were never able to see Von Braun and his comrades stand before a court of law. Even though they had walked the tunnels and had orchestrated the daily atrocities of the complex, these Nazis were never made accountable for the hell they had constructed.

These three pictures show the German citizens of Nordhausen burying the Dora-Mittlebau bodies. By order of General Eisenhower himself, it became the responsibility of the German townspeople to dispose of the concentration camp corpses - courtesy of University of Illinois Archives

Chapter 12
Making sense of two histories

St, Louis.17 Mo.
June 15th
1945

As a United States Citizen born and raised in St, Louis, Mo, and a taxpayer to the extent of approx $6,000.00 paid in federal taxes last year earnings and with 50% of my total assets invested in War Bonds.

Wish to report what I consider one of the most outrageous conditions that I have ever heard of existing at this time. In the 946th ENGINEERS AVAITION TOPOGRAPHICAL COMPANY at Will Rogers Field, Oklahoma City, Okla, under the command of Capt Eugene Chillemi.

1st I understand Capt Chillemi is physically disqualified or it is believed for overseas duty yet he has been living off taxpayers for approx four years...

Frank J Foster
1218 Arch Terrace Dr.
St, Louis 17 Mo.

The letter continues on from there for a full length of two pages. The conditions discussed describe a cyclone, a few incidents of possible negligence, and an overall rant about the incompetence, ignorance, and lack of duty shown by an Army Captain named Eugene Chillemi. Frank J. Foster only knew what he had admittedly heard, yet he was quite driven to defame the man as much as a letter could, because his son, James Norton Foster, was not allowed to go on leave by command of Captain Eugene

Chillemi. It has always been interesting to me how a man could start a letter in which the first sentence boasts his income taxes paid. Some men measure worth in such ways.

The letter itself should not mean much in the sense of this story, and the content of it should mean even less in respect to history and the real "outrageous conditions" existing in the year 1945. So, readers might inquire as to why I would include it at all. Well, the fact of the matter is, no one is born to only one set of grandparents. My mother was born a Foster, and I myself was once considered a pseudo part of that family.

The reason I bring it up at all, was to make a broader and more important point. Forks should not be feared. Plastic forks work easily enough. Yet two, even three hand crafted polished silver forks present a Rubik's cube of mealtime deductive reasoning, but why? Why must a man acquire such wealth as to concern himself with such a trite and priggish waste of time? Ah, but what is wealth for, but to waste time and money on such foolishness? Me, I like paper plates, plastic forks (just one each), and perhaps a napkin decorated with a symbol harkening to the holiday. Such napkins might include pictures of old Saint Nick, a turkey, Elmerfudd hunting turkey, a happy spring rabbit gathering eggs, and so on.

At Grandpa and Grandma Baczewski's home, everyone had one fork each. Now, you could get another; say if one fell on the floor. There were always extra forks for such eventualities. These forks were of many types, sizes, colors, and even materials, yet there was no confusion as to their purpose for they were quite versatile. Such forks could be used for salad, entrée, desert and whatever else you might desire to fork with that said fork. It was great; Grandpa and Grandma Baczewski's forks did it all.

Now as for the others side's forks, they could be quite deceiving, there were more of them, and their skills and talents were few as per instruction. As a child, I never saw the point. As an adult I see even less of one. My mother's family would have regal meals on occasion. Meals in which servants would set the napkin in your lap and with just the right mix of disdain and subservience written on their faces. I myself don't like strange people shoving things into my crotch and asking me lots of questions about my meal and such. As an adolescent, it was even more fun. They were great people mind you, but it was just different, and I was raised seeing the good in both families.

The problem was though, that the two sides of my family were not comparable even in the sense of apples and oranges or even apples and orangutans. The strange thing was that, my nuclear family, even at its conception, was diametrically opposed to itself, as it was equal parts patrician and plebian, lord and serf, half John Rockefeller half Woody Guthrie. No side was perfect. No side ever is. I found that for myself, high culture, etiquette, pomp and circumstance, were not realms in which I belonged or aspired to dwell in. Additionally, the trappings of everyday blue-collar existence seemed just as troublesome at times. What I eventually discovered was that each side of my family taught me volumes about life. I just had to grow to see it. Perhaps it was the contrast between the two that divulged the most truth.

Grandpa and Grandma Foster were very good to me and my family in many respects. I have to thank them in so many ways. They introduced me to art and history and culture. They were particular about how any daily task should be done (especially my Grandmother) and they taught me to respect and take care of what I had. Grandma was strict and stern in regards to manners and behavior, but through this, she taught my brother and sisters and I how to carry ourselves with dignity and respect to others. I do believe a good deal of my interest in history and art and culture stems from my Foster side. Because of what my Grandmother and Grandfather exposed me to, I have never contented myself to only fish or hunt or camp, or do the things that my Father's side exposed me to. I consider myself lucky; for my youth was spent with people I loved who spanned the spectrum of class and society. I have a healthy love, respect, and slight disdain for both sides of my family coin. Neither side of our family could really understand the other and we (my siblings) unfortunately sat in the middle of this silent debate. Both sides were ignorant of the other, and it seems both wanted to keep it that way. The Baczewski's cared little for the Foster snobbery, and the Fosters cared little for the Baczewski's lack of culture and polish. Being Polish doesn't necessarily mean that you have polish.

The Fosters reserved the worst of their disdain for my Father (a good deal of it deserved) and he dealt with it in the same stubborn manner as his adversary. Frankly, the old man relished the negative attention. To this day, I feel like my Father has never felt anything but pride in being a working class man, a union man: but neither trait counted for much on my mother's side. I can recall many occasions, when my dad would purposely drive his old work truck down the curvy driveway of one of my most pompous relative's home. His old rusted up red and black GMC would wobble its way to a squeaky stop. Dad had a good job, and we lived with all the amenities of an average middle class family, yet Dad liked to pretend as if he was more of a vagabond than he really was, just to piss off the relatives. Sure, we had a nicer vehicle at the time, but, my dad just loved to drive the beater. His goal was to pull it right up in front of the million dollar massive house nestled in a gated and ridiculously opulent St Louis neighborhood. Dad would saunter out in his characteristic gait, pull at his beard and bibs a bit, and greet the uncomfortable relatives. Then as

236

soon as possible, he would pat the oxidized truck hood and sarcastically say, "well just seventeen more payments and this baby is all mine."

Although he joked about it, my Father was raised in relative poverty and recalled times when the whole family had to hide from bill collectors because Grandpa was out of work. He once told me, that he had never stepped into a restaurant until he was 16 years old. Later in life, my Dad did well for himself as a union electrician and my mother had a good job teaching grade school. In my youth, we were lucky and we had everything a kid could want or need.

When My Grandpa Foster passed away, I was in my early 20's and working to finish a degree in history at Eastern Illinois University. Sometime later, my Grandmother knowing my interest in history decided to give me all of the letters that Grandpa Foster sent home during the war. His mother had saved them. They had sat in a box for years in a dusty basement full of random antiquity. Grandpa never threw anything away, and it was in that basement where Grandpa had given me his 8th Air Force jacket and helmet when I was a boy. Later when I received all of his letters, I dove into them with great interest. I had already started the project on my Grandpa Baczewski, and thought this would be a great addition or perhaps a different project all together. After reading a good deal of the letters however, I became bewildered and sadly disappointed. Despite how much I loved and respected my grandpa Foster, I had a hard time accepting just how easy he had it. This didn't make him any less of a man to me. I still thought the world of him and my grandmother, but the truth was that he just had a pretty mild experience throughout the war. Not everyone was so lucky.

I had to admit that he was in truth a typical rich kid: his letters home discuss only the most mundane experiences and his complaints over minor privations. He sent letters home begging for money to buy cars and trinkets and random oddities. The letter my Great-Grandfather sent to Will Rogers Field that started this chapter seemed to sum it all up. The worst part of the whole thing was that while my grandfather Foster was complaining about conditions at Will Roger's Field, (which amounted to some mere discomforts and a lack of leave) my Grandpa Baczewski was liberating Nordhausen Barracks, which was crowded with thousands of dead and dying.

To this day, I have never heard my Grandpa Baczewski complain about any aspect of his life, or suggest that at any time he experienced was anything akin to "the most outrageous conditions ever existing at this time," as Great Grandpa Foster's letter had done. My family history has shown me that far too many people are too removed from the real hardship and horror that is war or poverty for that matter. It is foolish and pointless to compare hardships as a means of judging a person and it is not my goal to say that one person here was somehow better for dealing with adversity and horror. Yet, I cannot deny the stark contrast in experiences between one side of my family and the other in all respects. At the least, I hope I can derive some lessons and wisdom for my own life by looking deeply at my own social dialectic. Around the same time I received my grandfather's letters, my mom gave me a box full of old toys that were my Grandpa Foster's as well. The box was immense. There were cast iron trains and wagons and trucks, planes, and on and on.

When I started interviewing my Grandpa Baczewski about the Depression and his childhood, I found out that in his youth, he had never possessed one toy. For Christmas he said he might have received a piece of fruit or a new pair of overalls, but he never once had an actual toy. He grew up in total poverty along with many others in his hometown. The strange thing was, he never looked back on these times with disenchantment or lament. As far as I could tell, he just figured it was the way it was, you just dealt with it.

Grandpa told me that on one boyhood occasion he, his brother Joe, and a few of his friends Dave Pagan, Mel Weber, Stanley Cravens, John Hustava, and Louis Moss were sitting around their camp on Shoal Creek, when one friend sarcastically summed it up. They had their usual minor provisions and were lying around the campfire killing time before they would run their lines again. They sat quietly among the broken ramparts and rusty remnants of an old mill dam. Dressed in dirty overalls and lying on their tattered homemade bedrolls and coats, they watched the flickering light of the fire. Then, out of the blue, Grandpa's buddy Louis Moss looked at Grandpa through the fire light and said, "Ya know Louch, I wonder what the poor people are doing tonight." They all quickly broke out laughing.

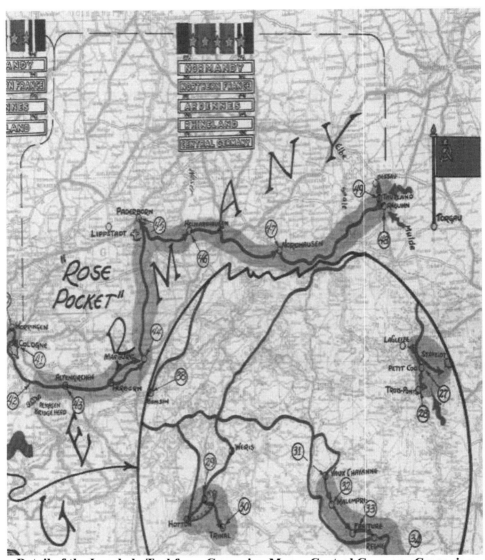

Detail of the Lovelady Taskforce Campaign Map – Central Germany Campaign
(#5 of 5 Campaign Stars)

Chapter 13
"They are looking for the Polish GI"

American history is longer, larger, more various,
more beautiful, and more terrible than anything
anyone has ever said about it.

James Baldwin

In January of 1945, roughly three months before the 3rd Armored
Division took the town of Nordhausen and the Dora factory complex, the
entire division enjoyed some much needed rest from the Battle of the
Bulge. Between the 22nd of January and the 4th of February, the division
refitted, repaired, and rejuvenated itself. Soon, the division received
orders to move back to the Roer region of Germany – the location of the
still ongoing Huertgen Campaign. The "reconnaissance in force" effort
made by 7th Corps was a dogged failure; this "push" was essentially stuck
in the same place that the 3rd Armored Division had left it in mid-
December. The Huertgen Campaign had continued from when Taskforce
Lovelady first crossed the German border and when they returned from
the Battle of the Bulge in early February. The Lovelady Taskforce ended
up right back in Stolberg.

Months earlier in the area around Stolberg, D Company had
experienced a drudging see-saw of battle lines and a constant rotation - in
and out of the meat grinder. Yet even in the worst places and in the worst
times, my grandfather somehow found his way back home; at least in
spirit. In a way that seemed like conveniently conjured fiction, my

grandfather found traces of his boyhood home even in the midst of the longest and most costly American campaign of the war.

Back in November, Lou and his tank crew fought on the fringes of Stolberg. While preparing for a German counterattack, Lou saw something that must have seemed like a mirage. In front of his tank, infantrymen from the 36th Armored Infantry Regiment dug in, anticipating a German attack. Artillery struck around them as they frantically scraped at the frozen ground. "We was there [outside Stolberg] holding and I was looking out through my periscope; cause artillery is coming in and everything. We'd get blasted with artillery every once in a while. And here, there's this guy digging a fox hole, I kept watching him, and watching him, and I thought, boy that looks like Mel Weber." After studying the man for a time, Louch called over the radio to Sgt. Cady. He told Cady that he recognized one of the infantrymen ahead of the tank, and that he really thought he was a fishing buddy of his from Pokey. Cady immediately replied, 'Lou you're full of shit." Cady thought that Lou might be losing it. Regardless, he climbed out of his drivers hatch and walked towards the infantry soldier. As Lou walked up, the infantry man turned and looked right at him and said, "Goddamn-it Louch what in the hell are you doing here?" It was Mel Weber. He was one of grandpa's Shoal Creek fishing buddies. Mel lived only a few blocks away from Louch's boyhood home in Pokey.

Lou replied, "what are you doing here?" "This is one hell of a place to meet one another," Mel returned. They shook hands and laughed and spoke briefly about home, about Pokey. Pokey was worlds away from the snowy industrial war torn landscape they now occupied, yet with the chance meeting, their hearts filled with the warmth of home. The emotion was overwhelming. "Ya just don't see things like that. Ya know? Who in the world would ever think that you's gonna see somebody from your hometown? Ya know that you was raised with," Louch smiled and continued, "Something like that and it gives you a good feeling, like damn! there's somebody from Pokey."

Mel was an infantryman in the 36th Armored Infantry, which was tied to the 33rd Armored Regiment, they had fought side by side throughout the war, but had never known it until that day in Stolberg. Like Louch, Mel was lucky enough to survive the war unscathed. Louch and Mel had grown up together in their microscopic hometown, and Mel lived merely a short walk from Lou's doorstep. It was an absolutely fantastic coincidence that they found each other half way across the globe in the middle of a battle. After the war, Grandpa and Mel would purposefully meet in the Leisure Lounge tavern in Pokey; and they did so on a frequent basis. Louch said, "Me and Mel, we drank a lot of beers over that one!"

Before the war, they had hung around as friends and fished Shoal Creek together. Grandpa recalled that Mel used to fish with dough balls for carp and catfish. If there were dough balls left on his lines in the morning, Mel would eat those dough balls right out of the muddy water, right off the line. Upon seeing the spectacle, Louch told him, "You're crazy." Mel responded, "No, they're good that way - nice and soft."

Reminders of Pocahontas Illinois and of Shoal Creek always seemed to find him throughout his life, even during the war. Grandpa's buddies Mel Weber and Dave Pagan were able to survive the war, but his two friends Stanley Cravens and John Hustava were not as lucky. Stanley had lost his life back in France, but not before he and the other 33rd Combat Engineers had helped cut off the German forces and construct a pontoon bridge across the massive Seine River. That very bridge allowed my grandfather's outfit to cross the Seine.

**(in front from left to right) John Hustava and Dave Pagan,
(in back on bridge rail) Stanley Cravens, Louie Sandretto, & Louch
on the Shoal Creek bridge outside Pokey – circa 1939**

In yet another remarkable coincidence, John Hustava's outfit actually fought alongside Grandpa's cadre as well. The 504th Airborne Regiment was part of the 82nd Airborne and they fought bitterly in late December to push back the 1st SS Panzer Division during the Battle of the

Bulge. By that point however, Corporal John P. Hustava had already become a casualty, as he never survived Operation Market Garden. John had been in a great deal of combat up to that point, as he had served in North Africa, Sicily, and participated in the drop at the Anzio beachhead. His final jump would set him down in Holland, with a mission to secure the Nijmegan bridge, as part of Montgomery's audacious plan.

In a memoir written by, Private Edwin M. Clemens of the 504th Regiment, B Company, Clemens mentions Hustava days after the 504ths aerial drop –days of constant combat. The 504th seized its objective. The paratroopers of 504th had a difficult mission. They had to take the Nijmegan Bridge intact and hold it, until reinforcements could arrive. The fighting was bitter and costly. Supplies were low as they were either exhausted or dropped in the wrong locations. Paratroopers like Clemens and Hustava were hungry and running on little sleep. According to Clemens, right after the 504th finally took the bridge, he and Hustava walked into a German kitchen mess. A huge kettle of steaming soup was still cooking over a fire. The Germans had retreated at this point. Clemens stirred the pot and checked the contents. At first glance, he thought it looked disgusting. He described it as a, "green soup-like concoction…with strange red and white pieces of something floating in it." Despite how hungry Clemens was, he didn't even want to try it.

Pokey native John Hustava took one glance at that steaming pot, and said, "We have enough pea soup to feed the whole company." He quickly told Clemens to quit being a pansy, "Eat some and then tell me you don't like it." Clemens reluctantly loaded up his canteen full. He stated, "It was delicious, it was the best tasting meal I'd had in the Army."[1] Just like Mel Weber eating dough balls out of the creek water, it seemed like those boys from Pokey would eat almost anything, they weren't afraid. John, Mel, Louch, Stanley, and Dave Pagan had grown up cooking over a campfire on the creek, so when it came to eating squirrels, rabbits, catfish, stolen chickens, or commandeered vegetables from farmers or German soldiers, they were by no means squeamish. To a poor boy from Pokey, food was food.

Shortly after this incident however, John Hustava was killed in action on the 11th of October 1944. An article in the Pocahontas, _News Patriot_, announced the loss of yet "another Pocahontas lad on the battlefield." John's last letter to his parents spoke to the warm welcome that he received from civilians in Holland, and that, "They gave the US soldiers apples and pears to eat, because that was all they had to offer." John Hustava's body was shipped back to the US, and buried in the Pocahontas cemetery. A parachute is carved into his gravestone. He would have been 20 years old in November of 1944.

By February of 1945, Lou's outfit had seen its fair share of death and combat, but their part in the war was far from over. Once they regrouped in the Stolberg area they were again called on to push further into Germany. Strangely enough, the deeper Louch pushed into Germany, the closer he came to yet another old friend from Pokey, as he would meet Dave Pagan in Frankfurt, Germany after the war's end. Yet between late February and April of 1945, a great deal of fighting was yet to be seen by D Company. They would also soon see the macabre remnants of SS handiwork, when they discovered the Nordhousen barracks of the Dora-Mittlebau work camp.

On February 26th just after midnight, Taskforce Lovelady moved into attack position and in the early morning hours they pushed east initially hitting little resistance. The 33rd Regiment along with the 32nd Regiment and the rest of the 3rd Armored Division drove further into

Germany. The break from combat lasting more than a month had been both out of necessity for the men and material. Additionally, German demolition of the Roer Dams flooded the river bottoms and blocked passage for a considerable time. On the east bank of the Roer, the Germans had considerable positions which were, "thoroughly organized with numerous continuous trench systems"...[2] The 3rd Armored's mission was to support other units of 1st Army's 7th Corps in seizing the bridgehead over the Roer and then pushing on to the Erft Canal.

Lou had by this time moved into the command tank of Lieutenant Alford. As he recalled, "Just before the end of the war, they gave me a break, and I went to driving for the CO. Cause, I was one of the oldest drivers that survived, so the CO asked me if I would drive for him. That was about a month before the war was over." Baczewski's former tanker commander, Lt. Burns was wounded immediately following the disastrous attack on Cherain. At the time, Burns was on foot, and as a tank destroyer drove by him, the TD struck a mine. Burns was wounded and never seen again by D Company, much to the relief of Sgt. Baczewski. In fact, after the engagement in Cherain, there were few experienced tankers left. By wars end both Virgil Decker and Pat Gillespie of Lou's original tank crew accepted promotions to become tank commanders. Despite similar offers, Lou and Les both declined to become tank commanders. Neither one of them wanted the job, so Lou stayed a driver and Les remained a gunner until the end of the war.

PARENTS NOTIFIED THAT CPL. JOHN HUSTAVA LOST LIFE IN ACTION OCT. 11

News Patriot Nov. 3, 1944

This community was again saddened Tuesday afternoon when the news of the death of another Pocahontas lad on the battle field was received here.

Mr. and Mrs. Paul Hustava, Sr., received a telegram about three o'clock Tuesday afternoon informing them of the death of their son, Cpl. John Hustava, in action in Holland. The message reads as follows: "The secretary of war desires me to express his deep regret that your son Corporal John P. Hustava was killed in action on eleven October in Holland. Letter follows." It was signed J. A. Ulio, The Adj. General

It is known that Corporal Hustava landed in Holand on September 17, but little is known as to what part of the country he was in or his activities since his landing. He was a paratrooper. He would have been 20 years old on November 30th.

John's last letter to his parents was written October 1st. In that letter he told them Holland is a pretty country. He said the people were mighty glad to see them and they gave the U. S. soldiers all the apples and pears they could eat. That was all they had to offer our boys. He said there was little he could write them that would not be military information.

John entered military service with a Bond county group on May 6, 1943. He took his basic training at Camp Croft, S. C., with William Tepatti, Harry White and Charles Moss. He volunteered for paratroop training and was sent to Fort Benning, Georgia, in September.

After completing his parachute training he came home on fullough, arriving here December 1, 1943, and remaining for ten days. A month later, in Januard, 1944, he went overseas, going to north Africa. Later he went to Sicily and then to Italy, landing at Anzio beach. He was sent to Eng'and in April, 1944, and remained there until he jumped in Holland about September 17.

The family has the deep sympathy of the entire community in their great loss.

CORPORAL JOHN P. HUSTAVA

248

In late February, Taskforce Lovelady (Combat Command B, 33rd Armored Regiment) pushed on past the bridgehead on the Roer at Duren and on toward Worringen. Lovelady's men were some of the first American soldiers to reach the Rhine River in Germany on the 4th of March 1945. By the 5th, the division reached the outskirts of Cologne. The taskforce supported the northern flank of the city and reinforced Combat Command A (CCA) of the 3rd Armored as they battled the internal chaos and street fighting in Cologne.

As CCA worked their way down the streets of Cologne, they were now equipped with a new implement of warfare. The 3rd Armored had finally received a M26 Pershing. The Pershing was the tank that the 3rd Armored should have had all along. Yet despite the frequent requests for these tanks from General Rose, Patton's influence slowed the change to such a degree, that the Pershing only arrived mere months before the end of the war. Patton's pressure had pushed back Pershing production and saddled all American armored divisions with inferior tanks. With a 90 mm cannon and vastly improved armor, the Pershing proved itself to be a better tank than anything even the Germans had to offer.

On the streets of Cologne, the Pershing tank proved its vast superiority. Richard Tregaskis, who had been a companion of the 3rd Armored since its historic entrance into Germany, wrote about the event. According to Tregaskis, "In the shadow of Cologne's great cathedral, a Panther, which had just destroyed one of the Spearhead's older tanks, a Sherman (killing the three American crewmen) was hit by an armor-piercing round of a new M26. The German tank burst into flames and exploded. The tankers were wildly eager to meet the German Panzers now and even old scores." In fact, rare film footage exists documenting this exact battle. Just as Tregaskis described, a flaming Sherman tank crew meets its demise before the massive Cologne cathedral. The tank commander, soon to die, struggles to dismount the flaming Sherman. He now possesses only one full leg. His other partial limb flails about, literally smoking from its abrupt removal.

3rd AD tankers "bailing out" in Cologne, 1945 (3ad.com)

Shortly afterwards, the Pershing opens fire and destroys the Panther tank. In further insult to 1st Army's Sherman tank crews, the original film opens with the words the "3rd Army in Cologne," instead of the 3rd Armored Division, thus giving additional undue credit to Patton. Tragically, if not for Patton's insistence, men like the Sherman's commander might well have survived. Had Patton not pushed to make the

Sherman the main battle tank of the US Army thousands of American tankers lives could have been saved.

Panther tank destroyed in Cologne by a Pershing (3ad.com)

Louch and an unknown soldier standing next to a Pershing tank, after the end of the war

251

Bitter fighting continued throughout the city through the 5th 6th and 7th of March. Cologne was for the greater part devastated, the once beautiful city sat reduced to piles of rubble. Additionally the towns all around Cologne looked just the same, as they were part of the Ruhr industrial region and had been carpet bombed to destroy German manufacturing capability. In fact, it was on the 6th of March, that the 1st battalion encountered another German Ford Motor Company, just like the one Lou Baczewski had walked through in Stolberg. The Ford-Werke Motor Company possessed plants in both Hamburg and Cologne. The March 6th After Action Report of 2nd Battalion confirms that the 1st Battalion, Combat Command A (CCA) 32rd Armored Regiment, "had cleaned up the Ford Plant…" In yet another desperate irony, the M26 Pershing tank which proved itself so valuable on the streets of Cologne, possessed a Ford engine, made in the USA.

By March 8th, the taskforce was again relieved and it hovered around Cologne "resting and reorganizing." Within the city of Cologne itself, the Staats Gefangt Prison for political prisoners of the Third Reich was liberated on the same day. According to the Spearhead's history, the prisoners were, "eighty-five miserable human beings, some of them so weak that they were unable to move, and others who had been hiding in the inner recesses of the building, were all that remained of an original 800." It was yet another reminder to 3rd Armored Division soldiers as to why it had been so necessary to eradicate the Nazi regime.

By March 24th, the Taskforce moved past the city and over the bridgehead at Remagen. The division continued to rest after crossing the Rhine until they were called upon again. On the 25th of March, The 3rd

252

Armored led the attack for 7th Corps of 1st Army. The 3rd teamed up with the famous 1st Infantry Division, the BIG RED ONE. While working their way toward Altenkirchen, the division gained twelve miles of ground in the first day alone; it was the beginning of a historic drive through Germany. In general, heavy resistance was spotty, and the division rolled through town to town, pushing back the scattered remnants of once mighty SS panzer divisions. During this period the roads filled with refugees, former captives, and slave laborers of all European nations; each of them now trying to find their way home. Many Polish laborers, cheered as the 3rd rolled its way through the now liberated towns. Having been raised speaking Polish, my grandfather found himself excited to see and speak to Polish people. They were in turn very thankful to see American soldiers rolling through Germany. During the drive Eaton Roberts fondly recalled that, "French, Belgian, English, Polish, and Russian prisoners of war lined the roads by the thousands, waving and shouting "Viva l' Amerique!" in all variations."

On the 29th of March, the division pushed so feverishly, that it made a one-hundred mile drive through Germany, setting a record in mechanized warfare. This still stands as the longest one day push through enemy territory in history. Celebration for the accomplishment was short lived however, because on the 30th of March, a combined force of Hitler youth and SS troopers dug in at Kirchborchen, and refused to yield to the 3rd's advanced elements. Heavy rocket, panzerfaust, and small arms fire roared out of their defensive positions, waves of 36th Armored Infantry soldiers met their fate during the day. In a hellish night of combat that followed, many Sherman tankers and infantry soldiers died in an attempt to secure the village. Battling to hold their fatherland, Hitler Youth and SS soldiers fought to the death in Kirchborchen. When it seemed like it could not get any worse for the remaining 36th Infantry soldiers pinned down there, as the morning sun finally rose, three German Panther tanks rolled in with the dawn.

Upon sight of the Panther tanks squeaking down the road, Captain Libby of the 36th Infantry turned and joked to his men that, "Well boys, maybe we'll be in the same camp together."[3] Luckily for Captain Libby and his men, the Tank destroyers of the 703rd Battalion knocked out the Panthers before they inflicted too much damage. Yet on that same bloody night a tragic event occurred, one which hit the entire 3rd Armored Division at its core.

North of Kirchborchen, General Rose's column was suddenly cut. A group of Tiger and Panther tanks sliced through the General's party as it followed Taskforce Welborne. In the confusion that followed, the commander of the 3rd Armored Division was killed. After being overwhelmed by the German tank group, General Rose attempted to surrender. As he tried to hand over his pistol, an antsy German tanker shot him down. His death was considered an assignation, which led into a full military court inquiry at the war's end. Following his death, the battle area for the Ruhr encirclement was henceforth named the "Rose Pocket" in his honor. Maurice Rose was never given the credit he deserved for all the 3rd Armored's tactical moves and overall accomplishments. He was mourned by his men, as he was a tanker's General. He had led from the front throughout the war, risking his own life on numerous occasions. Grandpa remarked that General Rose, "Was a good commander, he was well liked, and we all respected him." Rose was buried in Ittenbach, Germany. In further insult to his legacy, he was mistakenly buried with a Christian service and a Christian headstone marked his grave - despite his Jewish faith. He was the only US Major General to die in combat in WWII.

Ironically, in this combat pocket where General Maurice Rose was killed attempting to surrender, 380,000 German soldiers acquiesced to the Americans peacefully. This was the largest grouping of German prisoners ever captured.[4]

Even thought they had been in Germany since September, the Allied forces and the 3rd Armored included, had taken staggering losses, at times it seemed like the combat might never end. When D Company entered Marburg on the 27th of March, they halted before what Eaton Robert's described as, "An earthen road block, covered with infantry forces armed with small weapons, grenades and panzerfausts, and well zeroed in mortars."[5] By the next day however, Marburg fell, and so swiftly that many of the defenders were taken by surprise. Marburg had not sustained the damage that was inflicted upon cities like Cologne by way of Allied bombing raids. Consequently, the city's 13th century Cathedral, hospitals, and University built in 1527 had been spared from total decimation.[6] These hospitals contained many captured Allied wounded soldiers who were soon shipped back into American hands.

In Marburg, D company captured a vast cache of liquor. Lou's tank crew alone commandeered a huge case of white lightning. On the back of the tank, Louch secured a wooden case of moonshine bottles. From then on, D Company tankers and all their infantry support were well stocked with booze. Between the liquor and some available "Frauleins," D Company got a bit out of hand in Marburg. "They had a big warehouse there with all kind of liquor in it and they had women all around there and so the guys was running around all night," Lou recalled. "This CP guy that checked them road blocks the next morning had a meeting, and they got all the tank commanders together and he said, 'If the German's would have counter attacked us, they would have wiped out this whole damn outfit, cause there wasn't hardly anybody in any of the damn tanks. You guys were running around.' It is damn lucky that the German's didn't counterattack cause, we would have been wiped out. Hell, everybody was out looking for stuff, chasing women, and drinking."

Soon afterwards, the men of D Company gathered themselves together, rubbed their blood shot eyes, cursed their headaches and pushed on to Paderborn. In a short time, Eaton Roberts would again be surprised by the increased severity of combat and damage done to the taskforce. By the 4th of April, Roberts lamented that the entire taskforce, "Only had 16 Sherman's and 4 light tanks." After being reequipped on the 11th of April, the taskforce made its way into the Harz Mountains and the city of Nordhausen. There, they would discover the horrors of the Dora-Mittlebau complex and the stacks of corpses in Blocke Kaserne. For the man of Taskforce Lovelady, reminders of Nazi cruelty were ever present.

By the 12th of April, the taskforce moved out of Nordhausen and further into Germany, working their way towards the Elbe River. At the time, the German forces proved disorganized and were generally in a route. Pockets of resistance concentrated in only a handful of towns. The German lines fell back so quickly that their own messengers became over run trying to find their command posts. In one incident that seemed more like a Benny Hill episode than a real event Lou witnessed a German motorcycle messenger surrender in the most awkward manner.

"We was on a road block, and the road curved, and here come this motorcycle right straight for us. As soon as he came around that corner he seen us, and he was staring right at a tank, and he started going like this [lifting his hands up and down from the handlebars]. He kept grabbing it and steering it, and putting his hands up, and then trying to guide it. It just got him by surprise…" As soon as the German messenger saw the tank, he was trying to somehow hold onto the handlebars and keep the bike from crashing, while also surrendering at the same time. The desperate waving motions produced quite a scene, and the tankers and infantrymen at the roadblock got quite a laugh at the poor messenger's frantic movements. According to Lou, after a few good laughs, "They took him prisoner. And he told em, [headquarters] that his CP [Command Post] was there the night before, right where we was."

Even in these late days in April, the fighting was still rigid in pockets. The taskforce quickly took the towns of Haringen, Kelbra, and Tilleda. Yet, once they reached Unterrissdorf, resistance stiffened, specifically for D Company, as they ran into a crossfire of anti-tank guns. Scattered towns here and there put up strong resistance, while others fell without a shot. It was difficult to know what to expect. After crossing the Saale River, the Taskforce spread itself too thinly. Eaton Roberts complained that Lovelady had again left his Command Post virtually defenseless, just like so many other times throughout the war. Lovelady's Command Post (CP) then located in Thurland, fell to a group of experienced German soldiers. According to Roberts the Germans had been tipped of as to the taskforce's exact location and strength by Nazi sympathizers, including the town's mayor.

So when the German's decided to seize the thinly protected CP, the few soldiers there were quickly overwhelmed and caught completely by surprise. Some found themselves forced to surrender, while others ran in a mad scramble to hide, or scatter in the chaos. Chief Warrant Officer Palfrey, was able to avoid capture by killing one German soldier with his side arm, and then hiding in a pile of potatoes until the Germans had left.[7] A few officers and soldiers were killed trying to resist in the precarious scramble, but most could not help but be easily captured.

Surgeon Eaton Roberts and 117 Americans along with some of their German captors were gathered up and jammed into a cellar. "Friendly Artillery" raked the town once word of the Command Post's capture was spread throughout the taskforce. "If it is true that, "misery loves company," there was an abundance of both, crowded into this tiny shelter," Roberts grimly recalled. Later when the artillery died down and they were able to leave the cramped shelter, "The burgermeister [mayor] was walking around his town in full glory, smoking an American cigar and wielding an American pistol," Roberts explained. "He supervised the distribution of panzerfausts and furnished whatever information that was needed. His attitude did not impress us favorably and eventually led to his inability to ever hold that office again. Our vehicles were thoroughly ransacked, and soon Germans were eating our "K" rations with apparent relish, drinking our coffee and smoking our cigarettes."

In a short time however, the Germans would realize that their position in Thurland was untenable, so they decided to move the bulk of captives and captured equipment to the nearby town of Raguhn. The Germans had assumed that Raughn was totally in the hands of their own soldiers, yet the village was occupied equally by both Germans and Americans. The German attempt to relocate their pilfered supplies and prisoners was chaotic and confusing to say the least; many died on both sides as the convoy of captured American vehicles rolled into Raughn. It was not long before the Americans were freed and many of the Germans became captives themselves. The rest of the remaining German forces eventually disappeared attempting to rejoin their own lines, which had fallen back across the Mulde River.

In the last days of the war, events were downright absurd and not just for the men of the CP (Command Post). Les Underwood could attest

258

to this chaos in those final days of the war, as he would escape death by the narrowest of margins once again. By this time, he had survived so many attacks and destroyed tanks, he felt somewhat invincible. Yet on his last day in combat, Les's perception caused him to assess his situation prematurely. He was standing outside of the tank near some houses along the Mulde River. Everything was surprisingly quiet and calm all around him and his tank group. Just as Les was telling the CP over the tank radio that everything was clear in their area, the situation changed drastically.

"On the last day of the war, I was calling on the tank radio [outside the tank] and I said, 'everything is good here.' I hung up, and saw a German soldier with a gun pointed right at me. He was about 70 yards away and he shouted, 'Kamerad!!' I had a 45 pistol with me and shot three times, but missed him, as he ran for cover." As he fired towards the German man he looked around to find some cover. There was a house right next to the tank, and Les scrambled to make his a way inside. As he did so, small arms were screaming all around him. He quickly realized that his comments on the radio had been a bit off the mark. "All hell broke loose, there were Germans everywhere. I could not get to the door, so I jumped through a plate glass window." Les's luck was such that after diving through the window he found himself crashing onto a bed. Later that day, he was able to make it back to the tank when the fighting died down. It was on that same day, that the war finally ended for the men of Taskforce Lovelady and the entire 3rd Armored Division. On the 24th of April, the 33rd Regiment fired its last shots and pulled back from the line. The final unconditional surrender of the Third Reich occurred only days later on the 8th of May, 1945.

In the days between the 24th of April and the final surrender, the men of Taskforce Lovelady's D Company took up residence in lodgings built for officers of the SS. The posh accommodations had been constructed as lodgings for those touring one of Germany's foremost historical military monuments; Kyffhauser. "Ironically enough, we were destined to sojourn under the majestic shadow of a titanic monument in memory of Germany's leader in World War I, Kaiser Wilhelm," recalled Eaton Roberts. "On the highest hill at Kyffhauser, it could be seen by all the troops in our taskforce and the massive lodges surrounding it, a luxurious haven for officers in the S.S. and their spouses, would soon be occupied by "D" Company." In fact, this massive structure was far more than a monument to Kaiser Wilhelm.

Amazingly, Lou had kept a picture of the place. The photo was folded and worn and tucked deep in his box of war souvenirs. It was a large German print. The commemorative photo was taken from a high vantage point overlooking a villa like structure. Behind the more modern structure there was a sizable medieval ruin. Initially the castle and its role presented a bit of a mystery. Lou and Les recalled that the inside of the main building was littered with Nazi regalia. Yet they knew little else about the significance of the place. In truth, this castle was not merely a resort for the SS in Thuringia. It had a very startling story to it, and its role in world history was as profound as it was puzzling.

The only tidbit of info I had to start with was written below the picture. In tiny lettering and extremely formal print, two main terms were discernable, Reichkreigerbund, and Kyffhauser. With some difficulty, I was able to find out a bit about these names. I discovered that the Reichkreigerbund was a Nazi organization. Its origins went back to Prussian roots. The original pre-Nazi name for the Reichkreigerbund was Kyffhauserbund, which was an association of veterans, most members were veterans of WWI. The name Kyffhauser in fact derived from the huge monument built nearby the Reichkreigerbund resort where D Company would stay at the wars end.

Reichkreigerbund Kyffhauser

The monument itself was dedicated in 1896, in honor of the veterans' organization and the Holy Roman King Frederick I Barbarossa (1122-1190). This monument still stands today, although its patrons have understandably distanced themselves from the Nazi era history of the monument, it is no less part of its past. In fact, it was the distant history and legend of King Barbarossa that drove Nazi's such as Himmler to this site. The lore of the mountain ruins spoke of a prophesy which foretold that the Ancient Germanic King Barbarossa would one day rise out of his mountain tomb and conquer the world in the name of Germany. Himmler and other believers in Gnostic runes and mysticism dedicated a great deal

261

of study to the Kyffhauser site. The National Socialist Reichkreigerbund 1944 booklet "Kameraden," includes a photograph of Himmler himself studying occult artifacts from the site.

Excavations and interpretations of the messages of the ancient Germans were mulled over, as Himmler, and other SS members were consumed in the belief that the ancient Germans were leaving them cryptic messages in the ruins of Thuringia and elsewhere. Some members of Himmler's staff, notably Karl Maria Wiligut SS Brigadefuhrer (brigadier general) even professed the clairvoyant ability to see into the past by thousands of years, and interpret the ancient messages.[8] Himmler and his SS colleagues firmly believed that the supernatural powers of their Aryan predecessors were guiding their way, pointing a path by which they would conquer, and return to their former glory as Aryan "god-men." Much like the fictional depictions in the Indiana Jones movies, Himmler actually sponsored archeological expeditions run by a select group of SS men. They were tasked with searching for holy relics related to the Aryans and ultimately finding justifications for conquest. Their searches even took SS men as far as Tibet in search of Aryan signs and historical artifacts.[9]

As for the Aryan messages at Kyffhauser and the legend of Frederick the First, they held such significance that Barbarossa's name became employed as the code name for the invasion of the Soviet Union. It was launched on the 22nd of June 1941. Despite the lore of the Thuringian King, the clairvoyant messages, and all the Gnostic root race clues, old Fred Barbarossa really didn't seem to help too much. The long bloody Barbarossa Operation would in fact spell the end of the Nazis. The push into the Soviet Union would turn into the largest military operation in all history, in regard to the numbers of soldiers involved as well as the military and civilian casualties. More people died in the battle for

262

Stalingrad then in all the wars ever fought by the United States up to Vietnam. Thankfully even with the help of Fred Barbarossa's ghost, the German Wehrmacht couldn't push past Stalingrad.

Apart from the mystical tales of the Kyffhauser site, it was in the practical sense the headquarters of the Reichkreigerbund, which was a very large group of German veterans among other things. In the US during the war, the Kyffhauserbund and German American Bund members were widely feared and considered to be spies and saboteurs. Congress actually debated rounding up all members of the Kyffhauserbund. The FBI declared any member of the Kyffhauserbund a suspected Nazi sympathizer. In some cases, the FBI discovered actual plots for sabotage and military action on US soil. On various occasions members of the Kyffhauserbund were rounded up and jailed by the FBI. Numerous raids in the early 1940's uncovered bombing plots, stashes of weapons, ammunition, and stolen US military uniforms.[10]

So, as Lou Baczewski and Les Underwood sat at the Reichkreigerbund headquarters and drank to the end of the war, they toasted to the end of such foolishness. In fact they drank the Nazi's booze. Lou and les dug out a tavern full of cognac, wine, and liquor that the former residents of the Reichkreigerbund Headquarters had buried in the bottom of a well. There were young Polish women in the resort who had worked as servants for the Nazis. Because Grandpa spoke Polish, he was able to communicate with them. The Polish women led both Lou and Les to a cache of bottles sunk just below the surface of a muddy hole. Lou, Les, and the rest of D Company lived it up in the Reichkreigerbund's Headquarters for a week or more and celebrated their victory and their survival of many hellish months of combat. According to Les, the resort contained chairs marked for high ranking Nazis, such as Hitler, Himmler,

263

Gobbles, and Goring. I am sure it was a fantastic feeling of relief to see those chairs now vacant, and never to be occupied again by their dark namesakes.

Kyffhauser Monument – Postcard From Lou Baczewski's war souvenirs

Top image - Reichsfurher Himmler w/ an unknown SS officer at the Kyffhauser Museum
Bottom image - Adolph Hitler and General Reinhard touring Kyffhauser Monument

SS run excavations at Kyffhauser circa 1930's

**D Company and D Company CO Lt. Alford
shaking hands with Louch (photo taken at Kyffhauser)**

Louch leaning on the D Company Command Post sign, at Kyffhauser, May 1945

They celebrated at Kyffhauser, but the weight of combat they saw could not be lifted. The costs in their company alone were staggering, "By

267

the end of the war there was hardly anybody left," Les explained. The original tankers who started out in France, were almost totally gone. "There was about 18 of us that never got a scratch, of the original guys. One hundred and fifty-two guys, and the biggest part of them was in headquarters, like cooks and that, and they was back [away from the front]. Now, there was probably some of them that was wounded that got back, but most of them were killed," Lou recalled with astonishment.

Both Les and Lou agreed that as a tanker it was hard to keep track of how many were lost and who was killed, given that they were in separate crews and spaced out during combat. Moreover, it was almost impossible to understand the larger picture when you were in combat each day. "Most often you're sitting there in the driver's seat, ya don't got any information, and ya can't see anything, and the only thing ya got is what the tank commander says. Ya know what I mean. Ya got your ear phones and a periscope, and that's it. Ya didn't know who got killed that day or nothing. Ya knowed that somebody got killed whenever there was a replacement," Lou sadly stated.

Even some of the toughest men in the outfit appeared broken by war's end. Sgt Eckdal who had made it all the way through the war, and whose tank helped closed the Falaise Gap, broke down under the pressure. On the very last day of the war as he prepared to head to the front, Sgt Eckdahl seemed to snap. "He was crying, and said that he just couldn't take it anymore. And they sent him back. Then the war was over, and I never seen him after that. He was crying like a baby." Les remembered. He added, "I wouldn't want to go through that again, that's all I gotta say."

Neither Lou nor Les would judge those who broke down, and they understood exactly why they did. They had witnessed so much carnage and loss along the way. The Division's losses in both men and material were of epic proportions, over 100 percent of the light tanks and an astonishing 580 percent of the Shermans were decimated. Every tank that the division had at full strength was destroyed and replaced roughly six times throughout the war. The 3rd Armored Division at full strength possessed 232 medium tanks. These tanks were replaced again and again throughout the war at such a rate that 1,350 tanks were destroyed before the war's end.[11] As the great bulk of these tank losses resulted in fatalities for the crew members, it was no wonder that the 3rd Armored's casualty rates were staggering. The fact that my grandfather survived the 3rd's entire series of campaigns is truly a miracle. After all, even the 3rd's own commanding General was lost.

3rd Armored Ordinance Officer Belton Cooper commented that, "Of all those assigned to the infantry, tanks, or engineers, or as artillery forward observers, I did not know of a single one who survived without being seriously wounded." Strangely, Lou and Les were two rare exceptions to this rule. The path that the 3rd Armored Division paved had been indescribably costly and gruesome; there was no glory to be found in its aftermath. Colonel John A Smith, Jr, 3rd Armored Division Chief of Staff quite eloquently stated that, "Back along the old, torn roads of conquest nearly 3,000 comrades lay beneath the white crosses of military cemeteries. Battle is never one sided. By that token the most famous of fighting divisions are store-houses of sorrow. The "Spearhead" was no exception."[12] There had been thousands more maimed, wounded and disfigured. All of them would forever carry scars on both mind and soul, regardless if they were physically wounded or not.

There was little time to reflect on such things, as there was still work to be done. Yet during the occupation period, Baczewski found some solace despite all of the carnage that he had witnessed. He certainly relished the fact that as soon as the war ended, he was able to help some poor Polish folks in Germany itself. In a small town on the banks of the Elbe River, Lou pulled some goodness out of all the misery around him. When my grandfather reflected on the following incident many years later, I could see that he never truly forgot why he and others had fought so hard along that long bloody road into Germany.

After leaving Kyffhauser, the 3rd Armored moved to an area near the river, there Louch met many Poles who had been living in Germany, and some may well have been slave laborers. He didn't know for certain, but he did know that many of them were starving. He was able to speak to them in fluent Polish, as he himself was raised speaking Polish alone. In fact, he did not learn to speak English until he started school in Pocahontas, Illinois.

On one particular day, their column was rolling through a small town just across the Mulde. Alongside the great line of tanks, trucks, jeeps and mounted infantry, a man ran along the column frantically pleading for help with his family following behind him. The problem was that no one could understand what the man said as he neither spoke German nor English. Vehicle after vehicle passed him by, until Sgt. Baczewski's tank pulled aside the commotion. With his hatch open Louch could overhear the man's frantic pleas for help, and he recognized his words as Polish.

"This one Polock, he came up to the tank. He said something in Polish, ya know. And I understood him, and I said Polsky? And he said, 'Yea, Polsky.' And then he told me that they wouldn't sell him any bread," Grandpa recalled. It seemed that the only source of food in the town was a baker shop which would neither barter nor sell bread to the Poles. The baker was run by a German who was content to let the local

Poles starve. Upon hearing this, Sgt. Baczewski, stopped his tank and grabbed his side arm and instructed the Polish man to follow. "So, I went in there and I said 'give him all the bread he wants." said Baczewski. The man foraged liberally at all the items in the shop, grabbing all he could. There was bread and other items there and grandpa watched as he pointed to this and that and loaded his arms full of food. With tears in his eyes he kept looking at Sgt Baczewski and saying "dziękuję!!, dziękuję!!," which is Polish for thank you.

I asked Grandpa if he had to pull his gun when he stepped in the baker shop. He replied that he had his side arm on, but he didn't need to use it. The German baker reluctantly complied with every demand. He stated, "Well, I had a gun with me but after [the surrender], they didn't give ya no problem, they didn't give ya no problem at all. Cause they knew - they had to do what ya told em to do." Louch watched as the Polish man loaded himself down with all he could carry and ran to his family outside.

The following day, Lou's commander Lt Alford, came to fetch him. The tank crew was staying in a German house outside of town, and it seemed that more Poles had come looking for Sgt. Baczewski. Lieutenant Alford stepped into the house with a big smile, and said, "Hey Lou, there are some folks out here looking for you. I think they're looking for the Polish GI. They keep saying Polsky GI, Polsky GI." When Louch stepped out of the house, there before him he saw thirty or more Poles. There were men, women, and children and they were all starving. They were all standing there waiting for him. In his own words he fondly recalled, "And here come a whole flock of Polocks. Cause ya know food, that stuff was critical during the war."

271

Louch grabbed his sidearm, gathered himself together and marched down to that same baker's shop, only now followed by an immense entourage of more than thirty Poles. In his tankers overalls and bowlegged swagger he walked into the baker shop. To the disdain of the proprietor; he insisted that this very baker should feed each and every one of these people behind him and for free - each one could take all they could carry. He said, "They didn't pay for nothing. I just told em, give them some bread, ya know. From then on they all got bread there. One would tell the other one and news got out." That day they cleaned the place out for free. The amazing thing was that Louch then told the baker that from that day on, no Pole should be refused from buying or bartering bread. Even as part of a conquering army, Louch was fair. He gave the baker a chance for redemption. He certainly could have beaten the man up or even killed him without repercussions: knowing full well that he was starving those people. Yet that just wasn't the kind of man that Louch was, and even a war didn't change that. He said that from then on the baker sold to all the Poles. In his own words he smiled and said, "They didn't give em no trouble after that."

Chapter14
"I thought this was a free country."

"I haven't much interest in military affairs. The truth
is I am more of a farmer than a soldier. Although I
have been in two wars,
I never entered the army without regret,
and never left it without pleasure"

Ulysses S. Grant
Stated unto Auto von Bismarck while Grant reviewed a
group of German troops following the US Civil War

When Louch was a sophomore in high school, he and his older brother Joe, along with his buddies Dave Pagan, and John Hustava all went rabbit hunting together. The problem was that the best rabbit hunting spot they could ever imagine was on a farmer's land where they were not allowed to hunt. They had asked on several occasions, but the farmer kept turning them down. So they decided to try and get away with it anyway. The brush was so thick with rabbits on that farm that they could hardly walk as they came out of the woods; their game bags were just too full of rabbits. They were making their way back to the road where Dave Pagan had parked his father's car, when they were met with the unwelcome gaze of the farmer. As Lou stated, "Well whenever we got done hunting, we walked out there on the road and there was the sheriff and that farmer, they said, 'you guys are trespassing we're gonna take you to the justice of the peace for trespassing.' That cop, Charlie Ward was his name; he was a real fat guy. Anyway, so they took us to Pocahontas. They didn't take our rabbits, they let us take our rabbits home and our guns home. And then they fined us nine dollars a piece..."

They were allowed to go home, clean all the rabbits and put all their hunting stuff away, then go back to the courthouse to receive their sentence. According to Dave and Louch, both the judge and town cop were both pretty big drunks, and they figured that nine dollars each was just going to end up turning into whiskey money in a short spell. Uncle Joe was working and could pay the nine dollars, but none of the boys, Lou, Dave, or John had the money. Lou stated, "The judge and the Pocahontas police they wanted the money to buy whiskey, ya know... Well we knew they drank and that judge he was half stewed most of the time. My dad said' I'm not paying no nine dollars for you,' cause ya know money was scarce then. He said,' I ain't gonna pay any money, you are just gonna have to do whatever they do.' And they [the sheriff and judge] said if ya can't pay the fine you are gonna have to go to jail." "So they took us to Greenville."

"[In Pocahontas], they had a jail but they didn't have no jailor there or nothing, so they took us to Greenville, the county seat...We had a heck of a time, it was me and Dave Pagan and John Hustava and we was throwing pillows and everything we had a heck of a time. And this jailor, the sheriff up there in Greenville, his name was John Brown. Why we ran around with his boys up in Greenville - we knew his boys. And so this sheriff's wife done the cooking and heck she cooked us meals out of this world, cause she knew us ...We had a heck of a time we got off of school two days. We was in jail for two days for trespassing. Well, when we went back to school ya had to sign an excuse to where you was, cause we was absent two days from school, so we had to sign the thing. So we signed the excuse, 'visited the county jail.' Every time you went to class you'd have to give your teacher [the form]. And then everybody'd bust out laughing cause the whole town knew where we was. And see I was playing basketball too see, and me and Dave Pagan we was on the first string. So we had a game Wednesday, we got out on Tuesday evening. And so you had to be at school the day before [to play in the game], so we was absent. So anyhow, we asked the coach, 'do we get to dress tonight or what?' He said, 'well I don't know.' So he let us dress. And you ought to heard that crowd, they kept hollering, Jailbird!! Jailbird!! [Later on] we won the sectional."

When my Grandpa told that story, my Grandmother was sitting at the table with us, and it became quickly apparent that she had never heard any of this. As Grandpa laughed about the incident, Grandma said, "that's not funny, you were in jail. Do you have a record?" Grandpa let a lot of stuff slide in that interview, and it was obvious that poor Grandma had never heard one bit of it. In fact, she asked me not to put the jail story in the book, but I couldn't help myself. Grandma had met Grandpa after the war, and by that time, Grandpa and Pocahontas had settled down quite a bit. According to Lou and Dave Pagan, Pokey had been a pretty rough place in many respects. Both Louch and Dave grew up together in Pocahontas through Prohibition and the Depression. In fact, there were a good deal of bootleggers, thugs, and common everyday criminals running around Pokey in the 1920's and 1930's. Lou and Dave witnessed a lot together as they had always been the closest of friends even into their eighties.

1940 Pocahontas High School Basketball Team, Sectional Champions
Front row (left to right) – Dave Pagan, Stanford Brown, Lou (Louch) Baczwski,
Walter Romy, Bill Tepatti, and Matt Koberczski. Back row – Gerald Jenner, Jim
Kesner, Bill Swofford, Ralph McCaslin, Bob Boyce, and Coach Joe Lucco

They were called the "Gold Dust Twins" around town, as they were almost inseparable and only lived two blocks apart. The name "Gold Dust Twins" came from the label on an old Fairbanks soap container, which showed two young boys side-by-side. Dave and Louch were best friends all through grade school and high school and they stirred up a good deal of trouble between them. They fished the creek together, worked on the same farms, chased the same girls, and backed each other up in more than one fist fight. The oddest thing was that they even found each other in Germany right after the war had come to a close.

Like the rest of the 3rd Armored's cadre Baczewski found himself stationed in Frankfurt during the occupation. The 3rd's soldiers took up

276

residence in a group of regal homes. They were the former homes of high ranking corporate heads and Nazi Party members. These homes all looked out over a huge wooded park, just south of Frankfurt. Both Les and Lou remembered fondly how peaceful and beautiful the park was. There they hunted, fished, and walked through the woods on their free time. The occupation forces still had plenty to do as they were trying to band-aid the communities back together, keep the peace, and provide some services to the German people.

Unlike the occupation of Iraq which was hastily planned in a few months, the occupation of Europe was thoroughly organized and mapped out over a period of years. History should have shown that it pays to plan, but none of our contemporaries seemed to look at such things. In the German occupation, the US forces immediately declared Martial Law in order to keep the peace and organize the districts and towns. In many cases, they used the existing mayors and politicians, in order to ease the transition to a new government. They also never disbanded the German Army, and consequently they had a disciplined labor force available, while also preventing an insurgency of unpaid soldiers. Additionally, the American occupational forces through calculated legal and historical consideration, created a constitution which is still in use in Germany today. Sadly, none of these lessons were heeded in Iraq and in most cases the exact opposite was done.

Because the planning and application was so thorough, Lou, Les, and all the occupational forces in Germany, were able to live without constant fear of insurgency and reprisal. Very few guerrilla actions took place in Germany, and in contrast to Iraq, insurgency was literally non-existent. As such, Lou and Les spent all of their free time exploring the areas around Frankfurt. Louch quickly realized that they had no more need

277

for grenades as there was no more war and no insurgency, so he chose to find more practical applications for them.

As he stated, "After the war, we was in Frankfurt, Germany. This canal was going through there and, so I thought well man, maybe I'll throw a few thermite [concussion] grenades in there and see what's in there." Once he said he dropped the grenades, "boy them fish started coming up and we was getting them fish. We didn't need them grenades anymore." He said as soon as word got out of what he had done, guys from D Company were all hunting through their tanks for concussion grenades to "fish with." Before too long, the whole company had run out of concussion grenades and the streams were about out of trout. Some men even started throwing shrapnel grenades in the canal, forcing everyone around to hit the deck to avoid the shrapnel. But like he said, whatever the case, every time they got a mess of fish, "then they'd bring em back to the mess hall and we'd cook em up."

At the same time while Louch was fishing with grenades, Dave Pagan was stationed just south of Frankfurt. Being the guys that they were, they were both trying to fish with explosives. Dave said," I was in Germany, about thirty miles from Frankfurt, there was this pond there, and I wanted to see if there was anything in it." Dave went a bit overboard, as he used TNT with a primer cord instead of grenades. He said that it, "blew all the water out of the pond." Afterwards he found that there were no fish in it. Or more likely, the few fish that were in there had been obliterated by the massive explosion. His Captain was reasonably irate after hearing and feeling the shockwave. Upon viewing the muddy aftermath, he flipped out even further. Dave said, "My Captain went berserk."

This same Captain had helped Dave out of many jams all through the war. This time he was understandably pissed, but still not enough to stop from helping Dave hitch a ride to Frankfurt. A few days after the explosion, and once his Captain had calmed down; Dave asked if he could somehow get to Frankfurt to see Louch. Dave Stated, "Yea my Captain, I was really in good with him and I told him, I got a buddy over here about 30 miles. And my Captain says, 'Lieutenant, take that jeep and take him wherever he wants to go."

Lou stated, "That lieutenant had dinner with us and everything, he spent all day with us. That same day, I was just south, on the outskirts of Frankfurt, and I took Dave for a ride in my tank, 'I said you want to go for a ride in the tank,' and he said 'yea ok,' and so I took him down through this park ya know. He spent the whole day with me there."

Although neither Dave nor Lou knew it, they had been right nearby each other all through the war. Dave was an artilleryman and part of the 78th Lightning Division, 309th Regiment Battery B, which was involved in the Huertgen Campaign. They had been part of the attack on the German town of Schmidt. While Louch and Mel Weber were fighting in Stolberg, Dave was only a few miles south of them outside of Schmidt. During the Battle of the Bulge, Dave's outfit stayed just north of the 3rd Armored Division. Dave had not seen the amount of combat that Grandpa had been through, but he saw his fair share of carnage.

Dave was quite a baseball player and as he played for an Army team, he was kept stateside for a great deal of the war. He entered the Army earlier than Lou, but spent most of the war years stateside playing baseball. He was actually the captain of the division's baseball team. One of his regimental Colonels was a ball player himself, and because of Dave's skill on the field, he stayed stateside for many years until the whole Division deployed. He was fairly well connected and able to get the best treatment and positions available. As he stated, "My Captain was from St Louis, and they called me the "Captain's boy. I got by with anything." On one occasion, he even ran over on his leave and should have been marked AWOL, but his Captain bailed him out.

Eventually when his whole outfit was sent overseas, just like Baczewski, he spent a good deal of time in England, but was not sent in to fight until the beginning of the Huertgen Campaign in September of 1944. As he and the rest of his unit crossed the channel, one of his close friends told him that he knew he would get killed before Christmas. Dave told him, "you are too goddamn crazy, you will never get killed." The man's words were prophetic however, as he was killed by shrapnel on the 24th of December 1944.

For the bulk of the war, Dave drove an M5 tractor which pulled a 155mm cannon. He was tasked with firing and maintaining the 155mm gun back behind the American lines in the Huertgen area of Germany. He and his battalion were subject to frequent attacks from German artillery fire. During those barrages, he saw many men lose their lives right next to him and on more than one occasion. He found out quickly that death was dealt out randomly. He had many close calls, but felt that one of the scariest things for him was crossing a pontoon bridge over the Rhine River. "The night before we crossed the Rhine though, me and another guy, me and him got to drinking on wine, we got in a wine cellar, cause we was crossing the Rhine the next day and ya didn't know whether you was gonna make it or not. And we got all boozed up and we found a bicycle built for two. We rolled it, turned it over and got all skinned up." After the war his Captain joked to him stating, "you got more skinned up on that damn bicycle then ya did all through the war."

Pontoon Bridge over the Rhine River (3ad.com)

Louch was just as lucky as Dave, perhaps more, given all that he had gone through. Unfortunately their two close friends, John Hustava, and Stanley Cravens, never returned home from the war. With the war finally finished, both Dave and Lou made it back to Pokey. It was only a short time before they went back to working and fishing the creek together, just as they had done before the war. Yet things would never be the same after losing their two boyhood friends. Stanley and John were not the only losses from their hometown. In Lou's high school class alone, four out of a class of seventeen died in the war.

Once he had the required amount of points for discharge, Louch was able to get his walking papers and leave Germany. In the winter of 1945, Lou loaded up on the liberty ship SS Stanford, and made his way back home. Upon arrival in New York, he made his way to the train station and bought a ticket to St Louis. At that point, his family did not know he was coming home. When Grandpa finally stepped back in Pokey, he surprised everyone. His brothers, mother and father were elated to see him finally home safe and sound. They clamored around their small home. The wooden screen door creaked and groaned as the family roared out of the little red house to greet him. That night he stayed up through the wee hours talking to his mother and father at the dinner table, they spoke only in Polish. There in the dim light of the kitchen, he and his father passed a bottle of whiskey back and forth while they talked about the war. Their youngest son was finally home, but the change in him was visible and his stories were as dark as the corners of the room that night. Somehow he had made it home, to Pokey, and Shoal Creek, and the little fake brick home on Union Street. Somehow he had made it through all of that carnage. He made it home, but he was a different man, and deep inside he was haunted by all that he had seen and done.

In the days that followed his return, he quickly realized that it was time to get back to work. He needed to find a job. For him, college was not even a thought because in his world only the smallest fraction of folks went to college. So, in a short time, both Dave Pagan and Lou were working at the same coal mine as Great Grandpa. The mine as always had been dangerous and the wages were relatively poor. So, neither Dave nor Lou wanted to stay working in the Pokey Coal Mine for very long.

Knowing a few friends who worked for the Laborers Union, out of East St Louis, they were able to get a connection to some work through the laborers hall. There was a Laborers Union bus that took men from Pocahontas to East St Louis everyday. Lou and Dave hitched a ride on a bus and started working in East St Louis in order to get away from the Pokey mine. The laborers union charged a dollar a day to ride the bus to work. So, each day, Lou and Dave paid the fee and rode to ESL where they poured concrete and worked as finishers.

In the months that followed, the local car dealer offered to sell Louch the first civilian car sold in Pocahontas since the onset of the war. In fact, he said he would save the car just for him. During the war, the production of civilian vehicles completely halted, as all factories retooled to help with the war effort. With his GI Bill, Lou bought the 1946 Chevy. He was quite certain that it was the first civilian car sold in Bond County, Illinois. "I bought the first car the Chevy dealer got after the war. See they couldn't get cars ya know what I mean. They couldn't get any cars. But that was the first car that he got in, a 46 Chevy. And so he let me have that car. He said Lou, "you want this first car, then you can have it," I paid one thousand seven hundred and forty five dollars for that car. One of these guys that belonged to the local down there in East Saint Louis, he said how about you driving down there to East St Louis? So, I and five more guys drove. Well, they had a bus driving down there, and some of the guys rode that bus. At one time they told me to quit hauling passengers down there; told me to get my ass on that bus. Oh, they beat up my neighbor in Pocahontas. They beat him up bad. They beat up a couple of guys that I know of for not riding the bus."

The truth was that the East St Louis Laborers were at the time quite corrupt, and widely considered to be connected to the local mob. The Business Agent (BA) at the time "Poud" Roberts, made a good deal of money off all those men riding the bus down to East St Louis every day. A dollar a day from a bus full of men added up to be a hefty sum in 1946. So, Poud sent his thugs around to make sure that everyone from Pokey who worked in East St Louis had to ride that bus. Otherwise, the thugs would rough them up and the union hall would cut them out of work. Lou and his friends had not realized that driving to work on their own would end up pushing them into a sticky situation with the union thugs.

Yet Lou and Dave were not new to seeing and dealing with gangsters. When they were young, Pokey was full of gangsters and bootleggers and everyday thugs. There was even a building occupied by a gang for the greater part of the time. They had a house full of women and another built like a fortress with gun-ports and the like. The Sheriff would turn a blind eye to it all, as he had little chance of dealing with them anyway. Lou said, "Hell they had machine guns and every damn thing. They robbed the bank a couple a times, and robbed the train." In fact, Lou's older brother, Joe was walking home from school one day when a group of local gangsters was robbing the Pocahontas Bank. As Joe walked by, he noticed a man standing out in front of the bank, with a shotgun in hand. He was guarding the door. Uncle Joe, being a bit too curious, walked right up in front of the door and started peering into the bank. The gunman out front took a couple steps towards him and gave him a swift kick in the ass, and said, "get home kid!" Right afterwards, the rest of the gang rolled out of the bank, hopped in a car, and sped away.

Lou and Dave recalled that there was plenty of crime to be found in Pokey apart from robbery as well. Gambling and booze could be easily had, even though they were both illegal at the time. Dave stated that, "Al Golden, he had that cigar store, and there wasn't a cigar in it. All it was; was crap games, and poker games. He didn't give a damn if you was twelve, or fourteen years old, he'd let ya go in there. He'd let you play cards if you had money and shoot dice, if your Dad wasn't already there." Lou and Dave would step into Al Golden's establishment on a frequent basis.

**Dave and Louch, standing in front of John DeLaurenti's general store
Pocahontas, Illinois - circa 1940**

Lou fondly remembered that even as a boy, he could get a drink
now and again from a local bootlegger. "Whenever I used to be 10 or 12
years old my dad would send me over to a bootleg place to get some
whiskey and some beer. I'd take a miners bucket (it had a lid on it), and
he'd say, "go over to Mason's and get this beer and get a pint of whiskey."
It was 50 cents for the whiskey and a quarter for the bucket of beer. They
sold it warm; they didn't have no refrigeration in them days. And then on
the way home, heck I'd sip off that bucket, I'd take a swig now and then.
There was several bootleggers. Right there, where Leisure Lounge [the
local tavern] is, there used to be a big house there, a two story house. That
was a bootleg place, and every once in a while, they would raid it. They
had a big rock back there in the back, and they would take all them there
cases of home brew out and throw em against that rock and bust them
bottles. The revenue guys [the Feds] ya know. And then they'd clean that
whole house out, they'd bust every bottle." Louch would watch all of this

go on, while he and other local boys sat hiding under the porch of the house. He said before too long, the house was back in business selling beer and whiskey. Most of the raids were all for show.

(left to right) Louch, Bill Kalous, and Dave Pagan,
standing in downtown Pokey - circa 1946

There were also a great deal of fights and occasionally a shooting as well. When I asked Dave why were there so many fights and shoot outs, he replied, "Hell they use to fight in Pokey just for the fun of it. They use to fight over anything." He recalled fights breaking out between men over as little as a nickel lost in a card game. At times there were even big shootouts between groups of rival gangsters, or gangsters and the Fed's. Most of Pokey's local Gangsters were more than likely affiliated with the

Shelton Gang, which controlled basically all of Southern Illinois bootlegging.[13]

The Shelton Gang's influence spread from Peoria to East St Louis and even as far south as Cairo. They had bloody turf wars with smaller rival gangs and with the Klu Klux Klan, which was a strong fixture in the "sundown towns" of Southern Illinois. The KKK was a strong political entity in Illinois, and they wanted to eliminate the Shelton's bootlegging; especially because the Shelton's were more than willing to sell alcohol to Catholics and Blacks. In fact, entire towns erupted in violence in Southern Illinois during disputes between the Sheltons and the KKK. According to Taylor Pensoneau, author of a book on the Shelton Gang, Al Capone himself was fearful of turf war with the Shelton's and thus kept his bootlegging operation strictly confined to the Chicago area. The brothers Carl, Bernie, and Big Earl Shelton had their hands in everything from bootlegging, gambling, women, and even unions. Many labor unions in East St Louis maintained ties to the Shelton Gang and later gang leader Frank "Buster" Wortman.

So, when Lou and his friends tried to save themselves money and ride to work in East St Louis after the war, they were tangling with some very rough characters indeed. Yet, after coming back from the war, Lou was not inclined to have someone push him around after all he had been through. He was also single and without a family. He had little to lose. After his friends had been beat up by Poud Robert's thugs, Lou was certain that he was next. He started carrying a gun to work. Eventually, while on the job one day, one of Poud's thugs, stepped up to him and told him that he was supposed to report to the union hall, to talk to the BA (Business Agent). Louch told him, "I said I went to the war and I fought

287

the German's and then I come back here and some son-of-a-bitch is trying to tell me what I can and can't do!"

When he went to the hall, he thought that they may well try to kill him. He walked into the hall and into the Business Agent's office, with a pistol concealed at his waist. He understood that he might have had to shoot his way out. He soon met with the gaze of Poud Roberts, who was flanked by a couple of his goons. Roberts immediately started to chew him out a bit, but when Lou spoke up, Roberts backed off. Lou told him, "All I am here to do is work, but you mean to tell me that I can't drive my own friends in my own car. Ya know, I thought this was a free country! " According to Lou, he let it be known that he had just come home from fighting in a war, and asked them where they had been through all of it. He made it known to all of them that he was not scared. Roberts let it drop and told him just to go, nothing more was ever said about it. He was cautious not to say anything too wild, as he knew he needed the work, but he certainly let them know how he felt about it. Because of his comments and the fact that some of the guys he was transporting had clout at the union hall, Roberts left him alone. Louch drove his friends to work without any problems after that.

Lou said, "they didn't mess with me. I thought that they was gonna work me over, but I had a 32 pistol I kept under my belt. They wanted to talk to me. I figured they was gonna work me over, so I thought to myself, somebody is going to get hurt. Me, coming home from fighting a war and everything, and somebody was gonna tell me what to do! Well, after that, they didn't bother me a bit. Evidently they must of smelled something. There was a lot of disputes about riding back and forth, cause he [Roberts] made money off the passengers on that bus, I think a dollar a day. Well heck! If he had a bus full every day, he was raking in money!

288

They [the laborers hall] had thugs, if they wanted somebody worked over, they'd call these guys and work somebody over if they didn't like how something was going."

"Laborers was all real crooked at that time, ya had to toe the line ya know. If ya didn't do what they'd tell ya, ya either got fired or else got worked over. But it was different then. They had mob connections ya know. Cause these mobsters would go on a job where they didn't have to work. Oh yea, they got these jobs where they sat around in the tool shed or something, easy jobs where they didn't have to do nothing. Half the time they'd go to the tavern during working hours - go to the tavern and drink beer! Well heck, I know me and Dave Pagan worked down there and heck several times the foreman would say, come on, 'Lou and Dave, let's go have a beer,' and he was the foreman on the job and we'd go to the tavern and drink beer for the rest of the day and still be on the clock. Well see, the boss kept our time. He put our time in, and we'd go drink beer, that's the way it was. The foreman would cover up for you if they liked you. They had something to do with the business agent and the mob. That's the way it used to be."

Getting work through the labor hall was always a shady deal, if you did not have connections in the hall you wouldn't always be put to work. Occasionally, some of the goons from the hall would come out to the jobs and ask all the guys to bet on the "numbers." They even had their own gambling pool. It was a numbers racket. If you did not bet on those numbers, then you took a different gamble on whether you would find work through the hall or not. Guys who did not throw in had a tough time getting sent out to work, as referrals to work were all in the BA's hands. Sadly, many unions at the time were overrun by thugs, because the unions needed men tough enough to tangle with the company's thugs. Everyone on both sides of the labor and management coin hired thugs to do their bidding. Nowadays, the preferred nomenclature for "thug" is pronounced, "Lawyer," and each side still has their own "group of thugs," or "Firm." It's not a thug with a club anymore working for the company, now it's a thug with a suit.

Lou would work for many years in the laborers union, until he moved up the chain and became a millwright and joined the steelworkers union, which was less prone to corruption. He eventually worked as a millwright for Kanalco, until his retirement. In fact, all of Grandpa's sons and some of his grandsons would all later become tradesmen and union members of various stripes, myself included. And despite some admitted problems with some unions, we grew up knowing that they did their fair share of good as well. One of Lou's grandsons would even become a lawyer, although I joke about lawyers, my brother Joe is one of those litigators who never forgot his roots. He sticks up for the everyday folks whenever he can. Just like with thugs, you need both kinds, and I am damn glad that my brother Joe is one of "them there" working class jurisdoctorate thugs.

Chapter 15
The Flowing Dao of Shoal Creek

The best are like water...choosing what others
avoid hence approaching the Tao, dwelling with earth,
thinking with depth, helping with kindness, speaking
with truth, governing with peace,
working with skill, moving with time.

Lao Tzu

As far back as I could remember we fished Shoal Creek each and every year. It was our pilgrimage, but it was on a variety of locations along Shoal Creek that we fished. Because certain spots would silt in or log jams would be washed away in the spring floods, fishing spots changed continuously. The water changed each year, but the process never did, because Grandpa had taught us to understand that the only constancy was change. Throughout my life, we fished under the I70 bridge, Hwy 140 bridge, at Mill Dam, at a cow farm near Carlyle, a cow farm off of old Rose Road, and at a guy named Cletus's place.

Bridges were the easiest sights to access, and since they were on state ground, they were typically places where we didn't have to worry about trespassing. Other places required permission, which was a whole different problem, so we tried to avoid it. 140 bridge was the old reliable. We had good water there for most of my youth and it was a good campsite, until the damn Corps of Engineers dumped a few hundred tons of massive riprap under the bridge and made the once comfortable sandy bottom campsite a damn field of boulders. It looked like a quarry. There wasn't even a flat place to set your beer down much less sleep. It sucked after that.

Although the location mattered, there were a lot of other considerations, poles, lines, gear, and bait were of equal significance. Yet few things in the whole operation were of greater importance than the lines themselves, and how they were eventually placed. The banklines had been handmade by various people in the family throughout the years. They were simple. A large stainless steel hook would be tied to roughly a 2 to 3 foot long piece of heavy nylon string. The hook was tied in a bowline knot or to a swivel, so it could be removed later if the hook straightened, rusted, or broke off. Around the string a large lead weight was fastened. The lead was either melted down and pressed around the string or wrapped tightly around the line with strips of sheet lead. The lead was many times scrap off old construction jobs when lead was used to seal cast iron plumbing fittings. Some of the lines we still use today are probably forty years old or more. Grandpa had made most of them. He had sat many evenings at his kitchen table sharpening hooks on a stone, tying lines, and making up lead weights. It was an old tradition which dated back to his childhood.

When preparing for a creek trip, the lines were pretty easy to get together, if they were taken care of. Yet the worst aspect of getting set for the creek was cutting the willow poles. My Father, Grandfather, or my Uncle Dave would constantly search for shallow swamps full of willow trees. If and when one was found, we would head into the swamp, cleavers and hatchets in hand. I am sure it looked odd, and perhaps reasonably frightening to normal people, a bunch of Polocks brandishing bladed weapons in a swamp. I am sure most folks would wonder what good could come of that?

We would search for small straight willow trees about 1 inch in diameter at the base, and eight to ten feet in length. We would chop them down and throw them aside until we had cut perhaps fifty or more. If we had as Grandpa always said "good water" to fish that year, we might cut one-hundred poles and run lines in both directions up and down the creek. After we cut the poles, we would de-limb them except for perhaps a fork at the end to keep our lines from slipping off. It took a good deal of time to cut them all and bundle them up. By the time we were done, everyone was exhausted and dirtier than guys cutting down limbs in a swamp. Oh, wait a minute, that's what we were doing.

If cutting poles had not sucked enough, getting bait would make up for that for sure. The problem was, in order to catch the largest amount of fish, you needed large live minnows and lots of them. Grandpa had taught us two ways to do this: either catch a bunch with a cane pole, a small hook, and a red wiggler worm one by one, or seine them up in a two man minnow net. The first option was time consuming and tedious, but actually kind of fun. The later was quicker, but it was about as fun as getting a full frontal lobotomy, especially when it came to seining bait with Uncle Dave. My dad's youngest brother, Dave, was far enough apart in age with my Father that I always considered him more of an older brother than an uncle. Dave would always be the one to spout off the Shoal Creek catch phrase, "We're gonna run them all night." He meant that if the fish were biting well enough, we would keep running out on the boat and baiting up the lines all night. Yet this just about never happened, because we had usually succumbed to either consumption, or exhaustion sometime in the night. We almost never "ran em all night." Dave had a lot of crazy things to say, and was always a lot of fun. He is the kind of guy who could make anyone laugh, but he was militant about Shoal Creek and especially seining bait.

When seining bait, two people had to wade through the murky waters of a small creek holding two poles tied to the ends of a long net. The others there helping had to get the buckets ready and full of fresh water in order to keep the bait alive. Every time we went, Dave would invariably be barking orders and screaming about too little water in the bait, or how the net was set, and on and on. Eventually my cousin Mike and I started talking about Dave like he was a Nazi officer. We imitated him in our fake Nazi voices, right in front of him of course. "U carry zee buket now! Schnell!! Pik up zee net! Nein! Don't schpill zee bait!" That would go on and on. Eventually Dave would start laughing and lighten up.

When it came to doing things right on the creek, an outside observer might well think my Grandpa, Father, and Uncles were at times overly hard on my cousins and my brother Joe and I. We were not coddled, by any means. Yet as I have grown older, I have realized how much that taught me. I sure didn't appreciate being chewed out here and there for not doing things right, but I know I am a better person for it. My Grandpa, Father, and Uncles taught me a lot about life on the creek; I just had to grow up to see it for what it was. I had to grow a bit older before I could truly appreciate all that they had shown me.

Fishing the creek and all the effort involved was is in most people's minds utter misery. To many, it was a Herculean effort and with little reward besides a few catfish. However, as I grew up fishing in this manner, and was taught by men who regarded the steps and tasks with reverence, I never saw any bit of it as misery. The concept of misery only comes about when one fixates on the possibility that there is some place better to be at that given moment. When I find myself knee deep in a muddy creek carrying buckets full of bait, sweating like a pig in the

August heat, and being swarmed by horseflies and mosquitoes, I think about not spilling the bait. I think about what path I will take down the creek bank so as not to fall. I never long for climate controlled areas. I never lament for the comforts of home. Air-conditioned rooms are somewhere else and have now become none of my business. It becomes a matter of being here and in the now, with sand in my shoes and five gallon buckets in each hand. It becomes a matter of keeping my mind on the task and following the natural order of things. No one ever complained when fishing the creek, we just understood it for what it was. The hard work was not so much physical as mental. Once you got your "mind right," none of the ardors really mattered anymore, and there was no place else any of us would rather have been.

When my dad and Uncles were young, Louch would take them to Shoal Creek a few times a year. Grandpa never stopped fishing the creek until he was just physically unable to do it. After he arrived home from the war, he fished the creek as many times a year as he could. Upon his return, he moved back into his boyhood home in Pocahontas, Illinois. In 1947, Grandpa met my Grandmother, after being introduced through his cousin, Polly.

Grandpa and Grandma

Helen Tutka was a beautiful young girl from Madison, Illinois, and
from the way that both Grandma and Grandpa talked, it was love at first
sight. Grandma was quite a catch, as she was incredibly intelligent and
talented. She was actually a traditional Polish Dancer, and was quite a
singer as well. In my youth, she was always in the choir at Church, and
always encouraging everyone to sing at every family occasion. Louch
must have been tight lipped during the courtship and the bulk of the
marriage. It was obvious that he had not told Grandma about going to jail
for trespassing, sneaking into movies, or stealing chickens, or all the other
goofy things he had done as a boy. In fact, during one of my interviews, I
could see Grandma's astonishment as we both listened to grandpa's stories
of going to jail for rabbit hunting on private property, and him stealing
sips off his dad's beer as he came home from a bootlegger's place.
Grandma told Grandpa, "man you've got quite a past, I didn't know about
all this stuff," and she didn't mean that in a good way. When he told the

296

story about being in jail for trespassing, Grandpa and I were laughing hysterically, grandma half-jokingly interjected, "that's not funny, you were in jail! I didn't know about all this." I guess for grandpa's sake it was a good thing she hadn't.

Lou and Helen on their wedding day
April 3rd 1948

Lou and Helen with their oldest son
Stanley, circa 1949

When Helen and Lou married and lived in Pokey for a while, but later moved to Collinsville, Illinois. As time went on, Grandma and Grandpa would have five children, my father Stanley, Aunt Roseann, Uncle John, Aunt Mary Kay, and the youngest, Uncle Dave. My father, the eldest, was born on December 19th of 1948; Grandpa and Grandma named him Stanley in honor of Lou's father, Stanislaus Baczewski. Great Grandpa would not live much longer, and he died less than a month after little Stanley was born. My dad never had the opportunities I did. He never was able to get to know his own grandfather. He did however relish every moment he had with my Great Grandma Baczewski. She must have been something, because no one in the family could speak about her without shedding a few tears. Everyone missed her, especially Grandpa. She had unfortunately passed just a few years before I was born, but I grew up hearing stories about her. She had never learned to speak English fluently, and had never learned to read or write. She was never able to even read a cook book, but everyone agreed she was a fantastic cook with a sharp sense of humor and one heck of a work ethic. She made an impression on everyone she met, and I sure wish I could have known her.

Alexandria Baczewski (Great Grandma) holding her grandson Stanley Baczewski, circa 1949

The first time I realized how much great Grandma meant to everyone, was when my Uncle Paul created a charcoal drawing of my

Great-Grandmother and gave prints of it to all of her granddaughters and grandsons on Christmas Eve. Even though Christmas Eve was our most jubilant holiday, when Uncle Paul handed out those prints, every adult who knew her was instantly brought to tears. In my whole life I have still never seen so much emotion at a Christmas Eve gathering than what I witnessed on that year. Even though I was just a high school kid at the time, I saw just how much of an affect she had on our whole family.

When my dad and my uncle John were boys, they would stay with Great-Grandma in Pokey for weeks during their summer break. There in Pokey, they were able to run free, much like Louch did when he was a boy. They would fish the creek at night and hunt squirrels during the day. Dad recalled many times when he and John would wake up before dawn and ride their bikes out to the creek with shotguns and 22 rifles slung over their handle bars. Even when they returned in the middle of the day, no one in town would think anything of it, as they rode back towards the house with their guns in hand and hunting vests full of squirrels. They rolled down the roads in Pokey and back to Great-Grandma's. Dad said that when they returned to the house, Grandma would always say, "You catch um something," in her thick Polish accent. She would take whatever fish or squirrels they had and cook them up.

When my dad was a boy however, life wasn't perfect by any means, and neither was my grandfather. Lou came home from the war, and walked into another battle itself, whether it was union thugs, or unemployment, or mouths to feed at home; all of it added up on a man who had seen far too much violence and carnage. Grandpa was not the man I grew up with. Back in the day, he didn't have much patience or stillness. During the years that followed the war, Lou struggled to feed his family, find work, and make sense of his life. He was short tempered and prone to violent outbreaks. According to my dad, he was unreasonably rigid and incapable of communicating in more than commands. Honestly, decades passed before my Father and Grandfather got along very well. More than likely Lou had symptoms of post-traumatic stress disorder (PTSD). After all, he had seen far too much combat. To come home and somehow adjust to everyday life was an understandably difficult job. It was not until years later, that grandpa became the calm, sagacious man that I knew. I honestly think it took a lot of years of fishing to get there and it was a testament to the man's strength that he was able to transform at all. Far too many strong men and women never recover from the scars of war.

Even when Grandpa was younger, and still hard in his ways, the one place that he and my dad saw eye to eye was on Shoal Creek. Both Grandpa and my dad loved to fish Shoal Creek as much as anyone. Despite their differences, on the creek it didn't matter. When Dad was a boy, he and his brothers along with Louch's brothers Ed and Joe, they would fish the creek a few times a summer. Ed brought his boys as well. Uncle Joe unfortunately never had children, as his wife Aunt Gurtie, died at an early age of Lou Gehrig's disease. He never remarried, and moved back to Pokey to live with Great Grandma. He never entertained finding another wife, and always said, "There was only one Gurtie."

Uncle Joe came to the creek with Grandpa and everyone else, each and every time they fished; he was the favorite uncle. He was witty and unique, and blind as a bat. He had glasses thicker than Mama Cass. As a boy I can remember him coming to Christmas Eve in Grandpa's basement. Each year at an opportune point, he would recite this little limerick, "it was Christmas Eve and we were all feeling Mary, so Mary got mad and left, and we all jumped for Joy." He was quite a guy, old Uncle Joe. Sadly, he passed away when I started junior high.

Years later, I was looking through the family albums, and I saw a series of pictures which included Louch, great uncles, Joe and Ed, my dad, and his brothers, John and Dave, and brothers-in-law, Charlie and Paul. They were standing over a pile of catfish laid out on the old blue john boat. The strange thing was that they were all holding guns while they stood over the fish. I asked my Dad about it. With the picture in hand, I said, "What's with the guns?" He grinned at the photo and replied, "Ah, we were all drunk." They were standing around the fish brandishing guns as if they shot them.

(from left to right, in front kneeling) Louch, Charlie Lingua, John Baczewski, Stanley Baczewski, David Baczewski, (in back) Paul Tongay, and Ed Tutka. Photo taken on Shoal Creek.

They had caught the mess of fish the night before, but during the day that followed, the creek water rose at such a rate, that it came up above their lines. They couldn't run their poles even with the boat. Everything was under water, so they just resolved to get hammered. They went swimming and just goofed around. They made a mud slide on the steep banks, and all of them took turns. Grandpa actually dove off the bridge into the creek. Uncle Joe stripped down naked, and although legally blind and in his 60's he took off his coke bottle glasses and slid down the mud slide. When he stripped down naked, and got ready to slide, he said to his nephews, "here's how you're supposed to do it on Shoal Creek." Now although they certainly trusted Uncle Joe's judgment on Shoal Creek traditions, they choose to ignore the particulars and "naked" specifics of the mudslide art form.

**(left to right, up front kneeling) – John Baczewski, and David Baczewski
(middle row) Charlie Lingua, Ed Tutka, Stanley Baczewski
(in back) Paul Tongay**

When they ran out of beer, they all headed into Pokey, and ended up drinking at the Leisure Lounge Tavern. All ten of them bought T-shirts with the Leisure lounge logo and put them on immediately. In a short time, all the folks walking into the bar thought they were the Leisure Lounge softball team. They stayed there until they closed the bar down. As it was in the late 1970's before DUI's, the one Pokey cop stepped into the bar to make sure everyone there was okay to drive. Uncle John's buddy, Gary, was passed out hard with his forehead laying on the edge of the bar. The cop walked around, checking everyone out and sizing up their sobriety. Everyone talked with him and said their piece. Around the room, everyone said variations of, "I'm good," or "I'm ok to drive," and so on." Eventually, he spotted old Gary knocked out cold with the tip of his head resting on the bar, his eyes pointed at the ground. The rest of his body was precariously balanced on the stool. His arms hung lifeless at his sides. The cop turned to my Uncle John sitting next to him and asked, "Now what about him?" The whole tavern got quiet and everyone looked on as the officer waited for the answer. Uncle John, took a drink from his beer and dryly retorted, "Ah him, oh, he's just looking for his keys." The bar roared with laughter, and even the Pokey cop cracked a smile and shook his head.

My dad and my Uncles remember that trip with due fondness, just as I remembered every trip I took on Shoal Creek with Grandpa and the family. Each trip was an experience that made us who we were, and it was through Grandpa and his brothers that we saw the importance of Shoal Creek. Each time that we caught a mess of fish on Shoal, we would take them back to Grandpa's home in Collinsville. My uncle's good friend Dave Bohnensthel once stated that we buried so many fish guts in Louch's garden that if archeologists ever did dig up that sight, they would think there was once a fish cannery back there. When we caught fish, we always took them there, cleaned them, and buried their remains in the garden. As a boy the burying part usually became my job. I was always digging holes and burying fish guts. I wasn't a fan of it at the time, and I thought that someday I would be finished with this task, but I am still digging holes and burying fish guts in my own garden. Nowadays, I bury them in my own garden. Grandpa lives an hour away, so we don't bury so many fish there anymore.

From him we learned to bury fish and table scraps in the garden. Everything that broke down went back in the garden, as Grandpa and Grandma always had a huge garden throughout their lives. Many times when Grandpa and I went fishing, he would take all the small ones who swallowed the hooks or died for whatever reason, and toss them in the cooler. Each time he threw one in, he'd say, "I think I'll make a tomato out of him." He would bury a fish or two by each of his tomato plants every spring. It was almost a farm back there behind his home. He grew every vegetable possible, and the garden itself was always surrounded by immense rows of blackberries. His yard was and still is a veritable grocery store, with a pecan tree, a peach tree, a walnut tree, rows and rows of tomatoes, squash, brussel sprouts, peppers, green beans, garlic, onions, zucchini, cucumbers, squash, lettuce, herbs, and on and on.

He and Grandma always spent a great deal of their summer freezing, canning and tending the garden. He brewed his own wine from his innumerable blackberries and whatever else he could gather up. He even made dandelion, persimmon, huckleberry, peach, cherry, and strawberry wine. Every time I go over there he is still up to something, whether it's baking pies, working in the garden, or brewing wine, he has always been a busy man.

I had always looked up to my grandfather, and learned from him when possible. Yet, I realized in my late twenties I had to learn more from him, because I sadly knew that someday he would be gone. So, I started helping him make wine, and learned his steps. He gave me some equipment and I started brewing batches of my own. I started a garden and would call him every time I had a question about anything from tomato cages to types of pole beans. Grandpa had more than seventy years of

(left to right) Lou Baczewski, Stanley Baczewski, David Baczewski, standing over 65 catfish caught during one night of Shoal creek.
Photo taken in Louch's back yard by Joe Baczewski, the author's brother

gardening experience, from the garden he tended with his parents in Pokey to the one he built behind his home on Keebler Road. Before too long, I was making wine, growing a big garden, and canning, and freezing huge amounts of my own vegetables. Throughout his whole life, Louch had lived by providing a great deal of all his family ate, by growing it himself. He very rarely ate out. Up until the year 2000, he and Grandma didn't even know that they could order a pizza. They were amazed when they found out that someone would bring it to the house. Lou and Helen were children of the Great Depression; consequently they wasted nothing, and learned how to do almost everything on their own. I greatly admired this.

305

They were in many ways self-sufficient and "green" before green was "green."

I wanted to live up to my grandfather's way of living, and learn all I could from him. I had always wanted to live up to him, and to his name. But from an early age, everyone in the family called me Andy instead of my first name, Louis, my grandfather's name. Grandpa had named his oldest son Stanley, after his own father, and my father in turn, gave me the name of Louis in honor of that tradition.

The tough part for me was that even to my own namesake I was known as Andy, because my middle name stuck at an early age. In high school, I started insisting on being called Lou. It was difficult, and most people thought I was going crazy or something. For so many years people knew me as Andy alone. I felt like Prince, or the artist formerly known as Prince, but lacking a symbol. I thought perhaps maybe Prince had a Grandpa too, with a weird ass symbol for a name and maybe that's why he changed it. Who knows? Just the same, it was easy for me to change, but difficult for everyone else to comprehend. Eventually, I was able to save enough money to go away to school and I dropped the name of Andy, but it never left me alone. On my apartment answering machine, the message said, "You have reached the home of Andy and Lou, please leave a message. I lived alone. The name situation has never been resolved, but throughout the years, my Grandpa and I were always pretty close.

So, in 2009 when my grandfather decided to give me his boat, it was one of the most ambivalent moments I had ever experienced. My Grandmother's condition was deteriorating. He could no longer leave for more than an hour or so, given the condition of my Grandmother, so fishing now became out of the question. Tears welled up in his eyes when I latched the hitch to the ball and hooked up the safety chains to my pickup truck. He said, "I caught a lot of fish out of that boat, it ought to do you good."

In the material sense it was nothing special, just a 12 foot johnboat with a front deck and a few seats, but I do believe it was the best and worst gift I would ever receive in my life. To me the damn thing is priceless and a hard lesson in life just the same. I am certain, that between my Uncle Dave, my cousin Michael, Grandpa and I, literally thousands of fish were caught out of that very boat, and will continue to be.

By that time, my Grandmother was in the latent stages of Alzheimer's. It was hard to imagine that she of all people would have a cognitive disability, especially considering how bright she was throughout her whole life. She was one of those people who could do long division in her head, or multiply huge numbers without ever needing a pen or paper. Her work ethic and intellect allowed her to move up the ranks at Scott Air-Force Base. She worked on the staffs of various colonels and generals for twenty-five years. She won boxes full of awards for her accomplishments. She was even given a flag which flew over the US Capitol Building as a present for her retirement. Sadly, I waited too long to get all the details of her story, because within the last five years, her condition deteriorated so quickly that now she only recognizes my grandfather. When I go to see her now, she does not know who I am anymore.

For far too long Grandpa tried to take care of her on his own, but it started to wear him down. It got to the point that his doctors warned him that if he continued trying to take care of her alone, he was going to kill himself. He refused to even have a helper come by the house. No one wanted to put her in a home, but she just became too lost for Grandpa to take care of her. She needed special care. It was not until he himself fell ill with pneumonia that Grandma finally ended up being put in a facility. The home is dedicated to taking care of people with Alzheimer's and dementia. Grandpa now goes to see her every day as the home is just a short distance away.

It was amazing how tough and stubborn my Grandpa was when he tried for years to take care of Grandma alone. I can't imagine how hard it was for him to have to let go of his wife of sixty-five years. In fact, Grandma had become so sick, that she was not even able to attend my own wedding. It was hard to accept that she wouldn't have known what was going on. It was difficult to imagine not seeing grandma at the wedding, but at least Grandpa was able to make it, and in general we had a great time. Grandpa in fact provided all the wine for the reception, and since its strength is far greater than any old table wine, everyone there had a good time.

Shortly after the wedding when my wife (at the time) Sarah and I were on our honeymoon in Puerto Rico, we ran into a strange coincidence. We randomly picked a spot on the map and decided to drive there. It was a small fishing village, named Boceron. It was there that we met a man named Ian. It so happened that he was born and raised in Puerto Rico, but was actually from a Polish family. While making conversation with various local folks on the strip of downtown bars, we met Ian and a few of his friends. They congratulated us as we told them we had just been married. When we toasted to him and his companions shortly afterwards, I said, "Nostarovia," which is a Slavic toast which means "to your health." He immediately asked me if I was Polish, and I quickly nodded. He then went on to tell me that his Grandfather was a Polish native who had fought in the Polish Army. He had been a cavalry man and had rode with the lancers against the German Panzers. His comrades were slaughtered. Miraculously, he survived even after being captured by the Russians and

Germans, and escaped from both of his captors. He fought the rest of the war with the Canadians and Free Poles. It was strange to think that he might have even been one of those Poles that helped close the Falaise Gap. He might have been on the same battlefield as my grandfather. I told him a bit about my Grandpa's experience and about our family in general. He toasted to the both of us, and said, "We cannot forget that their blood flows in our veins." He was right, and I would never forget it. I did not forget it despite all the rum flowing through my veins that night as well. In fact, if he was right about the blood, I probably got a few of my ancestors drunk that night.

Chapter 16
The Honor Flight

The mystic chord of memory, stretching from every battlefield and patriot grave to every living heart and hearthstone all over this broad land, will yet swell the chorus of the Union, when again touched, as surely they will be, by the better angels of our nature.

Abraham Lincoln
First Inaugural Address

They were supposed to be at Lambert Airport by 5am, but being the men that they were, hell, they were checked in, had all their gear and shirts, and were sitting around waiting by 4:50. Everyone had shown up around or before 4:30 or so. These men along with their daughters, sons, grandsons, fellow veterans, and volunteers, had gathered together in the wee hours of the morning, to help a group of 29 WWII Veterans fly to Washington DC to see their own memorial. The Central Illinois Honor Flight was run by a very organized and contentious group of volunteers from Effingham Illinois. They had their jobs down pat and ran the flight from start to finish like a well-oiled machine. The Director, Don Niehart, along with his entire family worked tirelessly to insure that every veteran had all they needed and was ready to fly.

There were veterans from all over Illinois, from every branch of the service, and who served in both theatres and in a multitude of jobs. Many were physically mobile and some had to rely on wheelchairs, but all of them had an energy I could not even fathom. By the end of the day the "guardians," like myself, were absolutely exhausted. Yet the vets themselves, with ages ranging from 82 to 93 seemed completely unaffected – as if propelled by some unseen accelerant. It was amazing.

Lou Baczewski and fellow Battle of the Bulge Veteran Clyde J. Erb, waiting in the Lambert Airport

The day started at Lambert International National Airport in St Louis Missouri. I think the most chaotic part of the trip was getting many 80 to 90 year olds through security. Many of them had not flown in years and were unaware of all that needed to be done. Between the shoes and the bins, the knee, shoulder, and hip replacements, the internal bolts and screws, watches, rings, shrapnel, dog tags, missing belts, and falling down britches, we fought a pitched battle. The desperate clash between metal and detector, conveyor belt and scanner, raged on in fury.

In the battle through security, I briefly envisioned the TSA folks with German helmets on, set up in defensive positions. One TSA officer yelled, "Your papers please," in a thick German accent." Then, all hell broke loose. Suddenly, I imagined seeing the aged vets summoning the physical strength of their former selves. They became soldiers once again. A barrage rolled in. Artillery shells suddenly burst all around the X-ray machines. The everyday folks in the security area hit the deck, while the retired vets scrambled into action. Piles of blue plastic tote bins shattered from the barrage and ripped through the air. Battles raged on the conveyer belts between aged Vets and TSA officials. Bitter hand to hand struggles were waged across the line. Grenades were tossed into the scanners by the lead elements, who then waved on the other eighty-year old Vets. The supporting soldiers, some in wheel chairs and walkers, charged through the metal detectors with fixed bayonets laying waste to the TSA. I watched twenty-nine Vets punch a hole through the airport security line that day my friends. It was a horrible and beautiful sight. Somehow, we were fortunate enough to pass the TSA emplacements, tank traps, and pill boxes without losing one man. The damn thing was; we would have to face those friendly bastards yet again. After passing their line, we took solace in the fact that we were safe for now.

Eventually when I snapped back into reality, Grandpa and I took a seat at the gate and ate our breakfast. We made conversation with a few other vets and airport employees. Some workers in the airport came up and asked the vets about their stories. As they all sat near the gate eating their breakfast, the flight staff saluted the former soldiers over the airport intercom. Everyone around the terminal began to applaud, even Grandpa. So, I told him jokingly, "Grandpa they are clapping for you, you don't need to clap" He said, "oh, ok." He would clap throughout the day regardless, and I think it was because he was just so happy to be part of it. For weeks up until the flight, he would produce a grin that barely fit on his face whenever we spoke about the upcoming trip. We soon boarded the plane without a hitch. Excitement was thick in the air all around the veterans and the volunteers.

The flight went quite well, but little did I know what we would soon face in Washington DC. The TSA line in St Louis had been tough enough to break, but this was going to be altogether different. I was truly not prepared for what we would battle through when we landed in Reagan National Airport. When we departed the plane, the veterans walked off the tarmac and into a barrage of goodwill, respect, adulation, and thanks. We headed down a velvet roped line, some vets rode in wheel chairs, while others walked. Grandpa walked in his usual steady saunter. He bowleggedly moseyed through the crowd, shaking hands, touching shoulders and gleaming with pride. I was astonished to see so many men, women, children, soldiers, veterans, airport staff, and legionaries surrounding the vets in a gauntlet of thanks. Their flags were waving. Some folks whistled or exclaimed with praise. Many hands were extended, while others carried on in resounding in applause. They greeted the veterans with an uproarious and heartfelt welcome; the likes of which I have never seen in my life. One man was even playing a French horn sitting aside the velvet rope. For that moment, every one of those veterans felt like a rock star. They walked into the terminal as if on air. My Grandpa shook hands with cub scouts, women and children, countless men and women in uniform, and every random person who crossed his path. Every veteran commented on the welcome. Many said they never received anything like it when they originally came home from the war.

It made me think that every veteran, combat or non-combat, peacetime or wartime, deserves such a welcome home. It is a damn shame that so few have actually received it. The welcome continued through the airport as varied people extended their hands in thanks. Some patted the

314

veterans on the shoulder as they strolled past. So many went out of their way to tell the vets how thankful they were for their service. It was truly remarkable.

Earlier, when I was leaving the plane, I saw a hat sitting on one of the seats. It was one of the hats which had just been to the WWII veterans on our flight. Knowing that someone would be missing it, I picked it up. I hoped to find a hatless veteran somewhere in our party. After passing the warm welcome, I quickly saw one hatless members of our cadre. He was talking with a man in front of a store in the airport terminal. As I came closer, I could see that the man was handing the veteran a hat, it seemed that upon hearing that the veteran had lost his hat; the man ran into the nearby store and purchased him one. When I presented the vet with the original hat, the younger man commented in a thick Maryland accent that the glare off the WWII memorial was intense and that the man had to have a hat. The veteran Frederick Aljets, and myself were astonished at the gesture, and we both thanked him. Later, Mr. Aljets would comment on that incident to me and numerous others. He was just so touched by the man's concern.

We were guided by volunteers throughout the airport to the location of our bus. When we all made it on the bus, we found out that we had been sent some reinforcements. Three enlisted military personnel there representing every branch except the Air Force. Lieutenant Kathleen Craig, USN, Captain Mike Alabre, US Army, and PFC Christofer Baines, USMC, were on the bus ready to help us along the way. They were a great addition to our group and it was nice to see some younger soldiers interacting with all of these older veterans.

Our first destination was the WWII Memorial. We arrived there soon after leaving the airport. Once there, the act of getting off the bus was itself an undertaking. It was sad to think that more than sixty years ago these men were in the best of shape. They had been able to take on anything that was thrown at them. These were the men who helped beat the Axis powers. Yet now, many of these once abled warriors were slowly guided down the bus steps to the many wheel chairs awaiting them. Many were able to walk, but slowly and cautiously. Once we disembarked, I pushed my grandfather away from the bus as soon as he was settled into his chair. He was able to walk for the greater part, but the stiffness in his knees made him choose to take a chair – for which I was glad. It was hard to believe that in his late 60's and early 70's he was shimmying himself down the steep banks of Shoal Creek. He was always ready to paddle out in a johnboat to run the lines. Or, when I deer hunted with him in his 70's, he refused to get a ladder for his tree-stand, and instead choose to climb the tree every damn time.

My dad said that when he was young, he and Grandpa were hunting squirrels along Shoal Creek when they came to a spot in the creek which was too deep to cross without swimming. The good hunting was on the opposite side. My dad decided to head down stream to find a log to cross on, or a shallow riffle to wade through. Grandpa however, without blinking an eye, stripped down to nothing, wadded his clothes and shells and boots into his game vest, and swam across the creek with his entire wardrobe and shotgun in one hand. Without getting any of his gear wet, he arrived on the other side, dressed and went back to hunting. So, it was hard to see him in a wheel chair, that day at the World War II Memorial. I was soon happy that he chose to sit and ride though, because it gave us some mobility and we were able to see everything available to us. On that day, we toured the entirety of the WWII memorial, the Lincoln Memorial, The Mall, the Korean War memorial, and the Vietnam Wall.

Louis J. Baczewski and his grandson Louis A. Baczewski on the steps of the Lincoln Memorial, July 2010

Prior to the flight, Grandpa had hoped to find the names of some of his comrades on the WWII memorial itself, but we were both disappointed when we found out that there were no names on the WWII memorial. I suppose there were just too many to fit, but I felt, that if it is a true memorial it ought to include the names of every American man and woman who died in that horrible war; because, statues, stones, fountains, and brass wreaths do not show the cost of such things. If memorials are made to honor those who served and died, as well as educate future generations as to the price of war, they damn well should include every name of those who fell and paid the ultimate price in the service of their country.

Lou Baczewski sitting in front of the wall of stars commemorating all the lives lost in WWII

There was however one wall of stars there at the memorial, over 4,000 in fact, each star represents one hundred American soldiers lost in the war. My Grandpa looked at all those stars, shook his head and stated, "All those stars, and somehow I survived." He thinks about that quite often. The memorial did also possess a database, which included all known individuals who served in the armed forces during WWII. Additionally it listed all of those who had helped at home or abroad with the war effort. Most importantly, Grandpa wanted to find out what the registry stated in regards to his good friend and tank commander Joe Cady. According to the After Action Report of the 33rd Armored Regiment December 1944, headquarters marked Cady, Jr., Joe, missing in action as of December 21st 1944. My grandfather having witnessed his death, and after having, "laid his body in the snow" during the battle of the Bulge disagreed with that assessment. He was troubled with this discovery, ever

318

since he looked through his after action reports. He had long thought that Cady's family was aware that he was killed in action, but he never knew for sure if they understood what happened to him when he died. We looked up Cady in the registry there at the memorial, and Grandpa was at least relieved to see his status as KIA. Grandpa also wanted to look up the name of the original driver in his tank who Grandpa replaced. He was shot in the hedgerow country by a sniper when they mistakenly bailed out thinking their tank was compromised. Unfortunately, he was unable to find any information on this man. For many years, Grandpa had avoided thinking about the war. He did not try to contact other members of his company or regiment. I think he wanted to reflect very little on the war. I could see then that he regretted not trying to find some of his fellow company members earlier.

While still touring the memorial, I took a few pictures of Grandpa in front of the Atlantic section of the monument. Of the ten major battles listed at the edge of the fountain, Grandpa had fought in five of them. I could not help but tell people walking all around us, that this man had fought in all of those campaigns. He saw more combat than many other veterans present, and to him it was only luck and a lot of prayers that got him through it.

Central Illinois Honor Flight Veterans, 2009

Another veteran, (the only African-American Army veteran on the flight) told Grandpa as they bumped wheel chairs at the Vietnam memorial that, "he came home and found Christ," after the war. He then asked Grandpa if he was Christian and, and Grandpa replied, "I go to church almost every day." I told Mr. Hattie and his daughter pushing his chair, that, "heck, Grandpa is in church more than the priest." As it turned out, both men had served in similar areas in Belgium and Germany. Later, I wrote to Hattie's daughter and found out more about their father's experience. Timothy Hattie was a private in the 565th Quartermaster Company and he like so many other Quartermaster soldiers, held the responsibility of for supplying combat units. It was in fact African-American men who had supplied Grandpa and his cadre with fuel and ammunition each time they re-supplied the tank. Almost every night it was the African-American men of the Quartermaster's troops who pulled alongside the tanks and helped load ammunition, fuel, and supplies. They had been the logistical backbone of the 3rd Armored and so many other combat outfits. Men like Timothy Hattie, despite being considered second class citizens at the time, went to the war, and did his job just the same. He and other Quartermaster's were yet another group of unsung heroes in the war. Even in the heaviest fighting in the battle of the Bulge, it was the Quartermasters who had helped save Taskforce Lovelady, the 30th Infantry, and the 82nd Airborne's 504th Regiment. Amidst the fight for Staevlot, the Quartermaster's worked a miracle. In an amazing amount of time, the Quartermasters removed an entire fuel dump, keeping the 1st SS Division from refueling their massive tank force. Were it not for these men, the events in the Battle of the Bulge might have been far different. Jochen Peiper and "Hitler's Own" Division may well have carried the war on even longer, and at the cost of more lives on both sides.

Timothy Hattie himself was from East St Louis, and sadly after serving his country in Europe returned home once more to Illinois only to experience segregation and racial discrimination for many years to come. However, it was amazing to see all of these former soldiers sit tightly together for their Honor Flight picture and think, that in the 1940's, Timothy Hattie, would not have been able to stand next to these other service men. His unit was segregated, just like all "colored" units, until President Truman integrated the Army during the Korean War.

Earlier at the WWII Memorial, Grandpa and I were able to get a picture with Clyde Erb, an infantryman, who had also fought in the Battle of the Bulge, in the 26th Infantry Division, The 26th, was in support of the 4th Armored Division of 3rd Army under General George Patton. He and his comrades had been rerouted to fight at Bastogne and break through where the 101st Airborne was surrounded. In fact, he was a member of a group of Battle of the Bulge veterans who meet monthly in St Louis, and he encouraged Grandpa to join. They even found out that they had mutual friends in the chapter. Later on in the airport, they would talk at length about making wine, gardening, and many more light hearted things.

Grandpa was also able to talk with some of the soldiers on our tour, men and women presently serving in the military. He told Lieutenant Craig, about the men he had lost in his tank alone. He told her about Cady and how he died in the Battle of the Bulge. He spoke of how Cady revealed a premonition of his own death. Grandpa's comments were choked with loss and emotion. Lt Craig was visibly touched by his tale, and tears welled up in her eyes as Grandpa told her and PFC Baines some of his stories. He also spoke to them at some length about the present. He felt so sorry for all the men and women then serving in Iraq and Afghanistan. To him, he did not feel that we should be there in the first place, and it was no dishonor to bring those men home where they belong. He commented on how many times the men were being deployed and their inability to distinguish friend or foe. He kept saying, "I feel so sorry for those guys, cause I know what its like. I know what they are going through, and they're going back for four and five hitches, but I was only sent over one time. I don't know what we're doing over there."

In a short time, the whole group of veterans and volunteers were rounded up and led back onto the bus. After hitting all the spots on the mall, we were loading up to move on in the tour. We still had to hit the Marine monument, the Navy monument, and Arlington cemetery. While we were getting on the bus, a very raggedly clothed African American man walked past the bus looking on. I assumed he was homeless based on his appearance, and I wondered perhaps if he was a veteran himself,

322

especially given that according to the Veteran's Administration, "...nearly 200,000 veterans sleep on the streets of America, [and] 40,000 experience homelessness over the course of a year."[1] Twenty seven thousand homeless veterans live on the streets of LA alone.[2] According to Aaron Glantz, author of *The War Comes Home, Washington's Battle Against America's Veterans,* "one out of three homeless men sleeping in a doorway, alley, or box in our cities and rural communities has put on a uniform and served this country. Glantz revealed that, "about half of the estimated 400,000 homeless veterans served during the Vietnam years, but those who provide care to veterans note that they did not become homeless until nine to twelve years after their discharge. By contrast, some Iraq War veterans are becoming homeless almost immediately after returning home."

I wondered what recognition did all of these homeless veterans receive when they came home, and like these vets today, how long would it take to get some praise? It took sixty years for these men to get some recognition, and it was all done by work of volunteers and private donors. Our government itself has little to nothing to do with Honor Flight's activities. It had taken all of this time to "honor" these WWII vets even when they were in a popular war, and a war that almost everyone agreed had to be fought. Countless other conflicts since WWII have been costly, but would there be the same flights and honors for all those men? Where was the recognition for men who served in Korea, Vietnam, Panama, Grenada, Kuwait, Iraq, and Afghanistan?

One veteran I know, Ken Coonley, served two tours in Vietnam. Ken worked with my Father for many years as an electrician. Ken has been a good friend to the family for decades. In fact, almost every adult in the family from Grandpa on down, has stumbled out of Ken's tavern a time or two. He was a Marine, and he served in such horrible places as Khe Shan and Hue City during the 1968 Tet Offensive. One night in his tavern, he told me about his return to the states. He had just flown into a base on the east coast and was guided onto a bus. He quickly noticed that there was chicken wire strung up on all of the bus windows. He asked the driver what was the wire for, the driver lowered his head and told him apologetically, 'You'll see soon enough son. You'll see soon enough.' When the bus left the base, it was greeted by bottles and trash and people screaming baby-killer. For Ken, it was one of the worst days of his entire life. Men like Ken never had a welcome home.

Yet just as my grandfather was never a fan of the policies that led us into Iraq or Vietnam for that matter, he never confused the political debate with the men and women out there just doing their jobs. My grandfather of all people could criticize war, but he would be damned if he blamed the soldiers just mixed up in the thick of it. Sadly, it seems like some people on both sides of the political spectrum cannot understand the difference anymore, or they use it for their own political agenda. Yet, our soldiers are now coming home once again scarred from far too many deployments, once again scarred from fighting in wars that may well have been avoided. As such, we must guard against twisting the war itself into a noble cause, or conversely blaming those men and women in uniform for doing their jobs. Why can't we see in this country that nothing is black and white, and that there are no straight answers when it comes to war. Now, when I see everyone applaud in our airports and planes for our soldiers now serving, I can't help but think that maybe our politicians have learned nothing, but perhaps many everyday Americans have. In this same vein, The Honor Flight Association has recently started taking Korean War and Vietnam War veterans to Washington as well, to see their monuments. It's a step in the right direction, because we as a nation can never again forget the sacrifices of our service men and women, no matter the politics of the conflict.

Please Donate. The following veteran's charities have A+ records in regard to their dollar for dollar spending on veterans:

Honor Flight Association: *www.honorflight.org*

Fisher House Foundation: *www.fisherhouse.org*

Intrepid Fallen Heroes Fund : *www.fallenheroesfund.org*

Chapter 17
Third Armored Division Reunion

I have never seen a more sublime demonstration of
the totalitarian mind, a mind that might be likened
unto a system of gears whose teeth have been filed
off at random, such a snaggle–toothed thought
machine driven by a standard or even substandard
libido, whirls with the jerky noisy gaudy pointlessness
of a cuckoo clock in hell.
Kurt Vonnegutt Jr
(Author, Battle of the Bulge Veteran, & American POW)

At the 3rd Armored Division Reunion, I sat there with my

Grandfather and my dad, and I tried to listen. I certainly tried to give the

speaker the benefit of the doubt, but time after time he let me down. There

in the Holiday Inn conference room, General Brown talked for thirty-five

minutes. I know this for sure. I kept looking at my watch. Honestly, how

often does a person look at his or her watch when they are having a good

time? What was so astonishing was that in the audience before him, there

sat 27 veterans of the 3rd Armored Division, along with their families and

friends. They had come from all parts of this great country to be there that

night in Columbus, Georgia. They came there to see their friends, relive

good memories, and deal with the bad ones. Every man was in his eighties

at least, and some were in their nineties. They were grandpas and great

grandpas, they were retired farmers and plumbers, and millwrights, and

insurance men. They were the last of a great mass of great men leading

small but noble lives – they were there representing what was left of this

country's salt. But nothing would be mentioned of such things. It was to be the last formal reunion of the 3rd Armored Division and nothing noteworthy was said of this either.

His speech was a loosely connected tale of self. It was a rant. The speech only mentioned the 3rd Armored Division when he hoped to form a loose connection to his poorly constructed, odd, somewhat irrelevant, and seemingly baseless conclusion. He went on and on about General Abrams, artillery support, and serving in Cold War Germany. Nothing in his speech was human. Nothing was related to the sacrifices that these men had made. Nothing was said of the ultimate sacrifice made by thousands of 3rd Armored Division soldiers. I tossed in my chair. I fiddled with my empty whiskey and coke. I looked about the room at the people's reactions, and I could see similar fiddling and discomfort. He told senseless stories about Cold War tanks frozen in ice and running drills at crossroads in the dark. Nothing was about them, nothing thanked them, and little to nothing was even said about them as men - as soldiers. He expressed his stories with military jargon and a distant puppet master understanding of battle. It was as if he spoke of plastic soldiers and Lego tanks on Astroturf battlefields. He did not speak to these men, these soldiers, or the families of these soldiers; he spoke to himself as if no one else present had a story of their own. The damn thing was that all of them had a story, a plethora of stories, a galaxy of stories; stories far more interesting than anything this blowhard had to say. Yet he kept on talking, until I heard and briefly visualized crap continually shooting out of his mouth. His aptly given name was General Brown. He was full of himself, he was full of Brown. As far as I was concerned, he was a big steamy pile of Brown.

3rd Armored Division's "Final Roll Call," August 2010

Both my dad and I thought that the goal of Brown's speech was to suggest that the M1 Abrams tank was the legacy of these men and that it was made in response to the failures of the Sherman. Despite how well intentioned such a speech may have seemed to Brown, the poorly constructed conclusion he presented was perhaps the most misplaced sentiment I had ever heard in my life. He was completely removed from this room. He was far away unable to look out and see these former privates and sergeants and corporals and tell them anything relevant to them as men, as human beings. He couldn't look out into the small crowd before him and imagine these 80 year old men as the boys they once were, as soldiers who participated in the most immense and horrible war this earth has ever seen. He never mentioned anyone below the rank of Major. It was a thirty-five minute display of profound indifference to service, human suffering, and sacrifice. I was so aggravated by his speech that I tried to confront the man. I wanted to tell him what an ass he was, but as soon as his speech was over, he was gone.

I could not help but think then and now that it was men such as General Brown, consumed with self and incapable empathy that propel the obtuse warmongering of our recent times, and for that matter anytime. He had not seen real war except from afar. He was as fond of himself as he seemed to be fond of war and war games. General Dwight D Eisenhower once stated, "I hate war as only a soldier who has lived it can, only as one who has seen its brutality, its futility, its stupidity." Eisenhower knew quite well the costs of war and as his second term ended, he began to become more vocal as to the "grave implications" that lay ahead.

Our more recent president actually seemed to be indifferent to the suffering and destruction that comes with war, so much so that he boldly helped create more than one global conflict. Eisenhower on the other hand, thought long and hard about such actions. In fact, while president he presided over the only eight years in the entire 20th century where US military action did not occur. He stated, "The United States never lost a soldier or a foot of ground during my administration. We kept the peace. People asked how it happened - by God, it didn't just happen, I'll tell you that." Today, if a president or presidential hopeful expresses a desire to avoid war, they are regarded as weak. If they hope to spend American taxpayer money on domestic improvements such as roads, and infrastructure instead of defense spending they're lauded as dangers to the security of our nation.

No one would ever say that Ike was a pinko, or a socialist, but early in his first term as president, he expressed a concern that too much money was being spent uselessly on defense. As a Republican, he understood that militarism was a threat to democracy and that public money should be used for the "Public Good." Stealth Bombers don't fix levees in New Orleans, or stop bridges from collapsing in Minnesota, building either will put people to work.

Additionally, our country was not a nation with a vast military at all times, the founding fathers themselves feared militarism. They themselves had seen war and militarism first hand. They were aware of both the financial and social costs that these items posed to a democracy. Washington himself warned in his own farewell address to, "avoid the necessity of those overgrown military establishments which under any form of government, are inauspicious to liberty, and which are to be regarded as particularly hostile to republican liberty." Prior to the Second World War our nation had a standing army of 139,000 soldiers in uniform. Presently we as a nation have more than 1.5 million individuals in service. Our defense budget presently represents more than 40% of the US discretionary spending. Regardless of the growing political movement for "small government" and decreasing the role of the federal government there is a massive camouflage elephant in the room that neither political party chooses to recognize. Strangely we pretend as if this massive beast isn't there. In almost all political and economic discussion no one seems to confront the situation directly. We are instead invited to pull on either side the penny left in our discretionary budget not dedicated to what Eisenhower called, "the Military and Industrial Complex."

No one could argue that Eisenhower was weak. No one in their right mind would say that Ike was a softy, or a liberal. But throughout Eisenhower's presidency he spoke out against using too much public money for munitions which do not help the everyday American. On April 16th 1953, Eisenhower stated the following:

Every gun that is made, every warship launched, every rocket fired signifies, in the final sense, a theft from those who hunger and are not fed, those who are cold and not clothed. This world in arms is not spending money alone. It is spending the sweat of its laborers, the genius of its scientists, the hopes of its children.

The cost of one modern heavy bomber is this: a modern brick school in 30 cities. It is two electric power plants, each serving a town of 60,000 population. It is two fine fully equipped hospitals. It is some fifty miles of concrete pavement. We pay for a single fighter plane with half a million bushels of wheat.

We pay for a single destroyer with new homes that could have housed 8,000 people. This is, I repeat, the best way of life to be found on the road the world has been taking. This is not a way of life at all, in any true sense. Under the cloud of threatening war, it is humanity hanging from a cross of iron

Unfortunately in this country now, no Republican or Democrat would ever utter such words, unless they wished to commit complete political suicide. At the time however, the American people were sick of war and the effects of it were so pervasive that a great deal of the nation identified with Ike's statements with zeal. Lao Tzu once stated, "weapons are not a ruler's tools, he wields them when he has no choice."

Eisenhower's role as Allied Supreme Commander and President reflected this same sentiment. He was not only concerned about the financial costs of war, but more importantly the lives lost. He felt deeply for every life lost under his watch as Supreme Allied Commander, even when receiving an award from the British government, he stated the following. "Humility must always be the portion of any man who receives acclaim earned in the blood of his followers and the sacrifices of his friends."[3] I actually found this quote in a book sent by the British government to the parents of Corporal John P. Hustava, of the 82nd Airborne - the boyhood friend of my grandfather. The book's cover reads, *Britain's Homage to 28,000 American Dead.*

Eisenhower had a deep respect and admiration for all who served under him and the scores of US dead that resulted from WWII weighed heavily upon him. I cannot imagine the burden that must have been carried by Eisenhower: being haunted by so many ghosts. He had to send those men in, and they in-turn had to do their jobs. Yet all of these soldiers knew in their hearts, that they had to do this job even if they paid the ultimate price, because they had to rid the world of fascism.

The same spirits that swarmed about Eisenhower's conscience plagued the mass of soldiers who returned home after 1945. My grandfather for example, even in his 80's had nightmares of the war any night after he would speak to me at length about it. He was however sustained and soothed, by one unfaltering understanding that what he did, had to be done. The absurd gore and random chaos of war was an endless shroud that was laid over his entire life. He never escaped it. Yet, he was able to live the greatest part of his life as a normal man. The things that kept him on an even keel were his personal strength, the support of his wife, faith, family, fishing Shoal Creek, and the knowledge that the war he fought was a war of necessity. What nags at my grandfather is that the soldiers fighting today do not have the same knowledge that they are fighting for a clear and just goal. Our soldiers are being put into situations where "moral integrity" and "clarity of comprehension" as Eisenhower extolled, are sketchy at best. Eisenhower described these tenants in the end of his memoir and suggested that these pillars were necessary for our military to succeed and for the "free world to live and prosper."[4]

Although their backgrounds and educations were far different, my grandfather and Eisenhower seemed to resemble the same type of man to me. Eisenhower was the son of pacifist Mennonites, while Grandpa was the son of a Polish draft dodger. Despite their ironic origins, they were both soldiers, and men willing to defend their country at whatever cost. They crossed through many of the same battle fields (for clarity sake, Grandpa was out front, and Ike showed up later). Despite all the carnage they each saw, they did not become complete doves by any means, but they were also men who never actively sought or glamorized war. Their patriotism was not the cheap kind; it was the best kind, because it didn't come without thought. Patriotism without contemplation and critique can far too easily morph itself into goose steps and jack boots, both Eisenhower and my grandfather understood this. Just like my grandfather, Eisenhower was not a fan of preemptive war, and even in his final speech as president, he warned that, "We must guard against the acquisition of unwarranted influence, whether sought or unsought, by the military-industrial complex. The potential for the disastrous rise of misplaced power exists and will persist. We must never let the weight of this combination endanger our liberties or democratic processes. We should take nothing for granted. Only an alert and knowledgeable citizenry can compel the proper meshing of the huge industrial and military machinery of defense with our peaceful methods and goals."

On our trip down to the 3rd Armored reunion in Columbus, Georgia, Grandpa spoke to my father and I in detail about his experience in the war, but he also carried a heavy heart for all the soldiers who were then being deployed to Iraq and Afghanistan, over and over again. He talked about their deployments and spoke angrily as to why we were there in the first place. We came across many active US Army soldiers in the Atlanta airport, and Grandpa made an effort to speak to as many as he could. As we sat in the terminal awaiting our flight to Columbus, Georgia, there were soldiers all around us awaiting our same flight. At one point, Grandpa got up to walk to the bathroom. In his slow bowlegged saunter, he made his way past a fairly large soldier. Frankly, the guy looked like a refrigerator dressed in fatigues. When I first glanced at him, I thought to myself, "man I sure wouldn't want to mess with that guy." The towering Army man sat close to the aisle of the main walkway. His uniform was crisp and his movements mechanical. He sat partially leaned over at the waist, elbows resting on his legs, hands clasped at his chin. His face showed the marks of age and his eyes roamed as he scanned the terminal silently. All around us were the sounds and hustle and bustle of any given airport. As Grandpa passed the man, he gave him a wave and extended his hand. The man looked up to see Grandpa's WWII Vet ball cap which was decorated with pins of his various medals and campaign stars. Grandpa took his hand and they began to speak. Grandpa told him that we were heading to his 63rd Division Reunion and that he also had been an Army man. The man's formerly stern face turned into a half smile and he rose to his feet to speak to the fellow soldier.

Grandpa then told him that he felt for all soldiers right now, because of the amount of deployments and the unclear nature of their missions. He said, "Man I feel for you guys, cause I know what it's like, and I was only sent over one time." The soldier leaned his head closer and lower in toward Grandpa. Grandpa said a few more things to him, close into his ear. I could not hear what he said. This massive soldier who seemed like such an imposing figure, just seconds ago, then began to cry. Grandpa kept speaking into his ear. The soldier listened intently as his eyes welled with tears. The soldier whispered a few things as well, then he set one of his hands on Grandpa's shoulder, as the other shook Grandpa's hand. They said their goodbyes.

The soldier quickly composed himself, wiped his eyes, and looked around to see if anyone had seen. He gathered himself together, pulled his uniform tight and straight, and sat back down, eyes red, visibly changed. I never asked Grandpa what was said, that was between them. Here were two men who had never laid eyes on each other and who were 60 or more years apart in age, but for that moment, they were brothers. It seemed like they understood each other exactly.

For Grandpa the trip to Georgia was worthwhile for him, just in the fact that we met so many soldiers along the way. In fact, while waiting for our connecting flight from Atlanta to Columbus, we met a young African American woman who was returning from a ceremony held for her brother and others who had died in Afghanistan and Iraq. She was the last of her family and accepted a posthumously awarded Bronze Star, for his bravery in actions in Afghanistan. He was a Marine, and he died saving members of his company. She had the Bronze Star in a case there with her and a report of her brother's actions. She was kind enough to let me read it and she told me a bit about his story, as tears welled up in her eyes. We had flown from St. Louis to Atlanta, Georgia, and then to Columbus in an effort to attend the final Formal Reunion of the 3rd Armored Division. Even before we made it to the actual reunion, there were countless reminders of war and loss. They were all around us.

When we made it to our hotel, the lady at the main desk asked us if we were there for graduation. She assumed we were there to see one of the Army soldiers from Fort Benning who were that very weekend graduating from basic training. She was a tall middle aged African American woman, and she exuded kindness. It was like it came out of her pores, I swear I immediately felt like I was talking with someone I had known my whole life. My dad and I told her that we were all there to go with my grandfather to the 3rd Armored Division Reunion. My dad told her, as he pointed to me, "this is my son, and my dad is outside, he's the one we're here for." She looked at us both and smiled. In her rich Georgia accent she stated, "now, that's a blessing right there, three generations." I smiled and said, "yes ma'am, it certainly is." My dad shook his head in acknowledgement.

We had a few hours to kill before the reunion's banquet, so we drove to the Infantry Museum which was nearby. It was a large museum with plenty of displays, which included equipment and mannequins wearing uniforms from various eras of warfare. Sections were divided into the main wars and conflicts. As we walked through an intersection of displays where WWI, WWII, and Vietnam met, background sounds of combat were broadcast around us. Dad walked aside Grandpa as they passed along the eras of conflict, and stated, "We don't learn a goddamn thing do we?" Grandpa replied, "Sure don't seem like it, does it?"

Shortly after leaving the museum, we headed to the reunion, only to have the beginning open with General Brown's crappy speech. Despite

Brown's self-serving blabber session, Grandpa, my Father, and I had a great experience. Between meeting vets in the airport to talking with actual 3rd Armored vets, every aspect of the trip was a catharsis for Grandpa. We spoke with many who were in the headquarters and supply regiments; there were only a few actual tankers and infantrymen, and only one member of D Company. Daniel Bott was a replacement in D Company who arrived late in the war. He actually became part of Grandpa's former gunner's tank crew. Both Assistant driver Virgil Decker and Pat Gillespie became tank commanders at the end of the war. Grandpa had hoped to meet some of his crew mates or commanders, but unfortunately, none of them were there. It was quite hard for him accept the realization that most of them were all gone. He had known for some time that Pat Gillespie his gunner, had passed on, and that Virgil Decker was also deceased. He had briefly contacted them after the war, but lost contact over the years. He had hoped to see, Captain Stallings, Lt Alford, or Leslie Underwood, Octaviano Carrion, and others, but none of them were present and most of them had passed away. I believe he had a mixed experience, as he was able to meet others in the division, but felt somewhat alone because he longed to meet others who had served alongside him throughout that long campaign. All in all we had conversations with a variety of nice folks, and met division veterans from all across the country.

When the night ended, and we headed back to the hotel, Grandpa and my dad quickly headed to bed. I walked around a bit in the warm night air of Columbus Georgia. Eventually I grabbed a few beers, headed back to the hotel. I decided to sit down on the sweaty concrete walkway in front of our third floor room, and fire up my laptop. I figured I would drink a few beers and do a bit of writing given the events of the evening.

There were a lot of enlisted men and women moving about the parking lot and balconies of the hotel as I looked on. After sitting there for a time, in the thick Georgia night air, I noticed that occupants of the next room were celebrating something. One young man, probably in his late 20's kept coming out on the balcony to smoke. He was a tall solid figure with crisp features and haunting gaze. Every time he leaned on the rail, I could see that he was deep in thought. Eventually, I introduced myself and talked with him briefly. He told me that he was on leave from his third tour in Iraq.

I briefly explained what my purpose there was, and how I was writing a book about my grandfather. I told him about what Grandpa had done in the war. Being an army man himself, he immediately wanted to meet my grandfather, and became very excited at the prospect. Unfortunately, I had to tell him that Grandpa was sound asleep. He stared at the closed hotel room door, with a look of disappointment. Eventually, he began to tell me about Iraq, and how he had spent a good deal of his tours busting into people's homes drawing guns on fathers and sons in front of their families. Shooting people right in their homes. He described how hard it was to distinguish friend from foe. He suggested that Grandpa, was a real hero because he fought in his terms a "real war," and it was obvious that he didn't feel much like one himself. You could see the conflict written all over his face. I thanked him for his service, just the same, but didn't say much beyond that. Honestly, I really didn't know what the hell to say.

No one can debate that global terrorism is not a threat that should be pursued with extreme ferocity, but the manner in which we pursue it is treacherous. What concerns my grandfather is that our soldiers are fighting a war with no clear enemy, no clear mission, and no end in sight. Unlike

WWII these present conflicts lack clearly defined objectives and ultimate moral grounds, and this is tearing these soldiers apart from the inside. Dealing with the horror of war is enough on its own, much less if you add the moral and strategic ambiguity of these conflicts. As Grandpa later stated, "I want you to know I am completely against these wars. You shoot first and ask questions later, but these soldiers can't do that. I don't know why we are over there. Them people don't want democracy, just cause we're telling em to." He jokingly suggested that, "If we want to spread democracy why don't we invade Cuba, it's a lot closer ya know. I don't know why the hell we're over there [Iraq & Afghanistan], we ought to bring all our soldiers home and put all our troops on our borders."

Between the soldiers we met and the few remaining vets at the reunion the weekend gave us a lot to think about, there was a great deal to reflect on. The next day, we flew home, and I could tell that Grandpa was a bit disappointed with the trip, having gone so far without meeting any of his old comrades. Yet fate has its own ways, and for Grandpa, the real 3rd Armored Division reunion would take place the following spring in Collinsville, Illinois on the 16th of May, 2011.

When I began to look for surviving members of D Company and specifically Baczewski's tank crew, I looked up Les Underwood. Grandpa remembered more than 60 years after they had parted company that Les had lived near Lancaster, Pennsylvania before the war. So, I tried to find him there. Grandpa remembered distinctly where he had lived, but he had not heard from Les since they parted ways after the war in Frankfurt, Germany in 1945. After a short time of looking on the internet, I was able to find a number that seemed to fit the profile: Leslie Underwood 85, East Petersburg PA.

I called him up. After only a few short words were exchanged, I knew that I had found him. He spoke to me for almost an hour, and as I have come to learn from his family, he is never one to ever chat on the phone too much. Just like my grandfather, he is normally a man of few words. Yet when he spoke to me, he began to recall so many of the same incidents that my grandfather had told me about, and was able to speak in grave detail. I could hardly contain my excitement when I called Grandpa and told him that Les was alive and well and would soon contact him by phone. They had not spoken in 65 years, not because they ever had a falling out, but because both men wanted to leave the war behind them. When they returned to the states they just lost contact. After many passing years, it seemed like they were finally eager to look back on what they went through. They were both excited to talk to someone who really understood what the other had seen during the war; I felt quite honored to be part of it.

When I called Les a second time to set up a conference call, I reached his wife Vera. When I told her who I was, she quickly yelled exuberantly, "Les! It's that guy! It's that guy!" I could hear his energy as he made his way to the phone. Before he picked up the receiver, he exclaimed to his wife, "hurry up, get a pencil! Get a pencil!" After some frantic sounds of scratching and scraping, it was obvious that whatever writing utensil she handed him failed to work. I heard him speak loudly and excitedly again, "Get another one! This one doesn't work! Get another one!" Eventually they resolved the situation and he answered the phone breathing deep. We spoke for a good period again and set up a time when we could all talk together. My sister Ann set up the conference call a few weeks later, and Louch and Les spoke for some two hours, while I interjected with a question now and again. It had been years since I had seen my grandfather so overwhelmed with energy. The memories flowed from them like a flood.

I began to correspond with Les in 2009, and he was willing to be interviewed by phone and reply to questions via mail. He gave me a whole new perspective, because he had seen the same events as my grandfather, but he was many times at a very different vantage point.

On that day in May of 2011, a car with New Jersey plates pulled up the steep drive to Grandpa's home on Keebler Road. Leslie Baruffi had driven her mother and Father through the night from East Petersburg, Pennsylvania just to be there in that driveway. According to Leslie, her father was a stoic man and never one to reach heights in emotion - for good or bad. As far as she had known, he had never showed much in the way of anger or excitement for that matter. He had always been a man of purpose with a crisp demeanor. Yet when this trip was brought about, Leslie saw something in her father that she had never seen before. He was truly excited and almost giddy at the thought of seeing a soldier who he had fought side by side with throughout the war. Perhaps for the both of them (Grandpa and Les Underwood), this would be their catharsis, their point when they could finally face what they had seen in that horrible war. It took sixty-six years. These two men who had narrowly survived the war together had both wanted to put the war behind them, yet this day was different. They had both kept the war locked away inside them for far too long.

When they pulled in they were not sure if Grandpa was home, so Leslie called Grandpa's house on her cell. When he answered, she told him that she, her father, and mother were outside. Grandpa stammered as if he could not believe it. He said, "you are outside right now?" Leslie replied, "yes, we are right here outside." She could hear Grandpa's excitement as he said, "I'll be right there." In a few seconds he opened the door to greet Leslie. Les was making his way out of the car. Grandpa walked out of the door towards Les, while Les made his way up the porch. Grandpa just kept saying, "I just can't believe it," again and again. They met on the porch and gave each other a hug. Tears welled up in each of their eyes and soon ran down their cheeks. Grandpa said, "I can't believe I am seeing you, I wasn't even sure we would make it through the war and here you are on my porch."

Leslie Baruffti never imagined that the meeting would be so powerful, and it was the first time in her life that she saw her father cry. She had never heard her father speak about the war at all, and throughout the next two days she would hear more about her father's experiences than ever before. It seemed that years of pinned up emotion poured out of him. Both he and my grandfather walked around reminiscing as if they were fifty years younger. The memories and stories roared out of them.

Les remembering the gift he had for Grandpa, quickly scrambled back to the car. He yelled to his daughter to find the picture. After a short but frantic search through the vehicle, he produced an 8x12 photograph of Lou and Les together. The photo was taken in Belgium during the war. Grandpa still to this day has it prominently placed on his dinner table.

For the next two days, Lou and Les would just hang out trading stories and catching up on sixty-five years of lost time. It was as if they had never been apart, and Les's family, immediately felt like family as well. Both Leslie and her mother Vera, stayed with my dad and Stepmother Judy, who live right next to my grandfather. A lot of folks from the family came by and Dad made a bunch of chili. As Grandpa and Les sat at Dad's table eating, Grandpa smiled, and said, "Man Les, I can't believe you are at my son's house eating chili with me." They spoke on through the evening about stories of the war and about their lives since. Interestingly, Les just like my father and myself, had been an IBEW electrician, and had retired from electrical work many years prior.

After some conversation with everyone else, Lou and Les walked side by side, across my dad's yard and back to Grandpa's home. They spent the rest of the evening and the following day catching up alone. Grandpa cooked Les breakfast lunch and dinner and sat with Les all of the following day just talking about whatever came to mind. When I stopped by later with my brother Joe, they were sitting at Grandpa's table drinking coffee. Grandpa had pies baking in the oven and Les kept commenting on Grandpa's cooking skills.

Lou Baczewski & Les Underwood, Belgium 1944

Lou & Les - May, 2011

I asked them a bit about the war and why they lost contact afterwards. Les Underwood stated that when he returned home he put the war behind him and got on with his life. He never would speak about it or dwell on it. He and my grandfather both just felt that they had done their jobs and were lucky to make it home. Les said, "I pretty much forgot everything, unless I met someone who started talking about the war. I just never did think about it, but some people you know it just worked on their mind all the time." For the both of them, they had seen so much death that it was something that they shelved away deep inside themselves. When they returned home they put their heads down and went back to work. I asked Les, what "was the most positive moment of the war for you," he replied, "When they handed me those discharge papers."

Neither Les nor Lou, felt like military men, and neither considered staying in it. As soon as they could get out of the service they did so.

Neither one was a fan of war, but having seen all the remnants of the Nazi's handiwork firsthand, they both felt that it had to be done. In contrast, neither my grandfather nor Les Underwood agreed with the wars in Iraq or Afghanistan. They had not agreed with Korea, or Vietnam either, and felt that our country should not engage in war unless we were forced to defend ourselves as we had done in WWII. They are not pacifists, but both know all too well what war is all about. Just like Eisenhower, they had seen the wasteland of Europe and saw countless friends and foes fall before them. They did not want to see it again, unless it was absolutely necessary. They are living examples that it is truly possible to both support our soldiers and hate war. Sadly it seems in this country that we have forgotten about men like these. We have forgotten that there is no black and white when it comes to war. The costs of war are not only in dollars and cents, but in the bodies and minds of its youth. If WWII had been such a fantastic thing, then why had it taken sixty-six years for these two men to face it? Both Les and my grandfather, wanted to return to their homes and never look back on what they had done or seen. My grandfather just wanted to be an everyday man, raise a family, and hope that his sons and grandsons and great-grandsons would never have to experience what he had barely lived through. Thomas Jefferson once purported said, "I am a warrior, so that my son can be a farmer, and his son a poet." For me, that quote suits this tale exactly; because Louis J. Baczewski was a tanker, so that his son could be a tradesman, and his son, a writer.

In the process of researching and writing this book, I came to realize so much in regards to my family history and the lessons that we and so many others should garner from the justly branded "Greatest Generation." Given the present social and political mores, I could not help

346

but feel that we as a nation are failing to look deeply at our own history. Yet in each and every family in this country there are similar stories to that of my family's, which show how the events of the 1930's and 40's created deep rippling effects, and they still persist collectively today. Upon speaking to one WWII veteran and child of the Depression, he lamented that we today just cannot comprehend how pervasive and all-encompassing the effects of the Depression and the war were. The depression was felt on every level. Likewise, the commitment of every individual in this nation to the war effort was unprecedented before or since. No person in this nation or arguably the world was left untouched by the events of those two decades. Yet there are so many lessons of life and history that are being ignored and lost daily as these individuals pass on. We have celebrated the war and almost beat to death the subsequent glorious victory and our national rise to the rank of global heroes. Yet we have simultaneously glazed over many of the broader lessons, deep rooted wisdom, and collective desire to avoid war unless absolutely necessary. These members of the "Greatest Generation" have these concerns carved into their souls.

Chapter 18
"We're Gonna Run Em All Night"

The Tao is so empty, those who use it, never become
full again
and so deep as if it were the ancestor of us all
dulling our edges, untying out tangles,
softening our light, merging our dust,
and so clear as if it were present.

Lao Tzu

Long before the Honor flight or the Third Armored Division Reunion (or at least long in terms of my own life) it took many hard lessons for me to actually sit down and make a concerted effort to write this book. Sadly, bad things have to happen sometimes just to make people realize just how important family and history really is. Out of all of Grandpa's four grandsons, the two who I felt revered my grandfather and especially fishing the creek, were my cousin Michael and I. To the both of us, fishing the creek and everything related to our Grandfather was sacred. Michael took fishing the creek seriously, just as much as Grandpa and my dad and uncle Dave, my brother and I always have, but there was something else there as well. There was something about all of us fishing the creek that cannot be expressed in words, and was understood by only those who really and truly loved it, deep down in their bones.

Michael was tough, big and strong, and always witty. He lit up every family occasion and showed up in force at every family project. He was a hard drinking and hard joking man. He was never perfect by any stretch, but he did a great deal of good in his life and meant a great deal to the family. Michael was a Journeymen tree trimmer, who eventually became a union Lineman apprentice.

While he was on his way home from work, on a freezing cold windy night, he slid off the road before the edge of a highway 64 overpass. He was ejected from his truck and killed. It was a short time before Christmas, and his truck was full of presents for his son and the rest of the family. The wrecker, the repulsive ass that he was, stole many of these gifts as they were scattered by the road side. He plucked the packages from the snow and ice whilst they were mixed with bits and pieces of Michael's truck, which were strewn all along the highway ditch.

For the first time in my life, Christmas was darkness and the antithesis of a holiday. For years following the accident, Christmas was not the same. Every family occasion was not the same. Everyone felt the deep void in each and every room and on each and every occasion. Our greatest holiday was clouded by death, and it was hard to have fun anymore in Michael's absence. After Mike passed, our family was fishing the creek less and less. We went a few times, but it was hard to get back in the groove. Grandpa had stopped going due to his age, and we started to fear that the creek was getting more and more polluted. Folks in Pokey warned us not to eat what came out of there. According to most, there was too much farm run off. There was far too much spraying and livestock waste. On one incident, when we went to run our lines we found all of our minnows dead and floating in the live box. Every damn fish was dead. If only some were dead, then that could be natural, but every bait fish in the whole box was stone dead. When we shined our head lamps across the creek, we could see fish coming to the top of the water to breathe.

Something was in that water and it sure wasn't good. That was the last time we fished Shoal Creek.

For a few years there, I felt like the family just lost its way; we were having a hard time. Just when I thought it couldn't be worse, on Christmas day of 2004, my brother had to take me to the hospital. For months I had been in pain, and unable to feel like myself. The pain was excruciating and sometimes I felt like there was a mouse in my stomach with a dull knife. For months, that damn mouse would only stab when I least expected it, and I would fold up in a ball. It was the worst pain I had ever experienced, and I stubbornly lived through it for too long of a time. I had no idea what was going on.

I had been to the doctor, but was misdiagnosed and nothing seemed to help with the pain. On Christmas day I could hardly move, and the situation became dire. My sisters and brother saved my life, because they finally pushed me to go to the hospital. When I was admitted, I was in so much pain that I drifted in and out of consciousness. I do remember however, the doctor telling me the summary results of a CT scan while I laid in the ER. He told me with a solemn and apologetic look that I more than likely had a very severe case of Crohns Disease. I was showing all the signs, and my intestines were very close to rupturing. I was on death's doorstep. My brother was there at my bed side. Upon hearing the doctor's statement, Joe sardonically blurted out a comment. It was the all too common familial response to any distressful or implacable situation. He asked the doctor, "Is it chr-o-nic?" Translation: he was jokingly asking if it was a chronic disease, and placing a different emphasis on the "O" on purpose. The doctor looked at him like he was insane. I looked at the doctor and I looked at him, and I started to laugh. God, it hurt to laugh, but I did. I laughed and I smiled and said, "Damn Joe, ya have to make a joke

351

of everything." He immediately dropped his head and began saying over and over, "I shouldn't have said that." I immediately told him, "It's ok, I thought it was funny."

If you can't laugh about the worst events in life, you are just going to cry instead. If you had the right company, I was always up for the laughing. Hell, you can cry anytime, but laughing with others, that takes others who are willing to laugh. My family could always laugh about even the worst of things; hell even at my cousin Michael's funeral we broke out in laughter. There was no lack of crying, that's for certain. Yet we all felt that Michael, a person who had made us all laugh countless times throughout his life, had a divine hand in the incident. At just about the worst moment possible, when The Polish War Vets played *Taps* and fired their seven gun salute, and when some were red eyed, some weak, some weeping, and all of us overwhelmed with loss, the Polish War Vets played a crackly recorded version of the Polish national anthem to what sounded like bad rumba music. There we stood, all dressed up in the cold and the snow, laying one of our own into his grave, as the most unfitting rhythmic music gyrated through the snowy December air. The music seemed downright horrid, so much so, that everyone forgot for the briefest of moments that we were at a funeral. We began to look around at each other, and Uncle Dave said with tears in his eyes as the rhythmic rumba resounded, "Well, he got us again." We all started laughing. His closest friends and his family laughed, but the others, who did not know Michael as well as we did, looked at us like we were crazy. Even Michael's mother and wife laughed. I think for that moment we just felt his presence.

During the weeks I was in the hospital, I thought about things like this. I thought about Michael being gone. I thought how close I had come to meeting him. I realized how important my family was and how fragile

352

my life was. I crossed the divide where a young man who once felt invincible and immortal was now lumbering around in a weak bag of bones. I was hooked up to all kinds of crazy beeping things and intravenous liquids. I went in at 5'8"weighing 160lbs and came out weighing 120. When Grandpa and Grandma came to visit me, it felt so odd, they were in their early eighties and looking down at their twenty-seven year old Grandson who was now half dead, hooked up to a bank of blinking beeping machines and hoses. It was a strange juxtaposition.

When I finally started getting better and was released, I screwed up and tried to go back to work too soon. I was a residential electrician at the time, and I quickly found out that I was too worn down to do the work. One day, I was trying to bend some large wires into an electric meter on the side of a house, and I just couldn't do it. I tried and tried with everything I had. I was so weakened that I couldn't do it. I could not do what I had done hundreds of times. I was too weak. I was unable to perform my own trade. The realization came over me like a flood. I wondered how I was going to make a living, or even survive my condition, which was putting me in and out of the hospital all the time. I was standing in the mud next to that half built house and I started to cry. Up until that point in my life I never cried. I hardly ever shed a tear. I didn't even cry at my cousin's funeral, but I cried then. Something changed in me, right then and there. I have never been the same since. I was 27 years old, and worried that my life was over. I kept going in and out of the hospital, flare up after flare up.

It was a tough time for me, and so I stepped outside of my norm, because I didn't care about being cautious any more. Even though I didn't have a lot of money, I decided to say the hell with it. I was going to go see a good friend out West. Prior to getting sick, I had never taken a trip like that, and I just didn't know if I would have the opportunity again, considering how sick I had been. My buddy Greg had been inviting me to New Mexico for years. He wanted me to see some of the Southwest and go hiking and fishing in the Gila Wilderness. After doing a bit of research, I found out that the Gila River had catfish in it, flathead catfish even. So, I thought, what the hell. Maybe it would be like Shoal creek with mountains in the background, maybe it would help me gain some perspective.

When I flew into the El Paso airport to meet Greg, I was so skinny and worn out from my last stint in the hospital, that I could barely recognize myself. After a few weeks living on only a liquid supplement poured directly into my bloodstream; I looked something awful. I knew it. I decided to see if my friend since junior high would recognize me, so I walked past him in the terminal without saying a word. He was taller than I remembered and was standing by the gate in a cowboy hat. I walked right by him, just to see if he could tell who I was. He didn't see me at all, but he looked right at me. I kept walking for a few yards. I soon realized that he truly didn't know who I was, so I back tracked and turned around. I saw him looking down the terminal, studying the people. I walked up to him, stepped to his side, and tapped him on his shoulder. He flinched and stepped back. Even as he looked directly at me, he didn't know who I was until I said his name.

I said, "Greg, it's me." He blinked a bit and then awkwardly smiled. He looked at my skeletal remains, and after a few short moments and guesses, he finally saw the person he once knew. In a few short days we were up in the Gila Wilderness. When we finally stepped out of the truck and looked out on the Gila, I was amazed to find that willow trees grew on the banks. They were just like the willows my grandpa had taught me to fish with when I was a boy. Just in case, I had packed some of Grandpas pre-made lines, the same kind we used on the creek.

Fishing the Gila was a chance to do what I had grown up doing all my life, and just like my Grandpa had done as a boy. My buddy Greg and I parked by the river, and hiked up the banks to find a good campsite. Even though it was thousands of miles from Shoal Creek, the thought that there were flatheads in that river gave me an energy that I had not had since I fell ill. I cut a few nice willow poles and started searching for spots. I scoped out some holes early in the day, and tried as much as possible not to disturb the water. While scouting around, I noticed a log jam on a tight bend. When I looked at the conditions carefully, it was as if a divine beam of light shot out of the sky and blazed upon the hole. It was almost as if there was a voice in my head saying, "This is what all of your training was about; this is why you are here." I saw it. I could read the water like a book. I pointed towards the gleaming spectacle and said to Greg, "If there are flatheads in here, we'll catch some in that jam right there." Strangely, the fatigue from my illness and the ache from the hike were both gone. I channeled some primordial energy from the depths of my youth. I had to swim out across the whole river to set some lines in the log jam. I climbed around the convoluted web of limbs and logs to set the poles. Since we did not have all the normal tools for such an endeavor, we only set six poles.

By the end of the night, we caught three fish. One was probably about three pounds, another was about five, and the last was close to ten. I can't say for sure, we didn't have a scale, but I felt that from experience I was a fairly good judge. I had to swim to land each fish, and I did it without a net. The cold mountain water made me gasp for air, but I swam and caught each fish by hand and swam back to shore carrying the fish, it was a battle. The next day I cleaned all the fish and cooked up a banquet on the river bank. The filets from that mountain flathead were so clean and clear that I could not believe it. I swear it was the best catfish I ever ate.

**Lou Baczewski, grandson of Louch holding a flathead
on the Gila River, New Mexico 2008**

As we sat around the campfire that night, I told Greg stories about my grandfather, the war, and the creek. When the fire had died down to coals and I headed to sleep, I looked up into that vast band of stars and something clicked. I realized that I was going to be ok, my family was going to be ok and we could go anywhere and do what Grandpa had taught us. We didn't have to be on Shoal Creek – we just needed to remember where we came from. We needed to never forget. The lessons of Shoal were everywhere I went, they were written into my soul. I swore to myself, that as long as I was capable, I would fish like my Grandpa had shown me, no matter how arduous or archaic the method might be. There was something in it, and whatever it was, it helped me, just as much as it helped my grandfather escape from all the carnage he witnessed in the war. In the years that followed, I started getting better, and I went into full remission. Now I know fishing didn't cure it, but I feel it really helped me focus on what was important. I felt like the peace of mind and simplicity of my grandfather's traditions had helped me see clearly, and so I swore to never forget that.

Thankfully, between my brother, my Uncle and his boys Nick and Jon, and my dad and I, the tradition of bankline fishing would survive. We just had to find another place to go, another muddy stream in a now undisclosed location. None of us could deny that Grandpa's way of fishing made an indelible mark on us all. We also cannot help but think that each time we fish together, were it not for Louch's narrow survival, that none of us would even exist. This is something I often reflect upon. I will never forget all that Grandpa taught me, from fishing the creek to every last aspect of how a man should lead his life. The lessons of his life were chiseled into our bones on the creek.

In our family, some are gone, and some are too old to carry the burden, and some chose a different path. Yet as long as I am able, I will never say that anything he taught me is too much work, or not worth doing. It is a terrible thing to feel that if you don't do it, then no one else will. My uncle and my brother still like to run lines, but I fear that beyond us, no-one will carry this on. No one will be willing to work that hard just to catch some fish. Perhaps no one else will see the "noble truth" in it, but I and a few others always will.

Despite all the chaos and absurdity that was the war and Grandpa's day to day existence, the creek stood as his moment of Zen. The creek was not a place that mattered, what mattered was the process, and the act of simplifying life to a few basic principles. In this way, for the briefest of moments, the universe made sense and there was order in thought and action. Through Grandpa, the creek taught us something that cannot be expressed in words; it has to be experienced, year after year, dirty wet battle after battle.

There is an old Taoist maxim that states, "Before enlightenment, chop wood and carry water, after enlightenment, chop wood and carry water." That is what the creek means to me.

On numerous occasions as our boat floated along past the lines; we sat with our lights off and under the band of stars in the Milky-way galaxy. Uncle Dave would say, "This is the best it will ever get, right here, right now." There were no cell phones, no mechanized devices of any kind, nothing but a sense of accomplishment and the knowledge that all you had to do was run the lines. Life was simplified to a clear set of principles and Grandpa's process. To this day, I have found no other task that makes me feel more at peace than running bank lines. It is a fleeting moment. Yet there are times when I am knee deep in muck dragging a john boat over a riffle, or paddling through the dark, and all of a sudden the whole universe seems to make sense. As soon as you think about it, it goes away. It only makes sense when you don't care if it does or not. It seemed to me that on Shoal Creek, everything else in the world melted away from my grandfather, father, uncles, brother, and cousins. Shoal Creek ran through my grandfather. It flowed along his life and into the lives of his family. Despite all the hardships and horrors and suffering that he witnessed in his years, he could still return to the muddy waters of Shoal Creek and be a boy again. He simplified his task on earth to an archaic process, one which I swear to continue as long as I am able to do so.

In Shoal Creek's shallows we found depth. The word Shoal itself means shallow and the creek was indeed lacking in terms of nautical fathoms. It was not however shallow in its flow through our family and our lives. Shoal Creek was suffering for the everyday sort. If you recognized and let your mind fester on the suffering then you didn't belong at Shoal Creek. If one understood that our task to catch catfish was suffering and that we were there to do it, then therefore there was no suffering. Once you put air conditioned rooms and the comforts of home out of your mind, you were fine. Our job was to swelter in the heat, become covered in bugs, tear our skin on stinging weeds, stab ourselves with hooks and bait fish fins, immerse ourselves in dirt, live in primordial grime, and subsist in constant exhaustion. There was no suffering to be had.

Some nights when I go by myself and run banklines alone; I sit in my boat after dark and think of all of the ghosts of Shoal Creek. I think about all of those faces now long gone, all of those friends and relatives who once waded in its waters and climbed its banks. I imagine that in death we will all meet there. I imagine my uncle, brother, and I, with our lights off under a canopy of endless stars, listening to the creek flow. We pull our worn john boat ashore and load up our catch. We walk single file up the steep bank toward the glow of a flickering campfire. The fire will as always, paint its light around the ramparts of the 140 bridge. When we step closer, we hear their laughter. We see the faces in the firelight. They are all there, every last one, all the souls of Shoal Creek. The sandy ground gives way under our feet, and we drink deep of cold beer and homemade wine. We resolve to run the lines all night, but the sounds of the tree frogs, and the insects, and the cool night air soothes us into a deep, restful sleep.

THE END

Bibliography

Books

Ambrose, Steven E. <u>Eisenhower Soldier and President, The Renowned One</u>. New York: Simon & Schuster, 1990.

Ambrose, Steven E. <u>Citizen Soldiers, The US Army From the Normandy Beaches to the Bulge to the Surrender of Germany, June 7th 1944 to May 7th 1944</u>. New York: Simon & Schuster 1997

Astor, Gerald. <u>A Blood Dimmed Tide, The Battle of the Bulge by the Men Who Fought It</u>. New York, Dell Publishing, 1992.

Astor, Gerald. <u>The Bloody Forest, Battle for the Huertgen: September 1944- January 1945</u>. Novato: Presidio Press, 2000.

Bauerline, Mark. <u>The Dumbest Generation, How the Digital Age Stupefies Young Americans and Jeopardizes Our Future</u>. New York: Penguin Group Publishing, 2008.

Cooper, Belton Y. Death Traps, <u>The Survival of an American Armored Division in World War II.</u> New York: Ballantine Books, 1998.

Eisenhower, Dwight D. <u>Crusade in Europe</u>. Baltimore: Johns Hopkins University Press, 1948.

Ergenzinger, Fritz. <u>"Kameraden," Ein Bildbuch Vom NS. – Reichkreigerbund</u>. Frankfurt: Herausgegeben Von Der Propaganda–Abteilung des Reichkreigerbundes, 1940.

Hale, Christopher. <u>Himmler's Crusade, The Nazi Expedition to Find the Origins of The Aryan Race</u>. Hoboken: John Wiley and Sons, Inc. 2003.

Green, Michael, and Brown, James D. <u>M4 Sherman at War</u>. St Paul Minnesota: Zenith Press, 2006.

Glantz, Aaron. <u>The War Comes Home, Washington's Battle Against Americas Veterans</u>. Berkeley: University of California Press, 2009.

Goodrick-Clark Nicholas. <u>The Occult Roots of Nazism, Secret Aryan Cults and Their Influence on Nazi Ideology</u>. New York: New York University Press, 1992.

Ledbetter, James. <u>Unwarranted Influence, Dwight D Eisenhower and the Military Industrial Complex.</u> Grand Rapids: Yale University Press, 2011.

Ossad, Steven L. and Marsh, Don R. Major <u>General Maurice Rose, World War II's Greatest Forgotten Commander</u>. New York: Taylor Trade Publishing, 2006.

Pensoneau, Taylor. <u>Brothers Notorious, The Sheltons: Southern Illinois Legendary Gangsters.</u> New Berlin: Downstate Publications, 2002.

Reynolds, Michael. <u>The Devil's Adjutant, Jochen Peiper Panzer Leader</u>. New York: Sarpedon, 1995.

Sellier, Andre.' A History of the Dora Camp, <u>The Story of the Nazi Slave Labor Camp That Secretly Manufactured V2 Rockets</u>. Chicago: Ivan R. Dee, (Published in Association with the United States Holocaust Memorial Museum) 2003.

Schafft, Gretchen and Zeidler, Gerhard. <u>Commemorating Hell, The Public Memory of Mittelbau-Dora.</u> Urbana: University of Illinois Press, 2011

Theising, Andrew J. <u>East St Louis, Made in the USA</u>. St. Louis: Virginia Publishing, 2003.

Toland, John. <u>Battle, The Story of the Bulge</u>. Lincoln: University of Nebraska Press, 1999.

Tucker-Jones, Anthony. Falaise, <u>The Flawed Victory, The Destruction of Panzergruppe West August1944</u>. Barnsely South Yorkshire: Pen and Sword Military, 2008.

Zadeth, Ismael Hossein. <u>The Political Economy of US Militarism</u>. NewYork: Plagrave Macmillan, 2006.

Military Documents, Unit Histories, Narratives, Journals, Logs and After Action Reports

33rd Armored Regiment 3rd Armored Division CCB 2nd Battalion Log book

33rd Armored Regiment 3rd Armored Division After Action Reports

33rd Combat Engineer Regiment 7th Armored Division After Action Reports

36th Armored Infantry Regiment After Action Reports

Five Stars To Victory The Exploits of Task Force Lovelady 2nd Bn(Reinf), 33rd Arm'd Regt.,3rd Arm'd., Div. US. Army in the War Against Germany, A. Eaton Roberts Atlas Printing and Engraving Co. Birmingham Alabama. 1949

Official Report Number 2980 Headquarters European Theatre of Operations United States Army, "American Tankmen Recover from Ambush to Destroy German Armor."

Spearhead In The West, the History of the 3rd Armored Division 1941-1945

"The Devil's in Baggy Pants" – Combat Record of the 504th Parachute Infantry Regiment April 1943 – July 1945.

Newspapers, Magazines, Video & Online Resources

Engineering Disasters. Episode #9-49 "Sherman Tanks." (The recorded comments of Belton Cooper) Jupiter Entertainment, October 22nd 2002.

Dobbs, Michael, "Ford and GM Scrutinized for Alleged Nazi Collaboration." Washington DC *Washington Post*, 7 May 1998, sec. A p. 01.

"Registration bill goes to the president, house Accepts Senate Amendments and Final Action." *New York Times,* 29 January 1942, pg. 15.

"Where Barbarossa Dreamed, A Statue of William I. Placed in the Thuringian Forest." Berlin Dispatch to *The London Times*. Reprinted in the *New York Times,* Jul 5, 1896.

"FBI Gets 33 Aliens; 1 Was a NYA Teacher: Hungarian Once Instructor of Radio." *New York Times,* Aug 9, 1942.

"Nazi Coordination is accepted by all: Heil Hitler!' Is the Connecting Link in Regimentation By *The North American Newspaper Alliance*, Inc. Reprinted in the *New York Times (1923-Current file);* Apr 3, 1939, pg. 7

"64 Germans Arrested In New York," *The London Times*, Tuesday, Apr 14, 1942; sec A pg. 3.

"League Of German Soldiers Herr Friessner's Role," *The London Times* Wednesday, Oct 10, 1951; pg. 3; Issue 52128; col B

"Spearhead - Saga of the 3rd Armored" by Richard Tregaskis, Saga, Feb. 1963

St Louis (Missouri) Post-Dispatch, Special Edition, "Reprint of Eisenhower's Letter to All Soldiers, Sailors, Airmen," June - 5th 1994

Clemens, Edwin M. "*My Memories of Market Garden.*" [electronic journal] 1st Battalion, B Company, 1st Platoon, 504th Parachute Infantry Regiment, 82nd Airborne Division. Available @ MarketGarden.com

ENDNOTES

Chapter 2

[1] Green, Michael, and Brown, James D. <u>M4 Sherman at War</u>. St Paul Minnesota: Zenith Press, (2006): pg. 26

[2] Ibid, pg. 35

[3] Ibid, pg. 53

[4] Ibid, pg. 29

[5] St Louis (Missouri) Post-Dispatch, Special Edition, "Reprint of Eisenhower's Letter to All Soldiers, Sailors, Airmen," June - 5th 1994

Chapter 3

[6] 33rd Armored Regiment 3rd Armored Division CCB 2nd Battalion Log book, 21 June 44 – 23 June 44

[7] Cooper, Belton Y. Death Traps, <u>The Survival of an American Armored Division in World War II.</u> New York: Ballantine Books, 1998. pg. 41

[8] Ibid, pg. 43

[9] Ibid, pg 28

[10] Ibid, pg, 331

[2] Episode # 9-49, Engineering Disasters. "Sherman Tanks." (The recorded comments of Belton Cooper) Jupiter Entertainment, October 22nd 2002.

[11] Ossad, Steven L. and Marsh, Don R. Major <u>General Maurice Rose, World War II's Greatest Forgotten Commander</u>. New York: Taylor Trade Publishing, 2006, pg.198

Chapter 5

[1] Tucker-Jones, Anthony. Falaise, <u>The Flawed Victory, The Destruction of Panzergruppe West August1944</u>. Barnsely South Yorkshire: Pen and Sword Military, 2008. in preface & Acknowledgements vii

[14] Ibid, pg. 2

[2] Ibid, pg. 16

[16] Roberts, Eaton. Five Stars To Victory, The Exploits of Task Force Lovelady 2nd Bn(Reinf), 33rd Arm'd Regt.,3rd Arm'd., Div. US. Army in the War Against Germany, Atlas Printing and Engraving Co. Birmingham Alabama. 1949. pgs. 20 & 21

[17] Ibid, pgs. 20 & 21

[18] Ibid, pg 75

[19] Tucker – Jones, pg. 37

Chapter 6

[20] Roberts, pg. 86

[21] Hale, Christopher. <u>Himmler's Crusade, The Nazi Expedition to Find the Origins of The Aryan Race</u>. Hoboken: John Wiley and Sons, Inc. 2003. pg. 2

[22] Reynolds, Michael. <u>The Devil's Adjutant, Jochen Peiper Panzer Leader</u>. New York: Sarpedon, 1995, pg. 31

[23] Goodrick-Clark Nicholas. <u>The Occult Roots of Nazism, Secret Aryan Cults and Their Influence on Nazi Ideology</u>. New York: New York University Press, 1992. pg. 177

[24] Ibid, pg.195

[25] Ibid, pg. 197

[26] The DD-214 Discharge papers of Louis J Baczewski

Chapter 7

[27] After Action Report, 33rd Armored Engineer Battalion 7th Armored Division, August 22nd, August 24th & 25, 1944

[28] Ibid, Sept 18

Chapter 8

[29] Astor, Gerald. <u>The Bloody Forest, Battle for the Huertgen: September 1944- January 1945</u>. Novato: Presidio Press, 2000. pg. 51

[30] Dobbs, Michael, "Ford and GM Scrutinized for Alleged Nazi Collaboration." Washington DC *Washington Post*, 7 May 1998, sec. A p. 01.

[31] Astor, pg. 64

[32] Astor, pg. 9

[33] Astor, pg. 356

Chapter 9

[34] Toland, John. <u>Battle, The Story of the Bulge</u>. Lincoln: University of Nebraska Press, 1999. Author's Note, pg. i

[35] Toland, pg 12

[36] Cooper, Belton Y. Death Traps, <u>The Survival of an American Armored Division in World War II.</u> New York: Ballantine Books, 1998. pg. 191

[37] Ibid, pg. 187

Chapter 10

[38] Reynolds, Michael. The Devil's Adjutant, Jochen Peiper Panzer Leader. New York: Sarpedon, 1995. Reynolds, pg. 253
[39] Reynolds, pg. 27
[40] Roberts, Eaton, pg. 91
[41] Log book of the 2nd Battalion January 1945 pg 20.
[42] Cooper, Introduction, pg. xvii
[43] 33rd Armored Regiment After Action Report, 11 April 1945
[44] Eisenhower, Dwight D. Crusade in Europe. Baltimore: Johns Hopkins University Press, 1948. Pg. 409

Chapter 11

[45] Sellier, Andre.' A History of the Dora Camp, The Story of the Nazi Slave Labor Camp That Secretly Manufactured V2 Rockets. Chicago: Ivan R. Dee, (Published in Association with the United States Holocaust Memorial Museum) 2003. pg.108
[46] Sellier, pg. 237
[47] Sellier, pg. 455
[48] Sellier pg. 398
[49] Sellier pg. 404
[50] Sellier pg. 410
[51] Sellier pg. 411

Chapter 13

[1] MarketGarden. Com / Edwin M. Clemens, pvt 504th Parachute Infantry Regiment, 82nd Airborne
[2] 33rd Armored Regiment, After Combat Report February page 2 II Enemy Situation and General Plans for Attack
[3] Spearhead In The West, the History of the 3rd Armored Division 1941-1945, pg. 143
[4] Cooper, pg. 287
[5] Roberts, pg. 97
[6] Roberts, pg. 97
[7] Roberts, pg 108
[8] Goodrick-Clark pg. 179

[9] Hale, Himmler's Crusade

[10] "64 Germans Arrested In New York," *The London Times*, Tuesday, Apr 14, 1942; sec A pg. 3.

[11] Cooper, pg. 331

[12] Foreword to the "Spearhead in the West"

[13] Pensoneau, Taylor. Brothers Notorious, The Sheltons: Southern Illinois Legendary Gangsters. New Berlin: Downstate Publications, 2002.

Chapter 16

[1] Glantz, Aaron. The War Comes Home, Washington's Battle Against Americas Veterans. Berkeley: University of California Press, 2009. Aaron Glantz, pg. 159

[2] Glantz, pg. 158

[3] "Britians Homage to 28,000 American Dead," Eisenhower's speech

Chapter 18

[4] Eisenhower, Dwight D. Crusade in Europe. Baltimore: Johns Hopkins University Press, 1948., pg 478.